# CORPORATE SECURITY
## IN THE
# ASIA-PACIFIC REGION

*Crisis, Crime, Fraud, and Misconduct*

# CORPORATE SECURITY
## IN THE
# ASIA-PACIFIC REGION

*Crisis, Crime, Fraud, and Misconduct*

**Christopher J. Cubbage, CPP**

**David J. Brooks, PhD**

CRC Press
Taylor & Francis Group
Boca Raton London New York

CRC Press is an imprint of the
Taylor & Francis Group, an **informa** business

CRC Press
Taylor & Francis Group
6000 Broken Sound Parkway NW, Suite 300
Boca Raton, FL 33487-2742

First issued in paperback 2018

ISBN-13: 978-1-4398-9227-5 (hbk)
ISBN-13: 978-1-138-37464-5 (pbk)

---

**Library of Congress Cataloging-in-Publication Data**

---

Cubbage, Chris.
    Corporate security in the Asia-Pacific Region : crisis, crime, fraud & misconduct / Chris Cubbage, David Brooks.
       p. cm.
    Includes bibliographical references and index.
    ISBN 978-1-4398-9227-5 (alk. paper)
    1. Corporations--Security measures--Asia. 2. Corporations--Security measures--Pacific Region. I. Brooks, David. II. Title.

HV8291.A78C83 2013
658.4'7095--dc23
                                   2012017887

---

**Visit the Taylor & Francis Web site at**
**http://www.taylorandfrancis.com**

**and the CRC Press Web site at**
**http://www.crcpress.com**

# Contents

# Foreword

Dr. David Brooks and Chris Cubbage have presented a book for security managers, security administrators, crime fighters, and business analysts who operate within the Asia and Pacific regions. *Corporate Security in the Asia-Pacific Region: Crisis, Crime, Fraud and Misconduct* provides a detailed discussion of the current status of security in the Asia-Pacific region, and will prepare both security managers and security practitioners for the many risks and threats that populations and commercial organizations will encounter in international business and foreign affairs.

With regard to national security within the region, geopolitical, financial, legal, and nuclear security issues have been considered. Also, the security issues associated with corporate security in the Asian and Pacific regions have been presented in order that analysis will prepare readers for strategies that can be applied within their organizations. The consideration of security risk and security threat has been discussed according to aspects of crime and corruption in Asia and the Pacific. As a consequence, the application of security risk management to the protection of the people, the information, and the assets of large organizations in the Asian Pacific region has been presented for positive outcomes for the corporate organization. Discussions of internal corporate crime including fraud, internal theft, insider trading, ethical breaches, and political misconduct have been presented with analysis for prevention. Interestingly, workplace violence, food and product contamination, and the misuse of information have been included as corporate crimes that are trending upward.

This book will serve the purpose of guiding the security manager within the Asian Pacific areas to better protect the corporate organization and its assets. The authors are to be commended for the structure and analysis of the topics within the book, with comprehensive description and discussion of the need for asset protection and recovery. There is no comparable book on the international market and, as such, it is at the leading edge of advanced security management texts for the serious consideration of asset protection.

**Clifton Smith PhD, Hon. Professor of Security Science**
*Electron Science Research Institute, Edith Cowan University,*
*Perth, Western Australia*

# Preface

Security is a broad and multidisciplined function of management, which requires specialized skills and knowledge within risk management, technology, and business compliance. Nevertheless, security can also be extremely subjective, either not worthy of consideration or, at the other extreme, driven by fear. Include subjectivity of security and the diversity of the Asia-Pacific region, and most senior executives should have a degree of concern in what and how they are or are not protecting their people, organizations, and businesses within what is now considered the world's center of commerce.

What are the strategies and therefore corporate issues facing the Asia-Pacific region now and into the future? Will the current nation-state forum remain or will smaller states be consumed by the larger? Will the Association of Southeast Asian Nations (ASEAN) follow the European path or will it blaze its own regional path? What are the changing threats and risks in the region and does the region use risk management?

To manage these and many other issues, this publication provides a large number of real cases of corporate crime, fraud, misconduct, crisis, emergency management, and other security-related events within the Asia-Pacific region. Contemporary security risk issues are addressed for informed risk assessments and analysis of operational risk facing any company or organization from 2012 and beyond. The Asia-Pacific region has faced and will continue to face crises as its dominant nation-state security paradigms are found wanting.

The integration of corporate security risk management into regional and multinational company operations is increasingly a critical role involving the corporation's board and risk committees. Security professionals are increasingly communicating with their executives, and world events are driving a change in corporate security's positioning. In addition to comprehending security's broad body of knowledge, professionals need to be proficient in business, legal, and compliance obligations, constantly monitoring for emerging trends and technology.

Corporate security is a unique part of the general security domain; however, it is not public policing, private military security, or the security guard. Corporate security is a support function that for efficacy aligns with its corporation and assists in its success. To achieve this aim, corporate security has to encompass a number of clear areas of practice, such as security risk management, security management, business continuity management, and business as well as security technology. These have to be applied at an operational, a tactical, and, perhaps most important, a strategic level to align with corporate direction and profit protection.

This book is designed to be suitable for international corporate governance, risk, and security management aficionados, practitioners, and students or those with an interest in the Asia-Pacific region.

# Acknowledgments

Special thanks and gratitude to the following who provided assistance and critical feedback during the development of this publication: Professors Clifton Smith and Bill Hutchinson for their review and professional mentoring over many years; the staff at Amlec House Pty. Limited, namely Clint Tomlinson, security consultant, and Olivia Figueiredo, executive assistant, for assisting with the compilation of country reviews and author permissions. Thank you also to the Asia-Pacific security industry and the many professionals and practitioners who have provided invaluable input through their own publications and passing on their research, experience, and knowledge. Finally, our great appreciation to family, friends, and colleagues for their support, patience, and encouragement.

# About the Authors

**Chris Cubbage,** *BSc (Hons), CPP, GAICD, AdvDip BusMgt, Dip CI, Dip Pol,* is a corporate security and public safety consultant who has provided crisis and risk management advice, and has conducted security audits and investigations for government and private industry around the world. He has more than twenty years combined experience in criminal and civil investigations, in roles as homicide detective with the Western Australia Police Major Crime Squad and senior investigator at the Australian Crime Commission (ACC). Chris has lectured in security risk and physical security at Edith Cowan University, Perth, Australia, and has published research on the application and recognition of security risk management in Australian public companies. He is the executive editor of the *Asia-Pacific Security Magazine* and a presenter and producer of MySecurity TV. Through the media and his private consultancy company, Amlec House Pty. Limited, he continues to serve clients in the region and around the world. He is accredited as a Certified Protection Professional (CPP) with ASIS International.

**Dr. David Brooks,** *PhD, MSc (Security Science), BSc, ADipEng (Electronics),* is a senior security science academic with the Security Research Centre (SECAU) at Edith Cowan University in Western Australia. He conducts research and teaches security risk management, security management, resilience, and security technology evaluation. He is the academic chair of the Security Research Centre Annual Security and Intelligence Conference and is on the editorial committee of the *Security Journal.* In addition, Dr. Brooks has authored previous books on public space CCTV and the corporate security body of knowledge, and has numerous published articles in international journals and conference proceedings.

Dr. Brooks has been previously employed by the Australian Defence Department as the Western Australia regional fixed plant and equipment contract manager. During this period, he was primarily responsible for the development, implementation, and maintenance of the strategic process of facility plant maintenance and management. Other past employment included seven years within the commercial security environment as a technical consultant and thirteen years in the Royal Air Force (UK) as a development technician in defense radar systems.

# 1 Security in the Asia-Pacific Region

## INTRODUCTION

Much has been written in the context of security and the Asia Pacific; however, far less has been written within a regional context of corporate security. Many current books focus on and are therefore confined to the U.S. and European models of corporate security. As the world continues to rapidly change on many fronts, in particular, those of economic and population dominance, there is a sustained business focus on the Asia Pacific. The emergence of the Asia Pacific and its nation-states over the last two decades as a central, fast-developing region offers the world economic stability. Such stability comes at a time when the United States and Europe enter what many predict will be, at best, an economic crisis, or at worst, economic collapse.

The development and "Westernization" of the populations of China and India, representing over a third of the world's population, have allowed these two nation-states to reach out and influence the rest of the world to an extent approaching the influence of the United States. Inevitably, there will be an end to the world dominance of the United States as a global principal. The instability caused by such a "changing of the guard" carries a high degree of instability for business and industry. Nevertheless, U.S. and European companies are and will be increasingly attracted to the opportunities provided in the Asia Pacific, as their own local market and political stability stagnate or deteriorate.

The Western world, including Japan, is on life support. Contagion from Europe's underperforming and overspending economies remains a significant and unstable risk. In addition, the magnitude of the U.S. debt and deficit problems, which as of 2011 stand at US$14 trillion, is close to 100 percent of U.S. gross domestic product and continuing to grow. The U.S. government spends US$1.60 for every dollar it receives, which is unsustainable.

The central finance hubs of Singapore, Hong Kong, Tokyo, Sydney, and emerging Shanghai provide an ever-increasing percentage of world trade, to the expense of growth in traditional finance centers such as London, Paris, Frankfurt, and New York. The business transition to a new region as diverse as the Asia Pacific requires corporations to operate and adapt to myriad opportunities and risks. In particular, regional conflict, as seen in Afghanistan and Korea, or domestic instability, seen in Philippines and Thailand, requires corporate security strategy and operations to manage threats and risks not only on a regional level but also country by country. Food and energy security is an ever-present threat, caused by catastrophic natural disasters across the Pacific Ocean rim. A prominent example of an extreme worst-case scenario imaginable is the 2011 Japanese earthquake and tsunami, which killed many thousands of people, destroyed vast areas and infrastructure, and took out a nuclear power plant. Such an incident demonstrates the degree of threat and risk to be carried.

Many corporations are unprepared for difficult-to-foresee events, whether natural or human in origin. As Blackmore stated, "Fifteen years ago most companies would send a couple of good blokes who knew how to look after themselves into a country and tell them to get on with it." However, risk management has become far more sophisticated over the past 10 years, while corporations and governments have become more litigious and risk averse. As Evans, Petrofac's global head of emergency response and crisis management (Lyons cited in ASIS International 2011), suggested, the 2011 Middle Eastern uprising that commenced with Tunisia was difficult for organizations to deal with because it took place in a number of different nation-states.

Page Group's operations manager, Harry Collins, pointed out that it has never been more important for companies to assume responsibility for local employees in overseas nation-states as it is now. Large corporations cannot simply evacuate their international staff members in times of crisis and pretend that they do not have responsibility for those who have been left behind. Corporations that do business in potentially risky nation-states should take steps to prepare for a possible incident, including performing risk management, developing business continuity plans, and building strong relationships with the local community in order to mitigate unforeseen risks (Lyons cited in ASIS International 2011). Many of these corporate security issues are addressed in later chapters.

Nevertheless, a renewed approach to corporate risk management is necessary, in contrast to relying on traditionally designed and executed strategies based on U.S. and European standards and practice. Security and risk professionals need to have consideration and awareness of the Asia Pacific's unique regional environment, quite different from that of the United States and Europe. In contribution to this process, *Corporate Security in the Asia-Pacific Region* has been designed to encourage revised approaches for strategic and operational risk assessments in a corporate security context. Corporate security must be acknowledged as a necessary business practice to manage and minimize security risk exposures that are unique and dynamic to the Asia-Pacific region.

## THE ASIA-PACIFIC REGION: AN OVERVIEW

The Asia-Pacific region encompasses a heterogeneous group of states, extending from India in the west to Japan in the east, from China in the north to Australia and New Zealand in the south. Although an imprecise geographical descriptor, the term *Asia Pacific* became popular from the 1980s as the economies within this diverse and broad group of nation-states flourished due to increased regional capital flow, free trade, and other forms of economic and political interaction.

The region covers some 43,810,582 km$^2$, with an estimated population of 4.16 billion. Its nominal gross domestic product (GDP) is the world's third largest, with the highest purchasing power parity (PPP) in the world. According to the United Nations Office on Drugs and Crime (UNODC 2009) the region's population has fallen to the lowest of the developing world with a 1.1 percent per year growth rate, which is likely to be sustained. Nevertheless, the population is the largest in the world and many of the Asia-Pacific nation-states are becoming dominant or forecast to in the not too distant future. As of 2011, China became the world's second largest economy and is expected to surpass the United States by 2020 ("How to Gracefully Step Aside" 2011).

The region has a long history and diverse culture, with many influences over thousands of years. The term *Asia* is originally a Westernized concept, as the peoples of ancient *Asia* (Chinese, Japanese, Indians, Persians, Arabs) never conceived of themselves as a single collective. They were and still are extremely varied civilizations, contrary to past European belief. Such diversity leads to difficulty in most organizations attempting to operate in more than a limited number of these environments, without in-country understanding of nation-state culture, language, and business. Nevertheless, some nation-states are more Westernized than others. The risk is that a positive business experience can invariably lead to a corporate assumption that operations can move throughout the region unimpeded, which is far from a valid assumption.

The region and its culture are still reconciling their originality and identities from their Westernization experience, resulting in the adoption of regional and distinct agendas (Tow 2001). As Gilson suggests when considering Eastern Asia, it is not a legally definable entity nor is it bound by a common culture, heritage, or history (Gilson 2007); and here lies the difficulty in operating within the greater Asia-Pacific region. There is no Pan Asia, unlike Europe or North America. Each country has its own culture, regulatory, and currency regimes. Regulators are often comparatively judged only in terms of their capacity. Nevertheless, in this century the Asia Pacific has outpaced many other regional economies and, when combined with India, is becoming the world's center of gravity (Smith 2009, 8). Asia is forecast to be the dominant economic power of the century (Newman 2011), growing only more geographically and geopolitically powerful.

## ASIA-PACIFIC GEOPOLITICAL RELATIONSHIPS

The Asia-Pacific is home to four of the world's major powers and five of the world's largest militaries—the United States, Russia, China, India, and North Korea. In Australia's view, the United States has underwritten stability in the Asia-Pacific for the past half century and will continue to be the single most important strategic actor in our region for the foreseeable future, both in its own right and through its network of alliances and security relationships, including Australia. An ongoing United States presence in the Asia Pacific is essential to peace and stability in our region. Indeed, as the world moves to the Asia Pacific it is even more important that there is a United States presence, indeed an enhanced presence, in our region. (Australian Defence Minister the Hon. Stephen Smith, November 10, 2011, public speech)

Geopolitical relationships between respective Asia-Pacific nation-states and those of the world are fundamentally different from those experienced within European and U.S. history. Within Asia Pacific there are relationships with dictatorships of the past and with foes of the present. Current in-progress conflicts involve or are within Afghanistan, North Korea, China, Iran, Philippines, Thailand, Papua New Guinea, and Tibet, and Australia is involved as a U.S. ally. UN peacekeeping roles have also been led by Australia in East Timor and the Solomon Islands. The relationship between India and Pakistan is a constant strain on regional stability and can be compared to the loggerhead between Israel and a State of Palestine, although if an event occurs it could have a far more significant consequence.

Other, more diplomatic regional conflicts include a stretch of water around the Spratly Islands. The Philippines recently upgraded a military runway ("Phillipines Stirs Waters of the Spratlys" 2011), which sparked renewed territorial claims between China and the Philippines. China, Malaysia, Taiwan, Brunei, Vietnam, and the Philippines all contest all or part of the Spratly Islands, which are believed to have large hydrocarbon deposits.

However, internal Asia-Pacific relationships can cause concerns for those external to the region. For example, in 2011 Iran and Pakistan announced a cooperative agreement with the aim of boosting trade tenfold between the nation-states. Economic activities include increasing the supply of Iranian electricity and natural gas supplies to Pakistan, investment in infrastructure, and opening bank branches in each other's country. Both parties hope the initiatives will push trade between the states from US$1.2 billion per annum to US$10 billion. The agreement is the latest in a series between Iran and Pakistan, signaling increased ties. Such agreements are a concern for the United States, which is worried by the continued strengthening of ties as it further weakens U.S. attempts to isolate Iran. In addition, relations between Pakistan and the United States continue to decrease, compounded by accusations from Washington of the complicity of Pakistan's Directorate for Inter-Services Intelligence (ISI) and attacks on American forces in Afghanistan (Campbell 2011).

## NUCLEAR DEFENSE IN THE ASIA PACIFIC

There are a number of nuclear-capable and armed nation-states in the Asia Pacific, including China, India, Pakistan, North Korea, and Russia. Japan is nuclear capable, but limits the use of nuclear to power generation. Both India and Pakistan are nuclear armed and are two of only three nation-states not to be signatories to the Nuclear Non-Proliferation Treaty (NPT) (Figure 1.1). In addition, North Korea withdrew from the NPT altogether.

In April 2010, despite the United States imposing a new round of sanctions on Iran over its nuclear program, the key Asian powers of India and China opposed those sanctions. There is direct trading in defense between the Asia Pacific and the Middle East. In 2009, Asia emerged as the greatest consumer of Israeli defense goods, with the expenditure for India alone reaching US$3 billion. The three major Israeli arms export categories were missiles, sensors, and armored vehicles.

India remains the single largest consumer of Israeli defense goods, and China is one of Israel's principal trading partners, with bilateral trade between the two countries reaching US$6.7 billion in 2010. In light of these economic developments and trends between the two countries, China was defined by the Israeli Ministry of Industry, Trade, and Labor as an "Israeli Export Target Country." The main goal of this program is to encourage Israeli exports to China, especially in the fields of telecommunication and high-tech, agro-technology, security, environment, and infrastructures.

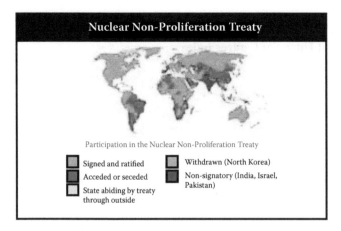

**FIGURE 1.1** **(See color insert.)** Nuclear Non-Proliferation Treaty of Nation-States. From "Asia Pacific Ramifications of the Arab Spring & Israel National Security," 2011. *Australian Security Magazine*, October/November 2011. With permission.

Australian intelligence agencies have held fears of an Israeli military strike on Iran for some time and that this action may trigger a nuclear war. Secret cables from the U.S. embassy in Canberra, provided to Australian media by WikiLeaks in 2010, revealed that Australian officials have previously raised the issue with their allies on several occasions. "The AIC's [Australian intelligence community's] leading concerns with respect to Iran's nuclear ambitions centre on understanding the timeframe of a possible weapons capability, and working with the United States to prevent Israel from independently launching uncoordinated military strikes against Iran," an embassy official in Canberra wrote to Washington in March 2009. "They are immediately concerned that Iran's pursuit of nuclear capabilities would lead to a conventional war—or even nuclear exchange—in the Middle East involving the United States that would draw Australia into a conflict."

Another cable sent four months earlier reported on Australia's concerns about a unilateral Israeli military strike against Iran and "the likelihood of an Israeli strike against Iranian nuclear facilities." Indeed, should such a nuclear exchange ever result in the Middle East, the profile of nuclear capabilities within the Asia Pacific, in particular those of India, Pakistan, and North Korea, will have a major influence on the region's risk, stability, and trade relations.

## ASIA-PACIFIC FINANCIAL CENTERS

The Global Financial Centres Index (GFCI), in its ninth edition in 2011 (Long Finance 2011), provided profiles, ratings, and rankings for 75 financial centers, drawing on two separate sources of data, namely instrumental factors (external indices) and responses to an online survey. The GFCI was first produced by Z/Yen Group in March 2007 and has subsequently been updated every six months. Successive growth in the number of respondents and data has enabled the study to highlight

**TABLE 1.1**

**The Global Financial Centres Index**

| Financial Center | GFCI 5 Rank | Changes in Bank since GFCI 4 | GFCI 5 Rating | Changes in Rating since GFCI 4 |
|---|---|---|---|---|
| London | 1 | → 0 | 781 | ↓ −10 |
| New York | 2 | → 0 | 768 | ↓ −6 |
| Singapore | 3 | → 0 | 687 | ↓ −14 |
| Hong Kong | 4 | → 0 | 684 | ↓ −16 |
| Zurich | 5 | → 0 | 659 | ↓ −17 |
| Geneva | 6 | → 0 | 638 | ↓ −7 |
| Chicago | 7 | ↑ 1 | 633 | ↓ −3 |
| Frankfurt | 8 | ↑ 1 | 618 | ↓ −3 |
| Boston | 9 | ↑ 2 | 618 | ↓ −7 |
| Dublin | 10 | ↑ 3 | 615 | ↓ −4 |
| Toronto | 11 | ↑ 1 | 615 | ↓ −9 |
| Guernsey | 12 | ↑ 4 | 613 | ↓ −7 |
| Jersey | 13 | ↑ 1 | 612 | ↓ −9 |
| Luxembourg | 14 | ↑ 1 | 611 | ↓ −10 |
| Tokyo | 15 | ↓ −8 | 610 | ↓ −31 |
| Sydney | 16 | ↓ −6 | 609 | ↓ −20 |
| San Francisco | 17 | → 0 | 601 | ↓ −11 |
| Isle of Man | 18 | ↑ 1 | 600 | ↓ −10 |
| Paris | 19 | ↑ 1 | 600 | ↓ −7 |
| Edinburgh | 20 | ↓ −2 | 596 | ↓ −14 |

*Note:* From Long Finance, 2011. With permission from Z/Yen.

the changing priorities and concerns of financial professionals over this time, in particular since the 2007 to 2008 financial crises.

Research indicates that many factors combine to make a financial center competitive. These factors can be grouped into five overarching "areas of competitiveness," such as people, business environment, infrastructure, market access, and general competitiveness. Evidence of a center's performance in these areas is drawn from a range of external measures. For example, evidence about a fair and just business environment is drawn from a corruption perception index and an opacity index.

In the Asia Pacific, there are a number of regional financial centers (Table 1.1) that aspire to be leading global centers. These include Singapore, Tokyo, and Hong Kong as the top three regional centers, but also Shanghai and Beijing. There is no consensus on which is the dominant regional center or whether a new global center will emerge. It may well be that there will continue to be a number of national centers with no one center emerging as a new global power.

There is some expectation that Shanghai and Beijing may well replace Singapore and Tokyo in importance within the next few years. Some expect Hong Kong to become relatively less important as more Chinese business is carried out directly in Shanghai or Beijing. The question remains as to whether there is a need for a Chinese "offshore center" in Hong Kong or (possibly) Singapore. Tokyo is seen as unlikely to become more important because of poor regulation and too much bureaucracy. Some believe that the future in Asia Pacific lies within China and that Shanghai will emerge as a new global financial center within the next 10 to 15 years. They argue that the sheer volume of capital that will pass through China will ensure this outcome.

A major determinant of what happens in the region is the political will of the Chinese government and what is allowed to happen within China. This somewhat "China-centric" view of Asia does not take account of India. The overall consensus seems to be that India will remain an inexpensive back office and IT center, and will develop its own national financial center, but this will not challenge the existing global financial centers. However, India should not be dismissed in such an arbitrary way due to its population size and social drive.

During the last decade, a large number of U.S. and European corporations have been systematically moving their back offices to cheaper places in the world, in particular Asia, while retaining their business people and senior management in the global centers of London and New York. The trend of outsourcing operations to India has been encouraged by a Security Exchange Commission (SEC) requirement that each major U.S. financial institution needs to have dual processing centers, in locations that are remote from each other. It is almost inevitable that the secondary, remote location should be a low-cost area, which for the majority of companies currently means India.

The 2011 GFCI (Table 1.2) indicated that Asia continued to exhibit enhanced competitiveness with 8 centers in the top 20 (against 6 North American centers and 5 European ones). In the 2007 GFCI there were just 3 Asian centers in the top 20. Seoul was the largest riser moving into 16th place, up 25 points in the ratings. Asia continues to feature very strongly and many expect to observe the most significant improvements in performance. Asian financial centers continue to perform well, and of the financial centers that are most likely to become more significant in the next few years, the top five mentioned were all Asian, namely Shanghai, Singapore, Seoul, Hong Kong, and Beijing (Table 1.3). Asian cities also filled the top six places when financial institutions indicated where their organizations are most likely to open new offices.

The U.S. dollar is likely to lose its reserve status. China and India will increasingly become the economic center of the world. Western military, financial, and cultural influence will go into relative decline. Developing economies will outperform large, developed ones and investment flows will adjust accordingly. The trend, already discernible, will gather momentum and it will challenge our beliefs and assail our comfort zones.

## ASIA-PACIFIC REGIONAL CENTERS

The Asia-Pacific region is made of a diverse group of nation-states with differing worldviews, cultures, and ways of business. Nevertheless, such uniqueness makes

**TABLE 1.2**
**Global Financial Centres Index World Rankings**

| | GFCI 9 Rank | GFCI 9 Rating | GFCI 8 Rank | GFCI 8 Rating | Change in Rank | Change in Rating |
|---|---|---|---|---|---|---|
| London | 1 | 775 | 1 | 772 | — | — |
| New York | 2 | 769 | 2 | 720 | — | ↑ 1 |
| Hong Kong | 3 | 759 | 3 | 760 | — | ↓ 1 |
| Singapore | 4 | 722 | 4 | 728 | — | ↓ 6 |
| Shanghai | =5 | 694 | 6 | 693 | ↑ 1 | ↑ 1 |
| Tokyo | =5 | 694 | 5 | 697 | — | ↓ 3 |
| Chicago | 7 | 673 | 7 | 678 | — | ↓ 5 |
| Zurich | 8 | 665 | 8 | 669 | — | ↓ 4 |
| Geneva | 9 | 659 | 9 | 661 | — | ↓ 2 |
| Sydney | =10 | 658 | 10 | 660 | — | ↓ 2 |
| Toronto | =10 | 658 | 12 | 656 | ↑ 2 | ↑ 2 |
| Boston | 12 | 656 | 13 | 655 | ↑ 1 | ↑ 1 |
| San Francisco | 13 | 655 | =14 | 654 | ↑ 1 | ↑ 1 |
| Frankfurt | 14 | 654 | 11 | 659 | ↓ 3 | ↓ 5 |
| Shenzhen | 15 | 653 | =14 | 654 | ↓ 1 | ↓ 1 |
| Seoul | 16 | 651 | 24 | 626 | ↑ 8 | ↑ 25 |
| Beijing | =17 | 650 | 16 | 653 | ↓ 1 | ↓ 3 |
| Washington | =17 | 650 | 17 | 649 | — | ↑ 1 |
| Taipei | 19 | 639 | 19 | 639 | — | 0 |
| Paris | 20 | 637 | 18 | 645 | ↓ 2 | ↓ 8 |

*Note:* From Long Finance, 2011. With permission from Z/Yen.

Asia Pacific what it is and will become, and why it is so difficult to operate across the broader region. For example, Australia is perhaps the most Westernized, being English speaking and with a large white British emigrant group. However, Singapore is also English speaking, but with a strong Asian culture and business approach. Operating in either country requires local understanding of social, cultural, business, and governance etiquette and requirements. Such issues are amplified when moving into non-English-speaking and far less Westernized nation-states.

## Australia: A Critical U.S. and UK Ally

Of the most Westernized countries in the region, Australia, a devout U.S. ally, has a significant role to play in leading the way with security and corporate governance standards, as it has previously done in the regulatory and monetary systems in many parts of Asia. The Singapore and Hong Kong regulators, in particular, have been publicly advocating improved corporate governance at board level. Notably, they are insisting on a move away from nepotism and interrelated multiple directorships, as well as limiting director tenures. Australia is still viewed in Asia as the leader in

**TABLE 1.3**
**Global Financial Centres Index—Leading Asian Centers**

|  | GFCI 9 Rank | GFCI Rating | GFCI 8 Rank | GFCI 8 Rating | Change in Rank | Change in Ranking |
|---|---|---|---|---|---|---|
| Hong Kong | 3 | 759 | 3 | 760 | — | ↑ 1 |
| Singapore | 4 | 722 | 4 | 728 | — | ↓ 6 |
| Shanghai | =5 | 694 | 6 | 693 | ↑ 1 | ↑ 1 |
| Tokyo | =5 | 694 | 5 | 697 | — | ↓ 3 |
| Shenzhen | 15 | 653 | =14 | 654 | ↓ 1 | ↓ 1 |
| Seoul | 16 | 651 | 24 | 626 | ↑ 8 | ↑ 25 |
| Beijing | =17 | 650 | 16 | 653 | ↓ 1 | ↓ 3 |
| Taipei | 19 | 639 | 19 | 639 | — | — |
| Osaka | 31 | 594 | 30 | 601 | ↓ 1 | ↓ 7 |
| Kuala Lumpur | 45 | 573 | 48 | 569 | ↑ 3 | ↑ 4 |
| Mumbai | 58 | 541 | 57 | 550 | ↓ 1 | ↓ 9 |
| Bangkok | 61 | 536 | 60 | 537 | ↓ 1 | ↓ 1 |
| Jakarta | 63 | 532 | =62 | 534 | ↓ 1 | ↓ 2 |
| Manila | 66 | 519 | 66 | 523 | — | ↓ 4 |

*Note:* From Long Finance, 2011. With permission from Z/Yen.

corporate governance and a number of international standards, with ISO 31000 Risk Management notably based on the Australian Standard 4360, originating in 1994.

Australia, currently one of the world's most economically resilient countries, provides political stability in the region and a competitive—but heavily regulated—business environment. The Australian state of New South Wales provides one-third of Australia's GDP, with an economy larger than Hong Kong SAR, Malaysia, or Singapore. Sydney's market trades ahead of Tokyo, Hong Kong, and Singapore. For example, in 2011 the Australian and Singaporean stock exchanges' AU$8.4 billion proposal to merge was rejected by the Australian federal treasurer, Mr. Wayne Swan, citing that "the merger was not in the nation's interest, and the ASX would effectively be a subsidiary to the SGX."

In 2011, Western Australia became the first Australian state to sign an agreement with the National Development and Reform Commission (NDRC) for the People's Republic of China. The NDRC oversees restructuring of China's economy, formulates economic policy, including China's approach to key overseas investment markets, and approves major infrastructure projects. The NDRC reports directly to China's highest executive body, the States Council of the People's Republic of China. This agreement makes the establishment of a China–Western Australia investment facilitation working group a key plank for sustained economic activity in Western Australia and the whole of Australia.

Australia ranks first in the Asia-Pacific region for labor, agricultural, and industrial productivity per person employed, according to the IMD *World Competitiveness*

*Yearbook.* The 2006 OECD Economic Survey noted that living standards in Australia surpass those of all Group of Eight countries except the United States. In 2008, the education system was ranked second to Singapore in the Asia Pacific for meeting the needs of a competitive economy.

Nevertheless, some parts of Australia have suffered. For example, Sydney performed poorly in the GFCI 5 and declined six places from 10th to 16th. Examining the center's score among instrumental factors, the cost of living index rose by almost twice the average and there was also a significant change in the level of both share and bond trading. This change was accompanied by a large fall in the capitalization of its stock exchange.

## Singapore and Hong Kong Remain Key Finance Centers

Singapore is ranked over Hong Kong as a financial center and remains a solid economy with continuing high performance in all industry sector subindices and in all areas of competitiveness. Hong Kong is in third or fourth place in all industry sector subindices, except insurance, and in all areas of competitiveness. With only a few exceptions, most Asian banks continue to be able to finance loans with deposits, insulating Hong Kong from some of the direct impact of the past decade of financial crisis. However, as discussed, the importance and relevance of Hong Kong as an access point to the world's largest market could reduce over time. Some expect Hong Kong to become relatively less important as more Chinese business is carried out directly in Shanghai or Beijing. What remains to be determined is whether there is a need for a Chinese "offshore center" in Hong Kong.

## Tokyo: Westernized, but Falling

Tokyo is now outside the top 10 global financial centers (GFCs) for the first time. Japan's banks suffered less from toxic debt problems than many of the other leading centers in the GFCI; nevertheless, Tokyo's decline is caused by more complex macroeconomic issues. In recent years, Japan's high export-driven income, in particular in the electronic, technology, and automotive sectors, has made it vulnerable to the global economic slowdown, as consumers reduce spending. Instrumental factors in the GFCI model indicate that consumer confidence has dropped and the Nikkei's 225-share average has reached a 26-year low. The Bank of Japan has cut interest rates from 0.5 percent to 0.3 percent and announced a fiscal stimulus package of approximately 1.4 percent of GDP. There is also a large rise in corporate and personal tax rates.

Tokyo suffers from negative perceptions among European, UK, and off-shore financial people, although Tokyo is perceived positively in North America, and very strongly in Asia. Many complain about restrictions, both legal and cultural, on access to international staff. As one New York-based banker stated, "Cultural acceptance of foreigners is very important to the ease of doing business in a country. Tokyo fares poorly in this regard."

The global financial turmoil raises a question about the global acceptance of the "Western" model of finance. It is apparent that Asian governments and businesses have vested interests in global financial recovery (particularly since much of their GDP is export driven). These governments have an opportunity to compete more strongly with established centers. GFCI respondents reinforced the potential in their positions. As a Sydney-based financial services consultant put it, "Hong Kong is best on the range of services available, quality of service, and tax; Singapore is also improving; London is falling in competitiveness."

### CHINA: EMERGENCE OF BEIJING AND SHANGHAI

Among the Asia-Pacific region in the context of global financial markets, Shanghai and Singapore are in second and third places, respectively, in terms of likelihood of becoming more significant over the coming years. As one Geneva-based GFCI practitioner stated, the "development of financial centres in Middle East and Asia should not be underestimated by policy makers in the West" (Centre for the Study of Financial Innovation 2003).

The Corporation of London (CoL) examined views about whether the two GFCs of London and New York were all that the world economy needed or whether there was scope for a new, third GFC. Paris and Frankfurt were important regional financial centers, with a number of other cities being successful in individual subsectors of the industry. Views on a third GFC were split, but most foresaw that if a third one did develop it is most likely to be Shanghai. It is unlikely that Hong Kong, Singapore, or Tokyo would become more than large regional financial centers (Centre for the Study of Financial Innovation 2003). Shanghai will become more significant over the next decade, without doubt topping the other current centers to be the leading Asia-Pacific center.

Nevertheless, many parts of the Asia-Pacific do have concerns with the Chinese government's method of business. For example, the *Straits Times* (December 9, 2011, C16) reported a case where a private company developed and patented an advanced nylon ingredient for use in lubrication, diabetes drugs, and many other twenty-first-century processes. Backers had provided US$120 million and could have gained a significant return on their investment; however, the Chinese government provided a US$300 million loan to a past employee to open a own state-owned facility. The issue is currently in the courts, but it is suggested that the government-owned facility is replicating the original formula. Many suggest that this follows a disturbing pattern of state control and intervention of private (and overseas-funded) companies.

## ASIA-PACIFIC CITIES

Financial centers have existed throughout history from ancient, nearly legendary, entrepôts such as Babylon, Samarkand, Constantinople, Marrakech, and Timbuktu to London, New York, Paris, Tokyo, and Shanghai. It is difficult to determine what is the appropriate "unit of analysis" for financial centers and how this relates to corporate activity. As a guide, there should be an examination of the financial centers at the level of the culture (Anglo-Saxon, Han Chinese, Continental European, or Arab), or the nation-state level (United States, UK, Germany, or Japan), or at a regional level (Far East, Near East, South East, Europe, North America). One of the more interesting observations has been that cities rather than nation-states are the drivers

**TABLE 1.4**
**World Cities Rankings**

| Points | World Cities | | | | | | |
|---|---|---|---|---|---|---|---|
| | **Alpha World Cities** | | | | | | |
| 12 | London | New York | Paris | *Tokyo* | | | |
| 10 | Chicago | Frankfurt | *Hong Kong* | Milan | Los Angeles | *Singapore* | |
| | **Beta World Cities** | | | | | | |
| 9 | San Francisco | *Sydney* | Toronto | Zurich | | | |
| 8 | Brussels | Madrid | Mexico City | Sao Paulo | | | |
| 7 | Moscow | *Seoul* | | | | | |
| | **Gamma World Cities** | | | | | | |
| 6 | Amsterdam | Boston | Dallas | Dusseldorf | Geneva | Houston | *Jakarta* |
| 6 | Johannesburg | *Melbourne* | Osaka | Prague | Santiago | *Taipei* | Washington |
| 5 | *Bangkok* | *Beijing* | Montréal | Rome | Stockholm | Warsaw | |
| 4 | Atlanta | Barcelona | Berlin | Buenos Aires | Budapest | Copenhagen | Hamburg |
| 4 | Istanbul | *Kuala Lumpur* | *Manila* | Miami | Minneapolis | Munich | Shanghai |

*Note:* Asia Pacific cities are in italics. From Beaverstock, J. V., Smith, R. G., and Taylor, P. J., Taylor, *Cities* 16, 6, 1999. With permission.

of economies. Cities are where people live and trade. A city is a unique combination of residential, industrial, business, and administrative activity, closely tied with its governing and policy-making bodies.

In 2003, the CoL conducted a study to analyze the opinions of nearly 400 financial services people on financial centers. The Asia-Pacific's defined "global" cities included Bangkok, Beijing, Hong Kong, Mumbai, Seoul, Shanghai, Singapore, Sydney, and Tokyo. The CoL study took the unit of analysis for a financial center to be the "city." The Globalization and World Cities Study Group and Network at Loughborough University published an interesting research bulletin that ranked cities by importance, of which just over a quarter were in the Asia-Pacific region (Table 1.4).

## LEGAL ISSUES AND REGULATORY STRUCTURES IN THE ASIA-PACIFIC REGION

Diverse legal and market variance exists with regulations, taxation, and governance the most significant factors affecting performance in the middle-income economies of the Asia Pacific. For low-income economies, the availability of adequate or reliable critical infrastructure is significant. For example, uninterrupted electricity supplies, road, rail, shipping, and access to finance are the top reported constraints. These factors can have significant impact on corporate supply chains and subject business operations to localized civil disorder. Higher-income economies report much lower levels of constraints overall, although the regulatory framework seems to be the most binding.

There is great variation in enforcement regimes across and within individual Asia-Pacific countries, which translates into sizeable differences in economic outcomes, business practices, and related security risk requirements.

## BRIBERY AND CORRUPTION IN THE ASIA PACIFIC

Transparency International, a nongovernmental organization (NGO) that monitors and publicizes corporate and political corruption in international development, publishes an annual Corruption Perceptions Index (CPI). The CPI is a comparative listing of corruption worldwide that annually ranks nation-states by perceived levels of corruption, as determined by expert assessments and opinion surveys. The CPI generally defines corruption as "the misuse of public power for private benefit." As of 2010, the CPI ranked 178 nation-states "on a scale from 10 (very clean) to 0 (highly corrupt)" (Transparency International 2010).

Fewer than 25 Asia-Pacific nation-states (Figure 1.2) have a CPI rating of 5 or below with Afghanistan, Laos, Cambodia, and Papua New Guinea considered at high risk of corruption. New Zealand and Singapore rate equal first at 9.3, with Australia, Hong Kong, Japan, and Taiwan also rated positively.

The United Nations Convention against Corruption (UNCAC) is the first legally binding international anticorruption instrument. The UNCAC obliges its nation-states (Figure 1.3) to implement a wide and detailed range of anticorruption measures affecting their laws, institutions, and practices. These measures aim to promote prevention, criminalization, law enforcement, international cooperation, asset recovery, technical assistance and information exchange, as well as mechanisms for implementation.

The UNCAC adopted resolution 3/2 on the prevention of corruption, underscoring the role that the private sector needs to have in preventing and fighting corruption. The 10th principle adopted states that business should work against corruption in any form, including bribery and extortion. The role of the private sector in the fight against corruption is regarded as crucial.

A number of countries have also introduced respective anti-money laundering (AML) and proceeds of crime laws, and established Financial Transactions and Reports Analysis Centres (FinTRACs). AML legislation in the form of prevention of money laundering acts exists in India (2005) and Bangladesh (2002). The FinTRAC of Afghanistan (FinTRACA) was established in 2004 as a Financial Intelligence Unit (FIU). The main purpose of these laws is to protect the integrity of financial systems and to gain compliance with international treaties and conventions.

A joint publication by UNODC and PricewaterhouseCoopers, entitled *Anti-Corruption Policies and Measures of the Fortune Global 500* (UNODC 2009), outlined the following activities to be alert for:

- Types of payments that have become associated with money laundering, such as multiple money orders, travelers checks, or large amounts of cash

VERY CLEAN

9.0 - 10
8.0 - 8.9
7.0 - 7.9
6.0 - 6.9
5.0 - 5.9
4.0 - 4.9
3.0 - 3.9
2.0 - 2.9
1.0 - 1.9
0 - 0.9
No Data

HIGHLY CORRUPT

**FIGURE 1.2**   **(See color insert.)** Corruption Perceptions Index 2010 results. Transparency International, 2010. With permission.

- A customer or other third party who is reluctant to provide complete information, provides false or suspicious information, or is anxious to avoid reporting or record-keeping requirements
- Unusually favorable payment terms or unusual fund transfers to or from foreign countries unrelated to the transaction
- Structuring a transaction to avoid requirements, such as conducting multiple transactions below the reportable threshold amounts (UNODC 2009)

Recent legislation trends include the fact that Australian companies or individuals that bribe an official in a foreign country can be prosecuted under Australian law and the laws of foreign countries. Australian companies that register securities under U.S. law or, from July 1, 2011, carry on a business or part of a business in the United Kingdom (wherever it is incorporated or formed), have obligations under these and

FIGURE 1.3 **(See color insert.)** UNCAC signatories and ratification status—Asia Pacific. From UNDOC, November 2011. With permission.

Australia's foreign bribery laws. The six principles outlined in the act provide a sound risk management strategy framework with the following elements:

- Develop and implement clear bribery prevention policies and procedures.
- Develop and implement risk assessment procedures.
- Develop and implement due diligence procedures.
- Communicate and train individuals on the organization's bribery prevention policies and procedures.
- Monitor and review the policies and procedures and make improvements when necessary.

## OVERVIEW OF ILLICIT DRUGS IN THE ASIA PACIFIC

Often influenced or related in some way to trends in corruption and transnational organized crime is the illicit drug market involved, in the manufacture, distribution, and social use of illicit drugs. The Asia Pacific is a major supplier of illicit drugs to the world market, and trends in use (Figure 1.4) vary by country.

### Illicit Drug Use

Cannabis is the most widely consumed drug in Asia. Despite nation-state differences, overall cannabis use is rather low in Asia and below the global average. While cannabis resin is mostly used in Afghanistan, cannabis herb is mainly used in South and Southeast Asia. The second most widely consumed drug type in Asia is the

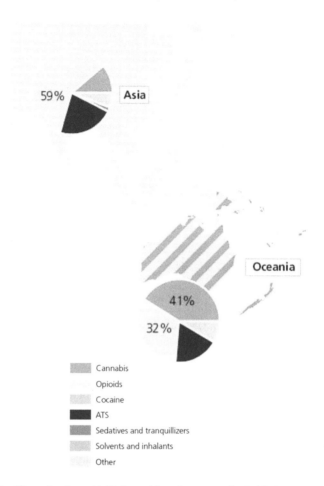

**FIGURE 1.4    (See color insert.)** Main problem drugs as reflected in treatment demand, by region, 2009. From UNODC, 2011. With permission.

amphetamines group, e.g., methamphetamine in East and Southeast Asia. Available information suggests that the use of amphetamines increased in recent years.

Asian countries reported mixed trends of ecstasy use with substances other than MDMA often sold as ecstasy in Asia. Significant amounts of ecstasy are still being smuggled into the Pacific region (notably Australia) from Europe and Southeast Asia, in addition to the domestic supply. It is estimated that more than half of the world's opiate-using population lives in Asia, with the highest estimates of opiate consumption found in the countries of Southwest Asia.

Cocaine use in Asia is still limited, though there are regular reports that organized crime groups are trying to develop the market, notably in some of the richer parts of Asia Pacific, where sufficient purchasing power exists. Due to the absence of regular prevalence studies for the majority of Asia-Pacific nation-states, information on nonmedical use of prescription drugs is scattered and limited. Available reports nonetheless indicate substantial nonmedicinal use of prescription opiates, tranquilizers, and amphetamines in many Asian Pacific states.

In Bangladesh, Nepal, and India, buprenorphine is commonly injected. In Southwest and Central Asia, among regular heroin users the nonmedical use of prescription opiates, barbiturates, and sedatives has been a commonly observed phenomenon. In Southeast Asia, along with the use of amphetamine-type stimulants (ATS), the nonmedical use of tranquilizers—especially benzodiazepines—is widely reported from various countries in the region, including Malaysia, Myanmar (formerly Burma), the Philippines, and Singapore. In the Republic of Korea and the Philippines, prescription opiates are the predominantly used opiates.

## Drug Production and Manufacture

The main illicit drug produced in Asia is opium with Afghanistan being the world's largest opium-producing country. Though the proportion of Asian opium production in the global total declined from 98 percent in 2007 to 87 percent in 2010, Asian opium continues to dominate the world opium market and thus also the world heroin market. While Afghan opium production declined over the 2007–10 period, production in Myanmar increased.

Cannabis production is widespread across Asia, including cannabis resin production in Afghanistan and its neighbors in Southwest Asia and Central Asia, and cannabis herb production in East and Southeast Asia, and South Asia. The preliminary UNODC/Government of Afghanistan cannabis survey found cannabis resin production of 1,200–3,700 mt (metric tonnes) in Afghanistan in 2010, and Afghanistan was worldwide the second most frequently mentioned source country for cannabis resin shipments after Morocco. Seizures of cannabis plants, an indirect indicator of cannabis eradication, were higher in Asia 2009 than in North America, Europe, or Oceania, with only South America showing higher figures.

Asia also plays a major role in the clandestine manufacture of ATS, notably methamphetamine. Methamphetamine manufacture is mainly concentrated in East and Southeast Asia, including the Philippines, China, Malaysia, and Myanmar. In addition, since 2009 the Islamic Republic of Iran appears to have emerged as a significant location for the clandestine manufacture of methamphetamine. Limited production of ecstasy also takes place in Asia, notably East and Southeast Asia, including Malaysia, China, and Indonesia. ATS production is mainly for consumption within the region.

## Drug Trafficking

Trafficking in Asia Pacific is dominated by opium and heroin (Figure 1.5), which are smuggled to final destinations within the region as well as to Europe (from Afghanistan) and China (from Myanmar), though some Afghan opiates also find their way to China (up to 30 percent of Chinese demand). Overall, Asian opium exports accounted for more than 99 percent of the world total. Similarly, morphine seizures made in Asia accounted for more than 99 percent of the world total. More than half of all heroin seizures (56 percent in 2009) were made by Asian countries. In line with the much larger opium production of Afghanistan compared to Myanmar, opiate seizures have been far larger for the countries surrounding

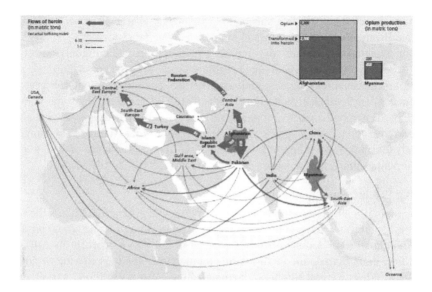

**FIGURE 1.5   (See color insert.)** Global heroin flows from Asian points of origin. From UNODC, *World Drug Report 2010.* With permission.

Afghanistan (notably the Islamic Republic of Iran and Pakistan) than for the countries surrounding Myanmar.

Cannabis herb seizures in Asia amounted to just 6 percent of the world total. In contrast, cannabis resin seizures accounted for 24 percent of the world total in 2009. Cannabis herb and resin seizures in Asia both showed upward trends over the 2005–9 period (60 percent and 30 percent, respectively). A breakdown shows that 98 percent of Asian cannabis resin seizures in 2009 took place in the Near and Middle East/Southwest Asia. Cannabis herb seizures, in contrast, occurred primarily in South Asia (53 percent of all Asian seizures) and in East and Southeast Asia (36 percent).

Cannabis production takes place in Australia, New Zealand, and most of the small island nation-states. Cannabis production is for local consumption and there is no information on exports to other regions. In addition, ATS production has started to gain prominence over the last decade, mainly methamphetamine and, to a lesser extent, ecstasy. In addition, some amphetamine is also produced. ATS production is concentrated in Australia and, to a lesser extent, New Zealand. The amounts of drugs seized in these countries tend to be very small by international standards. Seizures of cannabis herb continued to decline over the 2005–9 period and accounted for just 0.02 percent of the world total, far less than the share of the population of the Pacific region in the global total (0.5 percent). Such usage is surprising, as the Pacific has one of the world's highest cannabis use prevalence rates.

### Drug Law Enforcement Activity in the Asia Pacific
Asia Pacific has developed into a major production and trafficking hub for ATS, accounting for 64 percent of all such seizures worldwide in 2009. Amphetamine

seizures (mainly Captagon) happen primarily in the Near and Middle East, notably the Arabian peninsula, accounting for almost all Asian amphetamine seizures. Methamphetamine seizures, in contrast, affect primarily East and Southeast Asia (95 percent of all Asian methamphetamine seizures). Both amphetamine and methamphetamine seizures increased in Asia over the 2005–9 period (by 59 percent and 36 percent, respectively).

Ecstasy seizures, in contrast, declined over the 2005–9 period (down 58 percent), which is also in line with reports of improved ecstasy precursor controls. The importance of Asian ecstasy seizures in the global total (9 percent) is considered much lower than for the amphetamines.

A problem for states in East and Southeast Asia as well as South Asia is the increasing popularity of ketamine, a drug used mainly in veterinary medicine for its analgesic properties. It is not under international control and is sometimes sold as ecstasy or mixed with MDMA. Seizures of ketamine tripled over the 2005–9 period and in 2009 were some 20 times larger (in volume terms) than ecstasy seizures in Asia. Asia accounted for 99 percent of global ketamine seizures in 2009, with most of the ketamine produced in the region.

Cocaine seizures reported in Asia accounted for just 0.1 percent of the global total. Nonetheless, except for countries in Central Asia, all other subregions reported seizures of cocaine in recent years. Relative concentrations of cocaine trafficking seem to exist in East and Southeast Asia, as well as in the Near and Middle East.

## ASIA PACIFIC REGIONAL ORGANIZATIONS

There are a number of regional organizations that have formed within the Asia Pacific, based on both geographic and cultural alignment. Many of these organizations were formed to drive economic and political gain for their member nation-states. Of most prominence are the Asia Pacific Economic Cooperation (APEC), Association of Southeast Asian Nations (ASEAN), and Asia–Europe Meeting (ASEM).

### ASIA PACIFIC ECONOMIC COOPERATION (APEC)

APEC is the only intergovernmental grouping in the world operating on the basis of nonbinding commitments, open dialogue, and equal respect for the views of its participants, with no treaty obligations required of its participants. APEC is a primary forum for facilitating economic growth, cooperation, trade, and investment in the Asia-Pacific region. Decisions made within APEC are reached by consensus, and commitments are undertaken on a voluntary basis.

APEC nations represent approximately 54 percent of world GDP and about 44 percent of world trade. APEC's 21 member economies include Australia, Brunei Darussalam, Canada, Chile, People's Republic of China, Indonesia, Japan, Republic of Korea, Malaysia, Mexico, New Zealand, Papua New Guinea, Peru, the Republic of the Philippines, Russia, Singapore, Taipei, Thailand, the United States of America, and Vietnam.

One of APEC's key counterterrorism priorities is the Secure Trade in the APEC Region (STAR) initiative, which aims to secure and enhance the flow of goods and people through measures that protect cargo, ships, international aviation, and people in transit. The STAR programs are designed to include the private sector, in recognition of the fact that the engagement and active participation of business is fundamental to the success of APEC's secure-trade agenda. Annual APEC STAR conferences have been organized since 2003, bringing executives and government officials together to identify impediments to and solutions for promoting trade efficiency while ensuring security. A number of major counterterrorism initiatives related to secure trade, trade recovery, food defense, counterterrorism financing, aviation security, cyber security, and public–private partnerships were implemented in 2008.

In 2004, APEC members acknowledged that corruption poses a threat to governance and economic growth in the Asia Pacific. They agreed that APEC economies should nurture and sustain good governance, economic development, and prosperity by working together to fight corruption and ensure transparency. This focus resulted in the formation of the Anti-Corruption and Transparency Experts' Task Force, which considers that corruption is a major obstacle to social and economic development and increases the cost of doing business.

## ASSOCIATION OF SOUTHEAST ASIAN NATIONS (ASEAN)

Established in 1967, ASEAN aims to accelerate economic growth, social progress, and cultural development in the region and to promote regional peace and stability through the rule of law and adherence to the principles of a United Nations charter. The ASEAN Charter, which entered into force on December 15, 2008, provides a legal and institutional framework to support the realization of ASEAN's objectives, including regional integration.

ASEAN current membership (2010) comprises 10 nation-states, including Burma, Brunei Darussalam, Cambodia, Indonesia, Laos, Malaysia, Philippines, Singapore, Thailand, and Vietnam. In addition, ASEAN has 10 dialogue partners, which include Australia, Canada, China, the European Union, India, Japan, New Zealand, Republic of Korea, Russia, and the United States of America. The United Nations Development Program (UNDP) also has dialogue status.

The ASEAN Secretariat, based in Jakarta, Indonesia, coordinates, initiates, and implements ASEAN activities. The Secretariat is headed by the Secretary-General of ASEAN, who is appointed for a five-year term and accorded ministerial status. ASEAN has a core principle to develop a comprehensive approach to security (ASEAN Secretariat, 2004); however, this may be considered national or international security.

## ASIAN REGIONAL FORUM (ARF)

The ARF emphasizes the central role of ASEAN in regional security architecture, bringing together ASEAN members and facilitating dialogue between partners to discuss regional security issues and build mutual confidence.

## TABLE 1.5
## ASEM Nations-State Members

| Asia-Europe Meeting 2011 Member Nation-States | | | |
|---|---|---|---|
| Australia | European Community | Laos | Poland |
| Austria | Finland | Latvia | Portugal |
| ASEAN Secretariat | France | Lithuania | Romania |
| Belgium | Germany | Luxembourg | Russia |
| Brunei Darussalam | Greece | Malaysia | Singapore |
| Bulgaria | Hungary | Malta | Slovakia |
| Cambodia | Indonesia | Mongolia | Slovenia |
| China | India | Myanmar | Spain |
| Cyprus | Ireland | Netherlands | Sweden |
| Czech Republic | Italy | New Zealand | Thailand |
| Denmark | Japan | Pakistan | United Kingdom |
| Estonia | Korea | Philippines | Vietnam |

## ASIA–EUROPE MEETING (ASEM)

The ASEM is an informal process of dialogue and cooperation that brings together 27 European Union member states and the European Commission, with 19 Asian nation-states and the ASEAN Secretariat (Table 1.5). ASEM dialogue addresses political, economic, and cultural issues, with the objective of strengthening the relationship between the two regions, in a spirit of mutual respect and equal partnership.

The origins of the ASEM process developed out of the need for a mutual recognition, in both Asia and Europe, reflecting the new global context of the 1990s and the perspectives of the new century. In 1994, the European Commission had already published *Towards a New Strategy for Asia*, stressing the importance of modernizing Europe's relationship with Asia and reflecting its political, economic, and cultural significance. The Commission Communication of 2001, *Europe and Asia: A Strategic Framework for Enhanced Partnerships*, reaffirmed this objective (Asia-Europe Meeting n.d.).

## SOUTH ASIAN ASSOCIATION FOR REGIONAL COOPERATION (SAARC)

Founded in 1985, the SAARC is an organization of eight South Asian nation-states, namely Bangladesh, Bhutan, India, the Maldives, Nepal, Pakistan, Sri Lanka, and Afghanistan. The declaration reviews their commitment to alleviate poverty and reduce income inequalities within the societies and reaffirms their resolve to improve the quality of life and well-being of their people through people-centered sustainable development.

In the declaration, SAARC member states show their concerns about the continuing threat of terrorism in all its forms and manifestations, transnational organized crimes, especially illegal trafficking in narcotic drugs and psychotropic substances, trafficking in persons and small arms, and increased incidence of maritime piracy in the region; and reiterate their resolve to fight all such menaces. The declaration states that the nation-states are aware of the environmental degradation in the region and, in particular, the vulnerabilities of the region to the threat of climate change, and recognize the need to further strengthen the institutional mechanisms of SAARC in order to bolster and enhance regional cooperation.

Foreign ministers from SAARC member states have signed agreements on rapid response to natural disasters, a multilateral arrangement on recognition of conformity assessment, an implementation of regional standards, and a seed bank.

At the opening ceremony of the 2011 summit, Pakistani prime minister Yousuf Raza Gilani called for all SAARC nation-states to work together to eliminate terrorism. SAARC can also work together to promote culture and arts that can be used to promote tourism in the region.

Meanwhile, Indian prime minister Manmohan Singh pledged to promote fair trade in the region. He spoke positively of the progress made in SAARC, terming it as "impressive," and pointed out that many sectors including trade, transport, health, and education have benefited from it. "Our summit [2011] is taking place at a time when the West is having an economic crisis. In the meantime developing countries like ours will be squeezed for capital and markets and we should look for innovative solutions within South Asian region," he said.

Development within nation-states would attract foreign investors, and freeing of trade between SAARC members would create benefit for all nations. South Asia has been able to maintain a respectable growth rate, and this encouraging trend has resulted in the integration of SAARC and shows the region is on the right path (Xuequan 2011).

## OTHER FORUMS

There are other Asia Pacific forums, such as the East Asia–Latin American Forum (EALAF), which extends beyond Asia to include the Americas. Another is the East Asia Summit, which includes the United States, Russia, Singapore, India, Australia, Japan, China and South Korea.

## SECURITY ASSOCIATIONS IN THE ASIA PACIFIC

Industry associations that self-regulate their members may, to some degree, support industry professionalism (Penzarella and Cook 1998). As with the security industry itself, the security industry associations are fragmented and diverse, and generally represent only one or two sectors of the industry. The diversity of security associations may be demonstrated by the current active associations within the Asia-Pacific region. Such fragmentation increases the inability of associations to provide cohesion, leading to a lack of policy direction (Tate 1997). The drive of most security associations appears to be in the development and delivery of vocational training, rather than tertiary education (Manunta 1996).

According to Tate (1997), as an emerging industry, security has to establish an industry representative body to provide national policy and leadership. However, a review of Asia Pacific security associations shows that each nation-state has at least

## TABLE 1.6
## Asia Pacific Security Associations

**Example of Asia Pacific Security Associations**

| | |
|---|---|
| Australian Security Industry Association Ltd. | ASIS International |
| Risk Management Institution of Australasia | National Security Association Australasia |
| Asian Professional Security Association | China Security and Protection Association |
| Institute of Security Executives | Business Continuity Institute |
| Security Systems Association of Singapore | Transport Asset Protection Association |
| Australian Institute of Professional Intelligence Officers | Association of Certified Fraud Examiners |
| International Association of Bomb Technicians and Investigators | |

one or more industrial body representing narrow sectors of the security industry, with a linkage to their own representatives and training bodies. Consequently, this leads to opposing strategies and an inability to provide leadership, maintaining the disjointed nature of the security industry across the broader geopolitical Asia-Pacific region. This view was held by the National Academic Consortium for Homeland Security (n.d.), in the desire to promote the development of better-informed public policy and strategy regarding national security issues.

There are a number of security associations operating within the Asia-Pacific region (Table 1.6), although the list is far from comprehensive. These security associations are either directly or indirectly involved in the security industry. The listing demonstrates the diversity and breadth of the security industry. All security associations appeared to have one common goal, namely to promote improved standards and professionalism in the security industry. As security associations continue to develop and solidify, they will likely provide industrial cohesion, be instrumental in defining organizational security, and provide consensus in the presentation of a security body of knowledge.

## ASIS INTERNATIONAL

ASIS International was founded in 1955 and has an approximate membership of 35,000 and 205 chapters worldwide, with chapters in most major cities in the Asia Pacific. ASIS advocates the role and value of security management and its members to government, private organizations, media, and the public (ASIS International 2007). ASIS promotes and self-administers three certified programs in security, with the aim to "meet stringent, internationally accepted requirements for education, experience and examination" (ASIS International 2005, 6).

## ASIAN PROFESSIONAL SECURITY ASSOCIATION (APSA)

APSA has chapter associations in various nation-states such as Thailand, India, Philippines, Singapore, Malaysia, South Korea, Indonesia, China, and Hong

Kong. APSA's focus is the further development of the protection industry, and most important, its program for the benefit of safety and security sectors in Asia. The group purports to represent electronic security systems, physical security, and cash management elements of the security industry (Asian Professional Security Association n.d.).

### CHINA SECURITY AND PROTECTION INDUSTRY ASSOCIATION (CSPIA)

CSPIA's aim is to lead and support the Chinese electronic security and protection industry in the provision of security products and services. The association reports having "more than 4000 members who are responsible for more than 80 percent of China security business, including CCTV, access control, manned security, alarm, biometrics, physical security, video and audio intercom system" (CSPIA n.d.).

### SECURITY ASSOCIATION (SINGAPORE), SAS

The Private Investigation & Security Agency Act of 1973 was passed in the Singapore Parliament to regulate the security industry. To further regulate and to open dialogue with the government regulator, namely the Licensing Division, an association was formed in 1976, known as the Association of Licensed Security and Investigation Agencies (ALSIA). ALSIA constitutionally changed its name to the Security Association (Singapore), SAS. SAS members are from not only licensed security and private investigation agencies but also security, investigation, and safety professionals from other industries. To date, about 130 members form SAS and membership is growing (Security Association [Singapore] 2011).

### SECURITY SYSTEMS ASSOCIATION OF SINGAPORE (SSAS)

SSAS has 53 member companies, whose aim is to lead and support Singapore's electronic security industry.

### AUSTRALIAN SECURITY INDUSTRY ASSOCIATION LTD. (ASIAL)

ASIAL, founded in 1969, was formed by members of the industry in an attempt to "force shady operators out of the business" (Cowan 1999 1). In 1999, ASIAL had 2,500 corporate members (Cowan 1999) representing approximately 85 percent of the Australia security industry (ASIAL 2007), although this takes into account only the electronic installers and monitoring sectors.

### TRANSPORT ASSET PROTECTION ASSOCIATION (TAPA)

TAPA is an association of security personnel who focus on the threats surrounding the transportation of high-value electronic assets.

## Risk Management Institute of Australasia (RMIA)

RMIA, although not a specific security industry association, does actively promote cooperation between disciplines such as safety, health, education, fire, finance, security, and other industries (Risk Management Institute of Australasia 2007a). RMIA involvement in security is demonstrated through its development of the Security Risk Management Body of Knowledge document (Risk Management Institute of Australasia 2007b).

## Hong Kong Security and Guarding Services Industry Authority

The authority was established in 1995 under the Security and Guarding Services Ordinance (SGSO), Chapter 460, to administer a licensing scheme to regulate the security industry (Security Bureau 2010).

## Hong Kong Security Association (HKSA)

The Hong Kong Security Association (HKSA), founded in 1984, is the only Association of companies holding security licenses issued by the Security and Guarding Services Industry Authority. Our member companies are principally engaged in providing a variety of security services:

- Guarding services-commercial and residential
- Cash transport services by armoured vehicle
- Installation and maintenance of alarm systems and equipment
- Remote monitoring of alarms, fire alarm and CCTV systems
- Supply of security systems and products
- Investigation and security consultancy services

## Australian Institute of Professional Intelligence Officers (AIPIO)

AIPIO was founded in 1990 primarily for intelligence professionals. Its charter is to foster professionalism, and it comprises approximately 150 members. AIPIO holds an annual intelligence conference and publishes a related journal three times a year (Australian Institute of Professional Intelligence Officers 2006).

## CONCLUSION

As we have discussed, the Asia-Pacific region has great diversity, which leads to national and international security concerns in some of its nation-states. For example, issues of emancipation within Aceh and Papua have been a cause for concern for Indonesian security planners, as both have substantial secessionist activity (Aspinall and Chauvel 2007). China continues to have issues with Tibet. Furthermore, regional conflicts or strained relations between regional nation-states include those between South and North Korea, and between Pakistan and India, and over areas that have natural resources such as the Spratly Islands.

Many more of these security issues are expanded in subsequent chapters, such as the internal threats of corruption, fraud, crime, and misconduct, and the external threats, which include terrorism and politically motivated violence, kidnapping and extortion, civil unrest, regional conflict, organized transnational crime, and natural disasters and catastrophic incidents, just to name a few. In addition, an in-country synopsis in Chapter 9 provides an introduction to regional nation-states, supported with a summary of government structure, political nature and foreign affairs, geographical and economy details, concluding with local security issues.

## REFERENCES

Asia-Europe Meeting. n.d. "About ASEM." http://www.aseminfoboard.org/page. phtml?code=About (accessed October 26, 2011).
"Asia Pacific Ramifications of the Arab Spring & Israel National Security." 2011. *Australian Security Magazine*, October/November 12.
ASIAL. 2007. "Who Does ASIAL Represent." http://www.asial.com.au/about%20asial/ who+does+asial+represent (accessed June 25, 2007).
Asian Professional Security Association. n.d. "Welcome to APSA." http://www.apsa-india. org/ (accessed October 27, 2011).
ASIS International. 2005. *Career Opportunities in Security*. Alexandria, VA: ASIS International.
———. 2007. "History of ASIS." http://www.asisonline.org/about/history/index.xml (accessed June 25, 2007).
———. 2011. *The Tyranny of Events*. Alexandria, VA: ASIS International.
Aspinall, E., and R. Chauvel. 2007. "Constructing Separatist Threats: Security and Insecurity in Indonesion Aceh and Papua." In *Critical Security in Asia-Pacific*, edited by A. Burke and M. McDonald, 89–104. Manchester: Manchester University Press.
Australian Institute of Professional Intelligence Officers. 2006. "Australian Institute of Professional Intelligence Officers: About AIPIO." http://www.aipio.asn.au/about.html (accessed June 25, 2007).
Beaverstock, J. V., R. G. Smith, and P. J. Taylor. 1999. "A Roster of World Cities." *Cities* 16 (6): 445–58.
Campbell, A. 2011. "New Horizons in Iran-Pakistan Relations." Future Directions International. http://futuredirections.org.au/publications/indian-ocean/29-indian-ocean-swa/279-new-horizons-in-iran-pakistan-relations.html (accessed October 26, 2011).
Centre for the Study of Financial Innovation. 2003. "Sizing Up the City—London's Ranking as a Financial Centre." London: Corporation of London.
Cowan, R. 1999. *30 Years of Building an Industry and an Association*. Crows Nest, NSW: ASIAL.
CSPIA. n.d. About CSPIA. Retrieved April 15, 2012 from http://english.21csp.com.cn/article/ article_7793.html.
Gilson, J. 2007. "Regionalism and Security in East Asia." In *Critical Security in the Asia-Pacific*, edited by A. Burke and M. McDonald, pp. 56–71. Manchester: Manchester University Press.
"How to Gracefully Step Aside." 2011. *The Economist*, January 11. http://www.economist. com/node/21014562.
Long Finance. 2011. *The Global Financial Centres Index 9*. Financial Centre Futures. London: Z/Yen Group Limited.
Manunta, G. 1996. "The Case Against: Private Security Is Not a Profession." *International Journal of Risk, Security and Crime Prevention* 1 (3): 233–40.

National Academic Consortium for Homeland Security. n.d. http://homelandsecurity.osu.edu/NACHS/index.html (accessed January 18, 2006).

Newman, R. (2011). *4 Reasons To Cheer When China Overtakes America*. Retrieved May 5, 2012, from http://money.usnews.com/money/blogs/flowchart/2011/04/28/4-reasons-to-cheer-when-china-overtakes-america

Penzarella, R., and W. Cook. 1998. "Security Ethics Training: From Ethical Neutrality to Judgment." *Security Journal* 10 (1): 9–15.

"Philippines Stirs Waters of the Spratlys." 2011. *Straits Times*, March 31.

Risk Management Institute of Australasia. 2007a. "Mission of RMIA." http://rmia.org.au/aboutRMIA/Mission/tabid/210/Default.aspx (accessed June 25, 2007).

———. 2007b. "Security Risk Management Body of Knowledge." http://www.securityprofessionals.org.au/2007SRMBOK.htm (accessed January 24, 2007).

Security Association (Singapore). 2011. "About SAS." http://www.sas.org.sg/ (accessed October 27, 2011).

Security Bureau. 2010. "Security and Guarding Services Industry Authority." http://www.sb.gov.hk/eng/links/sgsia/scl.htm#type (accessed October 29, 2011).

Smith, S. 2009. "Nation Perfectly Positioned as the Asia-Pacific Takes Centre Stage." *The Australian*, November, 7–8.

Tate, P. W. 1997. *Report on the Security Industry Training: Case Study of an Emerging Industry*. Perth: Western Australian Department of Training, Western Australian Government Publications.

Tow, T. W. 2001. *Asia Pacfic Strategies: Seeking Convergence Security*. Singapore: Green Giant Press.

Transparency International. 2010. Corruption Perceptions Index 2010. Berlin: Transparency International.

UNODC. 2009. "Anti-Corruption Policies and Measures of the Fortune Global 500." http://www.unodc.org/unodc/en/frontpage/2009/September/how-companies-are-dealing-with-corruption.html (accessed January 17, 2012).

———. 2011a. Official UNCAC Status Ratification Map. Corruption and Economic Crime Branch. http://www.unodc.org/images/treaties/UNCAC/Status-Map/UNCAC_Status_Map_Current_Large.jpg (accessed January 17, 2012).

———. 2010b. UNODC. 2010. *World Drug Report 201D*. United Nations Office on Drugs and Crime. Vienna: United Nations.

Xuequan, Mu. 2011. "17th SAARC Summit Reaches Fruitful Decisions: Maldivian President." http://news.xinhuanet.com/english2010/world/2011-11/11/c_122269087.htm (accessed January 17, 2012).

# 2 Corporate Security

## INTRODUCTION

Corporate security is often a neglected management function; nevertheless, the need for directors and executives to have an understanding of their corporation's risk is becoming more prominent. For example, in Australia it is a director's responsibility to ensure that the organization has and maintains risk management. Factors such as managing a crisis now require senior corporate executives' involvement that demonstrates appropriate action with ever-decreasing margins for error. Therefore security has to be acknowledged by senior executives and requires professional, effective, and informed advice.

This chapter introduces corporate security at the company director level, with considerations of how security may support or impede Asia Pacific companies. This leads to the role of directors with security in the boardroom, considering such things as duties, responsibilities, regulatory issues, and ethics relevant to the organization's executive level. An issue that should be considered is the position of the security leader, often a manager with limited sway in the greater corporation ladder. There are clear skills that an effective security manager requires to ensure security leadership. Finally, communicating risk to senior executives and where security should be positioned in the organization conclude this chapter.

## PREVENTING BURSTING BUBBLES AND LEAKY BOATS

Shakespeare described a "bubble reputation," and contemporary illustrations are applied to the notion of a financial bubble, perfectly formed and free of gravitational market forces. But the implication of course is that there can be a day of reckoning, a time when it can grow too large to hold its shape, leaving it to implode with spectacular and significant consequences. An alternative notion is that of a ship slowly taking on water through a leak, which ultimately results in the ship's demise. In business, how does the bubble come to burst and where are the leaks most likely to occur?

Australian social commentator Hugh Mackay wrote about the moral maze people find themselves in and how they seem capable of behaving quite differently at work from the way they behave with their families and friends. Humans behave in a variety of ways and are strongly influenced by their environment, with a significant portion of their day being within the workplace. Many people are prone to recurrent stealing, lying, or cheating, and may suffer from intense fantasies, beliefs, sexual urges, or behaviors involving deceitful, sexual, or violent activity, while externally to others they appear to be upstanding and functional members of society. In particular, violence and fraud in the workplace are rarely impulsive and are typically the end result of an understandable and discernible process of thinking and behavior.

A CEO once described how when his business was small he could walk around the office and would know every employee by name and nature, but after a period of rapid growth in the business he was suddenly surrounded by five times the number of staff and it was not possible to get to know them all, let alone remember their names. Security risk management should consider the number of people employed and contrast that number with existing crime statistics to enhance awareness of the possibility of a variety of risks, including theft, fraud, damage, drug use, safety breach, misconduct, negligent act, policy breach, poor productivity, and poor morale. Having just 1 employee among 1,000 employees, or 0.01 percent, exhibiting inappropriate behavior will change the relevant risk ratio, meaning the possibility of a risk-related incident occurring and having a negative impact increases dramatically. A person's profile and daily behavior can impact in any one or more of the risks discussed, and the consequences range from minor irritating issues to fatal events, sometimes after warning signs were ignored. Accepting that one or more of these risks can and will occur at any time makes planning more focused and responses more appropriate and effective.

In Australia, for example, nearly one in two businesses reports suffering from some form of economic crime, namely theft, fraud, corruption, and bribery. Crime-related statistics demonstrate that many people are open to temptation, moral blindness, and indulgence. They are prone to making a bad decision. How many of you would take the opportunity of stealing money with the knowledge that it will go undetected? Crime and misconduct statistics indicate that many will take the money.

Consider insider trading, which has varying degrees of legislation across the Asia Pacific to combat such crime. Some estimates are that 1 in every 100 share transactions is related to some kind of insider information. It is understood to be a commonly committed crime, yet convictions are rare, hence little to no deterrence resulting in widespread abuse. Other statistical examples include findings that as many as one in three resumes contains false or misleading information about academic qualifications and job experience, or omits vital personal information such as criminal convictions. However, your corporate headquarters will be held liable for such failure in detecting fraud, and some nation-states have tough legislation.

## PREVENTION RATHER THAN REACTION

So do companies plan and prepare sufficiently? Most often do not until an incident occurs, which has highlighted the importance and then urgency of such action. There are plenty of examples of how companies reacted poorly in a crisis. If implemented correctly, corporate security should be a business contributor. Otherwise there will be an "over" spend or "under" spend, where obvious vulnerabilities exist and measures are costing money but failing to mitigate risk. Such an approach takes significantly greater resources and often results in a piecemeal approach to security mitigation. Combining business strategy and security risk management principles provides a layered protection strategy, which efficiently shields critical business operations. This strategy includes monitoring key performance indicators such as results from audits and investigations, staff morale ratings, staff turnover, recruitment and induction processes, and results from testing crisis, recovery, and business continuity plans.

In many cases, it is likely to be imperative that directors and executive managers inform themselves of critical crisis issues and provide preemptive guidance to management to have business protection response and strategy in place, at best to support growth strategies. It has been consistently shown that in the overall majority of cases where companies react and recover well from a crisis, the business is actually enhanced and contributes to higher productivity and profit. The business can become more robust, morale is improved, and staff and management are wiser for the experience. In other words, your organization becomes more resilient and learns from the experience to end in a better position. Responsibility for missing such an opportunity, through insufficient planning, ultimately rests with the board and results in a greater and prolonged impact on reputation and recovery activities.

There has been strong and consistent growth in the security and risk management industries, particularly servicing medium-size, fast-growing, and regulated companies, which often have high staff turnover or second-tier businesses relying on critical infrastructure industries, such as maritime, transport, banking, finance, and telecommunications. Small to medium-size businesses make up the largest portion of business in most Asia-Pacific countries, and they face a plethora of risks such as business crime, fraud, fire, natural disaster, staff turnover, misconduct, workplace violence, power failures, property loss or damage, as well as reputation and legal risks. These risks need to be managed in accordance with a broad set of national and state legislation, standards, guides, and codes.

Being in a position to treat such a variety of risks involves the need to provide for all aspects of the business—everything from reviewing recruitment and induction to considering the need for armed robbery and customer aggression training, travel advisories, security awareness promotion, through to business continuity and crisis management planning. There is a range of risk and incident management software systems available, and investigation and audit services provide guidance and learning.

Business risk management, involving corporate security, will in most cases be enhanced by a motivated, loyal, and happy work culture that has pride in what it is doing and is well informed and aware. This culture reduces the likelihood of internal theft and misconduct, enhancing the chance that someone will report anything of such a nature. It includes the promotion of corporate social responsibility, fraud and crime prevention awareness, sound corporate governance, good ethics, and compliance with the law, regulations, and codes of conduct.

Combining a range of well-considered mitigation strategies, a business can significantly enhance asset protection and loss prevention, thereby contributing to the triple bottom line. Businesses will also better learn to identify, analyze, evaluate, and treat all risks, as well as comply with various codes of practice, such as for workplace violence. The "it won't happen to me" mentality is no longer satisfactory in the modern world and in today's business, and will ultimately lead to costly insurance, liability, and legal issues in the long term.

**Workplace Violence still a high risk, but awareness growing**: The recently released 2011 Workplace Violence Fact Sheet shows that workplace homicides are the third leading cause of death at workplaces. In the US, there is an average of 590 workplace homicides each year. Those numbers do not include attempted workplace murders or suicides that happen at work, said Barry Nixon, the executive director of the National Institute for the Prevention of Workplace Violence. Nixon added that the number of incidents of workplace violence appears to be on the decline, in-part to decisions by the government and a number of organisations to boost funding for security. In addition, Nixon noted that companies seem to be learning that preventing acts of workplace violence is better than simply reacting to such incidents, as more companies are developing preventative and proactive programs (Leischen 2011, *Security Director News*, cited in *Security Management Weekly*, April 29, 2011).

As an example, an armed robbery will cost a business in lost time, lost trading, staff compensation, or litigation and can also be fatal. Yet there remain many businesses that have not provided any training to staff in what they should do to enhance their safety during a robbery. The preferred view is that it is an investment in staff and demonstrates a duty of care. The difference between having trained staff, who respond positively and productively following a crisis event, such as an armed robbery, will save money and protect profits over the longer term. It is even better if you have other security strategies to minimize the likelihood of an event occurring in the first place.

There are crisis events and major incidents constantly occurring (see Chapters 6 and 7), from armed robbers holding guns to staff heads, to internal theft, fraud, and corruption, in both public and private sectors. It continues to take time, often not until an event occurs, for business managers and directors think about implementing an appropriate mitigation strategy. Such action is then often done without thought or precision and in a panic response, because "they did not think it would happen to them." Resources are then wasted on the incorrect risk treatment and overcompensation for the risk, and the possibility of the original risk event occurring again is left untreated. No advantage is gained and an opportunity is lost.

There are great results to be had by getting diverse opinions and examining case studies, which are similar to the relevant business. This approach allows directors and managers to better understand and appreciate the need the business has in order to better protect it and reduce surprise events or react better when they occur. The creation of new business protection ideas can improve productivity, reducing longer-term general security costs and enhancing its effectiveness. Striking the balance between under- and over-investment in security contributes to the bottom line, but few companies actually audit their security or consider a protective or defensive strategy. Such a strategy should accompany and support growth and expansive business plans. The aim of corporate security is to create the necessary balance for smoother sailing, being leak-free, and reacting well should the bubble burst in a surprise event that threatens business functions or objectives.

## SECURITY ISSUES IMPEDING CORPORATIONS, CEOS, AND DIRECTORS

Until the 1990s academic textbooks on business management gave little attention to the role of the board, there were no courses in business schools on corporate governance, and the first dedicated book on corporate governance, in Canada, was not published until 1992 (Hansell 2003, iii). Training courses concentrated on technical and managerial areas rather than on the duties of directors, and developments only began in the late 1980s (Bosch 1995, 7).

Attention on the duties of directors has been aided by progressive court judgments since the 1990s, which have interpreted director's duties more stringently, placing more onerous and exacting legal responsibilities on company directors. Court cases that have arisen include those dealing with health, safety, environmental protection, and now corporate manslaughter. Directors must identify the issues that need to be addressed by the board, and they must deal with their responsibilities and record their decisions clearly (Bosch 1995, 41). It is argued that directors "are obliged to decide issues by identifying the personal and derivative rights of corporate stakeholders, giving paramountcy to the derivative rights that equate to the ongoing health of the company as a viable concern" (Dang 2000, 188). There is an emphasis that the need for management and the board to achieve sound financial performance ranked within the practice of sound corporate governance. Institutional investors are unlikely to simply invest in a well-governed company if its financial performance is poor, and therefore the focus of such performance will be on short-term measures (Dunk and Kilgore 1998).

The two primary duties a director has to the company are a *fiduciary duty* and a *duty of care*, both powerful legal concepts. Courts are likely to deal harshly with directors who act contrary to one or both of these duties, but will show restraint in questioning decisions made by directors that are consistent with these duties. The theory of these duties is "that if each director adheres to the appropriate standards of loyalty and care, board decisions which are properly motivated and appropriately thoughtful will follow" (Hansell 2003, 97). For example, Australian company directors and other officers have legal obligations, civil and criminal, pursuant to the Corporations Act 2001. The civil obligations are to act with care and due diligence, act in good faith, not to improperly use position to gain an advantage or cause a detriment, and not to improperly use information. They are criminally responsible, pursuant to section 184, if they are reckless or intentionally dishonest and fail to discharge their duties in good faith in the best interests of the corporation or for a proper purpose (Corporations Act 2001).

The ultimate responsibility for managing a company rests with the board and it is the board that determines how involved it should be in management. It is proposed that "the functions of the board and management result from the styles and personalities of the individuals who comprise the board and the management team as well as the challenges which the corporation faces over time" (Hansell 2003, 49). The board sets the ethics policies and expectations of the company; nevertheless, it is the CEO who sets the tone that will influence day-to-day behaviors. Directors should be independent enough to inquire or discuss whether the CEO's behavior demonstrates honesty and integrity. Boards should be alert to any indications that the CEO, other company officers, or directors are not conforming to the company's code of conduct (Cole 2004).

The role of a board is determined by the type of model the board functions within. Boards should not confine themselves to rigid methods, but be flexible in their approach, sliding back and forth across a scale of engagement as issues and circumstances do. The five models proposed are:

- The *passive board*, considered a traditional model that provides limited accountability and with the board's main function to ratify management decisions. "The board's activity and participation are minimal and at the CEO's discretion."
- The *certifying board* emphasizes credibility to shareholders and the importance of independent directors. The board oversees orderly succession plans, certifies management processes, and ensures the CEO meets the board's requirements.
- The *engaged board* provides insight, advice, and support on key decisions with the CEO. The board conducts substantive discussions on company issues and clearly defines its role and boundaries.
- The *intervening board* is commonly used in crisis as it becomes deeply involved in key decision making and holds more frequent, intense meetings.
- The *operating board* is considered to have strong, ongoing involvement, making key decisions for management to implement. Commonly used in early-stage business start-ups, where the board or top executives have specialized expertise but lack management experience (Nadler 2004, 9).

Boards can be packed with must-accomplish items to allow an in-depth examination of anyone. Directors must overcome frustration to dig deeper into meatier subjects, such as strategy, planning, and risk management. Frustration can be caused by poor communications between senior management and the board. Effective ways in which senior management can keep the board in the dark is by providing too little information or by providing too much (Nadler 2004), hiding significant information within a mass of irrelevant information. In David Nadler's (2004, 12) study, he found that only 28 percent of the directors surveyed had independent channels for obtaining useful information about their company. They rely on management to share the necessary information or what it chooses to share. Other boards suffered from feeling that information was missing or that they were being prevented from doing their jobs.

Boards are often provided with two sources of information. The first is retrospective data and trailing indicators of company performance and operations. The second is presentations by the CEO and senior management about the interpretation of financials and the continued vision of the company. Nadler (2004) asserts that "given those meager rations, it's no wonder companies get into deep trouble before their boards find out." Effective directors take positive steps to inform themselves about the industry and broader environment within which the company operates. Directors should not be dependent on management as the only source of information, otherwise external developments are considered only from the perspective of management (Hansell 2003, 9).

Cohen and Grace (2001, 116) suggest that accountability is important but is more narrow a notion than responsibility. Responsibility is proactive, involving the use of discretion and exercising sound judgment. To make decisions, responsibility and accountability for the decisions made need to be taken. The board retains the responsibility of ensuring appropriate policies are in place; and since circumstances are continually changing, it is likely that they will become outdated and therefore

periodic review is essential (Bosch 1995, 97). "Being complacent is not a good business decision" (Business Executives for National Security 2004, 25). The board has
a monitoring function that includes, among other functions, the oversight of the risk
management process. The board should reevaluate risk and related risk management
strategies on a regular basis. In opposition to corporate risk management is corporate
chance management, with the taking of risks an essential part of the business process and of transactions. The primary role of directors is to identify and benefit from
business chances when they present themselves (Hansell 2003, 6).

Company boards typically meet 12 times a year, with an average meeting time
of five hours (Bosch 2001, 5). There is a widening "expectation gap" between what
the public expects and what directors can realistically do. Directors must review the
business strategy and approve budgets, monitor business performance, evaluate the
chief executive, approve large investments and dividends, oversee management succession planning, approve executive remuneration, ensure major risks are identified
and managed, ensure accuracy of financial reporting, and oversee the management
of general and legal compliance. "That's quite a job for a few weeks in a year."
Boards may become risk adverse with the constant pressure for companies to perform and criticism of directors when they do not (Buffini 2004). Some disagree with
the view that boards are resistant to change and claim instead that boards are very
keen to do as well as they can. The mix around the board table is also changing, with
those becoming directors having the appropriate track records and experience, but
not necessarily knowing the others around the table (Pownall 2004, 14).

There is a widespread expectation that audit committees improve the standards of
corporate governance by, among other things, aiding in reducing fraud and misconduct by creating an environment of corporate discipline and control that effectively
reduces the opportunity for such practices, improving the effectiveness of both the
internal and external audit function (Dunk and Kilgore 1998, 148). Collier's (1997,
104) suggestion that the subjects dealt with by the audit committees were fairly consistent, with the main subjects being the examination of major accounting problems,
critical accounting decisions, adequacy of disclosures, and major audit problems.
In addition, the committee considered the nature and scope of the audit, issues
raised by the auditors, action taken on management concerns, and any major control
issues. Collier also determined that having at least one nonexecutive director with
an accounting qualification was extremely useful, but the presence of nonaccounting
members was also important, as different questions are asked, which occasionally
provides new insights (Collier 1997, 105).

An audit committee concerns itself with what has happened in the company. A
risk management committee should be aligned to look ahead at what may happen
to the company. Company management should concentrate on reducing risks, but
also know what level of risk is consistent with the business. Rather than turning
operational managers into risk managers, it is more productive for them to have risk
management procedures that advise them on areas of risk that impact their operations (Lawson 2004).

A KPMG review of the top 50 Australian ASX listed companies and 18 midsize companies showed that all had audit committees and risk management policies. In addition, 96 percent had clearly defined the different roles of directors

and management, and most had required charters, policies, and codes of conduct. However, only 66 percent had a majority of independent directors, one in two audit committees were not properly constituted, less than 20 percent reported that their CEO and CFO had signed off on accounts, and only 47 percent reviewed their own performance (Buffini 2004). Therefore it is of little surprise that security or security risk management finds its way across the board's table.

## SECURITY'S ROLE TO THE BOARD OF DIRECTORS

As discussed, attention to the duties of company directors has been aided by progressive court judgments that have interpreted their duties more stringently, placing more onerous and exacting legal responsibilities on directors. Provisions for taking *all reasonable care* as found in environmental protection and occupational health and safety legislation are just as applicable to a security function. Taking all reasonable care serves as a process in which directors and management put in place systems and procedures necessary to enable the corporation to comply with statutory and industry obligations, and to monitor the operation of those systems to ensure that they continue to achieve compliance objectives (Hansell 2003, 144).

Class action litigation in the United States has seen courts alter the legal definition of a *foreseeable event* to indicate that a "terrorist act" and "computer viruses and worms" are such events. In actions brought against airlines, airport security companies, and airplane manufacturers following 9/11, the court determined that "the danger of a plane crashing if unauthorized individuals invaded the cockpit was a risk that the plane manufacturer should reasonably have foreseen." Computer viruses were determined to be foreseeable due to the number and regularity of bulletins issued by software companies (Cook 2004) regarding viruses, worms, and computer attacks. These factors can lead to exposure to corporate manslaughter, causing significant financial and incarceration penalties to be imposed

Warning signs prior to the collapse of large companies, from the likes of HIH to Lehman Brothers, were shown to have been ignored, misunderstood, or not sufficiently communicated to force preemptive action by the board. Warning signs included concerns raised by regulators, downgrading of credit ratings, and conference papers (White 2001, 59). Applying such warning signs to the security environment raises may indicate sustained increase in fraud, computer crime, corporate espionage, and extortion. In addition are threats and attacks to corporate interests from special interest groups, and warnings from international security, police, and military experts of impending and changing political, social, and environmental aspects in parts of the Asia-Pacific region.

Most companies today, in particular larger companies, can demonstrate extensive and, at times, impressive risk management systems; nevertheless, these generally relate to financial risks, market risks, credit risks, workplace safety, and environmental risks. In contrast, the greatest risks have been shown to be the willful or ignorant misconduct of employees and management. Unethical and criminal misconduct is often difficult to detect and can directly result from organizational culture (Walter 2000, 34).

In the context of corporate security, company officers performing in a highly competitive market may be seen as a corporate risk, particularly with the potential for fraud and misuse of information. Security's role to the board should be to ensure that the company has in place strategies that apply systems to appropriately monitor and detect unauthorized conduct. In this context the board's security responsibility, as part of risk management, is to:

- Identify and review security risk from consultation with management and outside advisors.
- Evaluate all risks to determine appropriate security management strategies.
- Review the risk management strategy to satisfy themselves with the way management proposes to manage each of the principal risks.
- Monitor the security management process from management reports that should describe major occurrences or less significant occurrences that suggest a trend.
- Take remedial action for any material breach of the controls or pattern of immaterial breaches, discuss with management the remedial action required, and monitor the implementation and effectiveness of any action taken (Hansell 2003, 6; Pausenberger and Nassauer 2000, 265).

In the area of board decision making, security assessments can contribute to forecasts that determine the likelihood of realized outcomes. Risk is considered when selecting projects, and choices will be dependent on the board's attitude to risk (Appleby 1987, 82; Pausenberger and Nassauer 2000, 272). Having access to the security discipline at the board level provides diversity in contribution and specialist skill in security risk management applied to business risk management.

There must be security recognition at the board level offering senior management support in order to get things done. For example, in IT security the most overlooked aspects are often the most important such as passwords, training, and awareness. Security and IT managers need to demonstrate to company executives how to take better advantage of the systems the company already has by raising awareness and recognition of the security function. Often the most useful security skill is how to deliver the security message in a way management and nontechnical people within the company can understand and can support (Rohde 2004). The security message should highlight the benefit of the strategy, not be seen as a barrier.

Company reputation, uninterrupted reliability of critical and technical infrastructures, normal business processes, protection of physical and financial assets, employee safety, and shareholder confidence all rely, in some measure, upon the effectiveness of an accountable, senior security position. The potential conflicting objectives among mid-level managers, often dispersing accountability, is not suitable, and can lead to a decentralized and uncoordinated security function (ASIS International 2004).

By introducing security to corporate governance, the board is recognizing its accountability and responsibility to the security function. Security risk management should contribute to reducing the risk of financial distress and failure, and upon consideration of the market, is likely to result in an improved competitive position in the company's product and labor market. Employees and company agents have a demonstrated interest in the success of a company, as they also incur substantial costs should the company fail (Kaen 2000). All employees, from the board of directors downward, should have security awareness of signs of internal and external risk. Such an approach driven from the board creates a sustainable security culture, making any breach of conduct or procedures noticeable and reportable.

The application of security to corporate governance should involve the board or designated committee formulating the security policy of the organization and developing an appropriate security culture. Strategic security planning should be in line with corporate direction and key resources, directing the board and executive management in protecting all asset types, mitigating loss. and providing accountability for corporate governance. Governments and regulatory agencies should support the development and functioning of risk management products, like security, that assist managers and directors in carrying out their responsibilities. This support should be consistent with viewing the corporation as an institution, which promotes economic efficiency in the marketplace (Kaen 2000).

Company management should concentrate on reducing risks but also know what level of risk is consistent with the business. It is security's role to ensure that corporate security is effective, does not waste resources on security items the company does not need, and uses current security systems to their full potential. The provision of sound security analysis and management proposals to the board and executive management allows the company to consider and approve a balanced security plan. This promotes efficient spending to reduce under- or over-investment in security management systems, and provides board-approved security procedures to counter risks that can severely impact the company's reputation, intellectual and physical assets, and ability to recover from crisis.

## CORPORATE SECURITY RISK AND DIRECTOR ETHICS

The dominant similarity between the major regional corporate failures over the last several decades is the *surprise* response to the disclosure of the company's distress or unorthodox internal practices. As the recent global financial crisis) demonstrated, the size of the company does not equate to sound corporate governance, in particularly sound disclosure policies. As an example, the Australian Wheat Board bribery scandal dominated the international media landscape, with significant effect on that organization.

> **In a Class of Their Own**: The *Atlanta Journal-Constitution* reported that Coca-Cola, Home Depot, and many of America's other big corporations require their top executives to use corporate aircraft, even for vacations and trips to other companies' board meetings, citing personal safety and security. Critics, though, say security concerns are being used to justify an unnecessary perk that can cost thousands of dollars a year (McWilliams 2011, cited in *Security Management*, April 19, 2011).

When presented with any market-sensitive information that for a public company will fall under disclosure requirements, the presumption should always be that the information will have to be released. However, the timing of the disclosure is critically important and can determine how the information is received or perceived. Any attempt to cover up, misuse, sabotage, or destroy information is extremely high risk in all circumstances and likely to result in criminal or civil litigation, irrecoverable reputation damage, and potential catastrophe for the company. With today's increasing use of digital media such as e-mails, laptops, and mobile devices, the acceptance of digital documents as admissible court evidence results in cover-ups that are not going to be contained.

Examples are easily found once cases get to court. For example, in the Australian Federal Court a News Corporation executive, who played a vital role in allocating the 2000 pay TV broadcasting rights for the National Rugby League, is alleged to have leaked critical details of a rival network. In another, Pan Pharmaceuticals IT manager Karl Brooks gave evidence that he was ordered to wipe incriminating data from a hard drive to prevent auditors from discovering irregularities. In another example, an IT team was recruited for a "special project" at a financial services company. They were all forced to sign nondisclosure agreements, only to discover they were working on customer data that had clearly been stolen from a competing organization. One was quoted as saying, "When the issue was raised we were told in no uncertain terms the company would sue us into the ground. It never got off the ground because people just resigned because it was both illegal and badly managed."

These cases, and there are many others in Chapter 6, highlight that directors, executives, and employees are put in vicarious or tempting situations on a seemingly regular basis. In some examples it is a wonder how some directors and executives got their positions in the first place as their lack of judgment is astounding. As an additional note, companies are well advised to conduct thorough background checks and screening on all executives and directors, despite perceived reputations, detailed resumes, and outstanding qualifications—all the better for ensuring the person being recruited is top-shelf quality, not a fraud or at least not prepared to use false or misleading information for personal gain. Companies should not expect or rely on the recruiting agency to performing screening, as in most cases the agencies simply do not do so.

During the same period as directors' duties have become more stringent, to a similar degree security issues ranging from terrorism, organized crime, electronic crime, and economic crime have continued to grow. Such growth has become an international significant and recognized issue, which has an impact on nation-states and their industries and businesses, estimated to be many billions of dollars in the Asia-Pacific region.

There can be severe or even fatal financial impacts on a company should it fall victim to a major crime, such as a fraud, extortion, or sabotage, or be affected by a major disaster or terrorist attack within the next three to five years, the period that companies usually have business plans for. Directors should consider security strategies that protect the principal business against critical risks and ask how the company proposes to protect itself against its significant risks, including security and reputation risks. Failing to properly incorporate security issues into the risk management framework can leave an organization vulnerable to a public or financial crisis, crime or internal misconduct, and in many instances, liable for third-party losses from a judged lack of diligence or care.

White collar crime is grossly underreported, and most medium- to large-size companies could easily report having been a victim of crime, including vandalism, stealing, and burglary. There are also fraud and identity theft, two of the Asia Pacific's fastest-growing crimes. For example, fraud accounts for a third of the total cost of crime in Australia at A\$5 billion per annum. Company directors must consider and incorporate into strategic and risk planning how the company proposes to create a secure workplace, and protect its core functions and critical operations.

## MANAGING MARKET-SENSITIVE INFORMATION

One area of corporate responsibility that many public companies appear to have trouble with is the management and disclosure of market-sensitive information. How this relates, the type, and the significance the corporate security manager may have in this matter will very much depend on their ability to demonstrate corporate leadership, as discussed previously in this chapter.

Nevertheless, from a corporation's perspective there are clear guidelines that directors and executives must comply with. For example, in Australia the Corporations Act 2001 deals with continuous disclosure, and specifically, Section 674 creates the circumstances in which disclosure must occur, and an offense for contravention, incorporating civil and infringement penalties. This act requires all listed entities to notify the market operator, namely the relevant stock exchange, of information about specified events or matters as they arise for the purpose of the operator making that information available to participants in the market. The information about events or matters may be subjective, as such information is not generally available, but is information that a reasonable person would expect, if it were generally available, to have a material effect on the price or value of enhanced disclosure securities of the entity. The question then arises as to what is reasonable or what a reasonable person would expect. What advice could a corporate security manager give when asked by the board or executives for an opinion concerning the treatment of market-sensitive and potentially damaging information—information that if released is likely to have a negative effect on the short-term stock price or market position of the company? What security risks, if any, should be considered in such a scenario?

The first issue to consider is the company's ability to control the information and deal with it on a "need to know" basis. A distribution list should be compiled as to who knows, why they know, and when they were informed. This approach endeavors to lock down the information until a decision of release is reached and all those on the list are advised of their responsibility, both legal and moral, to maintain confidentiality or not to misuse the information. It is critical that a sufficient culture exists where these responsibilities are respected and adhered to, not ignored or just assumed to be the case. Recording this information early will prevent false claims and counterclaims down the track, which only adds to the embarrassing perception of confusion and mismanagement by the company once the information is in the public domain.

The impact of disclosure versus nondisclosure should be assessed for potential short- and long-term security risks. Security risks resulting from a poorly managed crisis or a corporate scandal, resulting from the nondisclosure of information, can be both internal and external. Externally, undue public exposure will affect reputation, which may attract the attention of activists, computer hackers, or extortionists. Internally, these issues often cause low morale and disgruntled employees, potentially giving rise to more information being leaked, or other events of sabotage and aggression. Outcomes such as this have the potential to add to an already sensitive or critical situation, and should be factored in to all disclosure decisions by the board and senior executives.

The culture of the company is critical and should be carefully monitored. If the company already has low morale and an unethical or noncompliant culture, any attempt to lock down sensitive information will have little or no reliability. In a majority of cases the information will inevitably be leaked out into the public domain, namely to journalists, regulators, or competitors. Any "cover-up" attempt has a high likelihood of being exposed, will be difficult to control or manage, and will only compound the negative attention the company is likely to receive following the discovery. Public companies go to great lengths, using public relations (PR) experts, to carefully craft sensitive market stock exchange releases. This approach is completely justifiable and prudent. Corporate security managers should be abreast of PR and marketing issues, and ensure that they can add value in decision making, in particular in communicating risk.

Following the Herron Pharmaceuticals extortion in 2000, after choosing to ignore two previous extortion threats, the company took an initial, incorrect stance in its handling of the media and PR, stating the situation was under control. Had Herron continued with its stance it would have been doomed to fail. Despite their initial mistake and following sound advice from specialists, they introduced an appropriate and carefully planned PR campaign. This campaign allowed Herron to gain empathy from the public and ultimately to regain market share once the crisis had passed. Corporate security managers should be aware of this and similar cases, so they have the ability to manage crises effectively and, if possible, capitalize on negative information or at least minimize the damage.

In the current market of expected high returns and high employment, companies making negative releases, such as profit downgrades or poor strategic decisions, can cause an immediate drop in the share price and therefore the value of the company. This share price reduction can have a considerable impact on market position, revenue, credit ratings, insurance, and indeed, sustainability.

At times, it is understandable why companies choose to delay disclosing information despite being required to make a release. One of the main reasons is that the directors are often surprised by the information themselves and need time to fully assess the situation. Regrettably some directors panic, often falling into the trap of procrastinating or pretending the information does not exist. There are no management textbooks that recommend this course of action. So why are directors inclined to take this path? One answer is that they are human beings and therefore prone to making mistakes and errors in judgment. Part of the corporate security manager's responsibility is to avoid or minimize these mistakes from appropriate and well-researched security and risk management advice, planning, and testing.

## SECURITY IN THE CORPORATE C-SUITE

Senior management experience will become an essential quality as the role of security moves up the food chain in corporate significance. In general, security is placed in mid-level management positions, which is a modest level given the current international security environment (Cavanagh 2004a, 6). The highest levels of an organization must be provided with the strategy and related benefits of the security function, and the nature and likelihood of catastrophic and significant security risk events (ASIS International 2004). A role for the security discipline at executive management level and within the corporate governance framework should be to add experience, a balanced view, and, importantly, value in addressing risk management, business continuity, and crisis management.

The security discipline should provide the company with the experience needed to perform rationally under stress, and to balance company protection with company officer entrepreneurialism and self-interests. Company failures and debacles are generally not random events; they are the result of failures in governance that grew out of the nature of business and, in particular, the nature of human beings. Corporate scandals have often been caused by the reliance on trusted directors or employees to do the right thing. It has been repeatedly shown that they do not always take this route (Walter 2000, 37). Matrix management, decentralization, and the encouragement of managerial entrepreneurialism have increased the scope for fraud and are relevant to fraud and embezzlement prevention and detection.

As the threat to business from security risks continues unabated, in particular, with the backdrop of climate change, food security, terrorism, and e-commerce crime, security will progressively become more important and vital for business longevity. In addition, security needs to span what are today many stovepiped functions such as risk management, business continuity, IT, facility management, physical security, and finance. As the corporate and business communities increasingly move to protect themselves, those remaining unprotected and less resilient will find their risk will increase as those protected drop off the vulnerability radar, leaving those left to the online predators and open to public liabilities in the event of a major security incident.

Following the 9/11 terrorist attacks in 2001, there was an expectation that there would be a widespread move to centralize the corporate security function that would report directly to the CEO. While there was a move toward improved coordination, security remains decentralized in most companies. Nevertheless, there are indications of an evolution, not a revolution, in regional corporate security management. A study by Cavanagh (2004a) determined that from all major regions in the United States, 47 percent of companies reported a drop in revenue following 9/11, with 80 percent reporting disruption to business, mainly from interrupted business travel. In comparison, a major U.S. power outage in August 2003 caused a 21 percent disruption to business travel and a 13 percent drop in revenues. These numbers reveal that a terrorist attack will have a greater impact on business and, as Cavanagh concludes, that future assessment of corporate vulnerabilities should bear these findings in mind.

Developments in the United States have created the position of a chief security officer (CSO), intended to be analogous to the "C-Suite," like that of the chief executive officer (CEO), chief financial officer (CFO), and the chief information officer (CIO). The CSO's role is to coordinate all security responsibilities throughout the organization, report to top management and the board, and control the security budget, so security spending can be managed more effectively. The CSO concept places accountability on a single person to oversee the many aspects of security operations across the whole organization, allowing better coordination and dissemination of information (Cavanagh 2004, 15). This approach provides an integrated security strategy with less duplication and lower cost (ASIS International 2004), providing a more resilient organization.

Many Asia-Pacific companies have realigned their health, safety, and emergency (HSE) managers into HSE and quality (HSEQ) managers, with others into HSE and security (HSES) managers. One company in Singapore has a position termed CRASHES, responsible for community relations, auditing, security, health, emergency response, and safety (Hayes and Truscott 2004, 37). Nevertheless, security professionals must be comfortable in the executive management arena as well as in operations. They must be able to articulate the case for security that can affect overall company policy and operations. "The business protection challenge is huge" (Cavanagh 2004, 27).

ASIS International CSO guidelines (ASIS International 2004, 9) propose that the CSO must have the skills to accomplish the following:

- Relate to and communicate with senior executives, the board of directors, and operating committees.
- Understand the strategic direction and goals of the business, and how security intertwines with strategic needs.
- Understand and assess the impact of external and internal changes on security risk.
- Ensure security and related ethical issues are appropriately investigated and resolved with limited impact on business operations.
- Facilitate the use of traditional and advanced scenario planning techniques for senior management, the board of directors, and employees.
- Successfully network and develop working relationships with external and internal resources.
- Promote organizational learning and knowledge sharing.
- Be politically astute, but not politically motivated.
- Be realistic and comprehend the need to assess financial, employee, and customer implications in plans and recommendations.
- Function as an integral partner of the senior management team.
- Develop sound organizational security awareness, which is appropriate for the business and organizational culture.

Cavanagh (2004b) surveyed nearly 100 chief executive and company officers in a wide range of midsize (annual revenues between US$20 million and US$1 billion) companies in the United States. The proposal that security provides value for the corporation and a positive return on investment was endorsed by 61 percent of respondents, with 39 percent regarding security as a cost that must be tightly controlled. Further results relating to contact between chief executives and security managers indicated that only 21 percent met at least once a week and 25 percent met at least monthly. In the remainder, 28 percent met only a few times a year and 26 percent had never met with the security manager at any time during the previous year.

Cavanagh's study (2004b) found that the smaller the company, the less likely its board will establish written security guidelines and have procedures in place to handle security situations. Seventy-one percent of midsize companies had board-approved written guidelines on disaster recovery and business continuity. Only a third reported board-approved written policies dealing with routine security issues.

A 2004 study by the Economist Intelligence Unit (EIU) (cited by Broersma 2004) conducted an online survey with 254 senior executives from Europe (40 percent), the United States (27 percent), and the Asia Pacific (21 percent) and found that 78 percent considered security to be the top network-related issue, while the same number admitted to opening e-mail attachments from unknown sources. Respondents indicated that 83 percent of their attacks were initiated internally, which included sabotage, espionage, and mistakes.

Senior management commitment is the single most important factor in the success or failure of any security program, which must include security risk management, and sets the style to the toleration of imprudent or unsupervised risk taking. There needs to be an overarching corporate culture, which leads to the issue of behavior modification techniques (Hayes and Truscott 2004, 37; Walter 2000, 25; ASIS International 2004, 5). Over the last several years the two major contributors to security incidents in business, industry, and government have been inadequate training and a poor security culture. Most organizations have security policies and procedures in place, but they are not being supported by effective training and security awareness. The biggest security challenge facing organizations is known to be changing attitudes and behavior, within a dynamic business environment.

A review in 2004 of the annual reports and corporate governance statements of 60 Australian public companies listed within the ASX/S&P200, Australia's largest companies, found that less than 30 percent disclosed governance policies relating to security, yet 85 percent disclosed policy relating to environment, health, and safety. It would seem that as corporate responsibilities increase, requiring greater compliance with national and international governance standards, and the nature of protective challenges evolves with new or emerging threats such as terrorism, there will be a need to establish a holistic approach in risk and governance management. Corporate responsibilities can blur across organizations of any size. Operations, finance, information technology, human resources, property, procurement, environment, health, and safety all have a stake in creating and maintaining the best possible risk reduction and mitigation plans. Security is often not included as a major contributor or implemented strategically, but is instead regarded as a cost center rather than a contributor to short- and long-term revenue.

In terms of implementing security into corporate governance, whatever the reasons, the message from the top down must be that the company wants to develop and maintain a security culture. If the message is that the company recognizes its need to develop security functions, security behavior, and a general security environment, and if the message is serious and sincere, then security issues become the focus for the conduct of organizational matters.

Security in corporate governance contributes to a favorable perception of the company by demonstrating that security risks are recognized as a significant business risk and the company has systems in place in the event of security events, up to and including a major incident on itself, a competitor, a client, or supplier. Articulating and championing the business case for security must be seen as an essential part of the role played by any corporate security director. This strategy may be more difficult if security is not directly reporting to top management; however, as security concerns become more integrated into strategic management, this should improve (Cavanagh 2004b).

## COMMUNICATING SECURITY RISK TO C-SUITE EXECUTIVES

Corporate security directors or managers must have a sound understanding of corporate governance principles to ensure the security function is integrated into the corporate governance framework. Primarily, corporate security should be ingrained into the company's risk management, and preferably, there should be a seat for the security champion on all risk management committees. Companies with operations in the Asia-Pacific region need to have enhanced risk management cultures, as poor corporate governance was identified as one of the root causes of the Asian financial crisis. It has been found that illegal practices in breach of trust, expropriations, embezzlement, and company theft appear to continue in many East Asian countries, but the punishment of such abuses remains largely weak.

Equally, it is suggested that many Asia-Pacific nation-states have weak systems of ensuring companies are adopting best practice in corporate governance. For example, Australia's recent cases include the Telstra director Steve Vizard and the National Australia Bank futures scandal. Steve Vizard was a director of Australia's largest telecommunications company, Telstra. Yet Telstra came out of the saga relatively unscathed and was not required to explain how one of its directors was able to misuse confidential board information for his personal gain. Were other Telstra directors conducting similar transactions, and what was the culture of the board that allowed this to occur, or at least gave Vizard the perception that he could act this way?

Stock exchanges in Australia, Singapore, Hong Kong, and Tokyo regulate corporate governance practices via listing rules. These rules require that the company must make a statement of the main corporate governance practices that it has in place during the reporting period. There is no mandatory compliance with any specified benchmarks. While most corporations voluntarily comply, there is evidence of a lack of conformity and uniformity, and a suggestion that the state's stock exchange requirements are simply used as a means of maintaining legitimacy and control, not necessarily to allay stakeholders' concerns. Many entities view the rules as a means of avoiding the threat of litigation and overlook the broader accountability objective of satisfying the need for public disclosure in order to promote stakeholder confidence.

Alan Kohler has highlighted the likely widespread existence of insider trading by company directors. He notes that as of 2007, there were 1,650 public companies listed on the Australian Stock Exchange, with about 7,000 directors or an average of 4.2 per board. In the previous financial year, company directors disclosed 7,602 trades, as required under the listing rules, about 1 trade per director per year. Of the 93,000 announcements made to the ASX, 22 percent were deemed "market sensitive," which equates to 1,715 share price-moving statements per month. This means that directors are regularly and consistently tempted to commit insider trading offenses by conducting share transactions while in possession of market-sensitive information that is not yet known by the market. How often are directors trading illegally through transactions that are conducted through affiliate but unconnected entities? Insider trading is a criminal offense under the Corporations Act 2001 and punishable with five years' imprisonment, though as the Vizard case demonstrates, that penalty is rarely applied.

The question for security managers is, if directors are or are perceived to be flouting the law, how can mid-level managers and employees be expected to comply and enforce codes of conduct and ethics policies? How can a culture of compliance become ingrained if employees are highly skeptical of director behavior? These cases give the perception of "Do as we say, not as we do." What this issue highlights is that the introduction of security policy and guidelines will make little difference if the corporate ethics culture is not right. Appropriate corporate governance is reliant on the basic principles of acting in good faith, viewing issues from other stakeholders' point of view, and taking responsibility for actions and decisions. Company security is equally reliant on these factors.

Confidence in corporate governance can first be enhanced by the disclosure of the role, responsibilities, and methods of appointment of the board of directors; second, the responsibility for the strategic direction, day-to-day management, and internal controls; and third, director remuneration. There is no single model for sound corporate governance, and practices will evolve with the changing circumstances of the company and national or international developments. Business decisions always carry risks that require effective management through oversight and internal controls. Enhanced board and management effectiveness come from keeping pace with the modern risks of business.

The challenge to maintain sound corporate security in line with relevant and ethical corporate governance relevant to the nation-state is currently so great that security issues should be on the agenda of every board. There should be holistic reviews of security to ensure a strategic implementation of internal security controls that range from theft, fraud, and IT protection through to corporate espionage, extortion threats, crisis response, and disaster recovery planning that also consider natural disasters and terrorist attacks that may impact on company operations, directly or indirectly.

Mid-level security management positions or adding security responsibilities onto an existing management portfolio with indirect contact to the CEO and board are not sufficient to ensure company resilience against security risks experienced in the Asia-Pacific region. Continued reluctance or ignorance by business toward the evolving security profession and its revenue-enhancing benefits will change as directors and companies are repeatedly reminded that no business is immune from falling victim to criminal and security breaches, attacks, and failures.

## SECURITY PERCEPTION, CULTURE, AND RISK MANAGEMENT

An effective security function is reliant on integration with the corporate structure and culture. Where the security function resides in an organization will determine its authority and power base, and in turn its ability to contribute to strategic policy and influence decision makers. What will be most encouraging for the executive and directors is that there is likely to be genuine interest by employees about issues of security, similar to safety concerns, with most accepting that security should be improved and maintained.

Employees often describe themselves as lazy with security, with keys left in cabinets, not used, or lost; and wide and open access to cash, valuables, and confidential information left lying around offices and on laptop computers. Alarms are left off and safes left open. But despite this, there is often a strong willingness to adopt new practices and improve general security, in particular with regard to information security, access control, and personal security. In most instances, employees simply need some awareness training and an understanding of their own responsibilities.

## WHERE SHOULD SECURITY BE IN THE CORPORATE STRUCTURE?

A role for the security discipline at the executive management level and within the corporate governance framework should be to compensate, not contribute to, asymmetric concern in dealing with risk management and business continuity management. Company failures and debacles are generally not random events; they are the result of failures in governance that grew out of the nature of the business and human beings. The security discipline should provide the company with the knowledge, skills, and experience needed to perform rationally under stress, and to balance company protection with company officer entrepreneurialism and self-interests.

Strong holistic security controls that are reported regularly to the board and designated committees will enable alert watch keeping of director, management, and employee behavior, critical infrastructure protection, operational security and loss mitigation monitoring, asset protection strategies, and external forces, all of which can cause severe stress on short- and long-term financial performance (Walter 2000, 37). It would seem that as social responsibilities increase and the nature of protective challenges evolves, the current demarcations in corporate responsibilities will further blur. Operations, finance, information technology, human resources, facilities, purchasing, and security departments all have a stake in creating and maintaining the best possible risk reduction and mitigation plans.

As discussed, developments in the United States have created the position of a CSO. The CSO's role is to coordinate all security responsibilities throughout the organization, report directly to senior management and the board, and control the security budget. The CSO concept places accountability on a single person to oversee the many aspects of strategic security operations, allowing better coordination, dissemination of information (Cavanagh 2004b, 15), and an integrated security strategy with less duplication and lower cost (ASIS International 2004).

However, access to the chief executive by the CSO has a direct impact on security spending. Seventy-five percent of companies that held weekly meetings with the

CSO reported an increase in security spending since 9/11, compared to 30 percent of those firms where there were no meetings (Cavanagh 2004b). The strongest support for security spending was in "critical industries," which included transportation, energy, utilities, financial services, media and telecommunications, information technology, and health care. Following the 9/11 attacks, 45 percent of respondents reported no increase in security spending and most reported little increase. Increases in security spending were lowest among smaller companies, with only 28 percent of midsize companies having off-site emergency operation centers. For many smaller companies, it would be difficult conducting business in the event of a prolonged power outage or closure of their primary facility.

## CONCLUSION

Corporate security is often considered a cost center, functioning only at the operational level with little strategic corporate or business focus. Security is often a neglected management function; nevertheless, there is a need for directors and executives to have an understanding of their corporation's risk. Within many Asia-Pacific nation-states it is a director's responsibility to ensure that the organization has and maintains a safe and secure working environment. Therefore security has to be acknowledged by senior executives and requires professional, effective, and informed advice. In addition, security managers have to take a leadership role to ensure that they drive and demonstrate business acumen at the executive level.

This chapter has introduced corporate security at the company's director level, with considerations of how security may support or impede Asia Pacific companies. The role of security in the boardroom has considered such issues as their duties, responsibilities, regularity, and ethics relevant to the organization's executive level. In essence, ensuring that reasonable security, driven through risk management, has been applied with a clear audit trail to the final decision-making outcome. With ever-increasing and stringent compliance and governance requirements, ethical behavior on the part of directors, executives, and security were considered along with such threats as insider trading and passing on commercially sensitive information. If directors are seen to be operating at an unethical level, there can be direct conflict between security and directors, as this impedes an appropriate security culture.

The need to increase the responsibility of the security group to the C-suite is important, as this provides a leader operating across the organization. In general, the position of the security leader is often a manager with limited sway in the greater corporation ladder. There are clear skills that an effective security manager requires to ensure security leadership, such as an ability to communicate at a high business level to the board, take a strategic approach, and develop broad networks, just to name a few.

## REFERENCES

Appleby, R. C. 1987. *Modern Business Administration*. London: Pitman.
ASIS International. 2004. *Chief Security Officer Guidelines*. Alexandria, VA. ASIS International.
Bosch, H. 1995. *The Director at Risk: Accountability in the Boardroom*. Melbourne: Pitman.

————. 2001. *Collapse Incorporated: Tales, Safeguards and Responsibilities of Corporate Australia*. Sydney: CCH.

Broersma, M. 2004. Study: Company execs admit IT idiocy. CSO. Retrieved April 15, 2012, from www.cso.com.au/article/14269/

Buffini, F.(2004. "Directors Face Even Greater Expectations." *Australian Financial Review*, March 11. http://afr.com/articles/2004/03/09/1078594355714.html (accessed September 19, 2004).

Business Executives for National Security. 2004. *Company Primer on Preparedness and Response Planning for Terrorist and Bioterrorist Attacks*. Atlanta, GA: BENS Metro Atlanta Region, Homeland Security Advisory Group.

Cavanagh, T. E. 2004a. *Corporate Security Management: Organization and Spending since 9/11*. Research report. no. 1333. New York: The Conference Board.

————. 2004b. *Security in Mid-market Companies: The View from the Top*. Executive Action no. 102. New York: The Conference Board.

Cohen, S., and D. Grace. 2001. "Ethics and the Sustainability of Business." In *Collapse Incorporated: Tales, Safeguards and Responsibilities of Corporate Australia*, 99–128. Sydney: CCH.

Collier, P. 1997. "Audit Committees in Smaller Listed Companies." In *Corporate Governance Responsibilities, Risks and Remuneration*, edited by K. Keasey and M. Wright, 93–119. Chichester, UK: Wiley.

Cole, C. 2004, August. "Think Your CEO Is Honest? How Would You Know?" *Directors Monthly* 28 (8). Washington, DC: National Association of Corporate Directors.

Cook, W. 2004. "A Foreseeable Future." CSO Online, September 30. http://www.csoonline.com.au/index.php?id=420533628&eid=-302 (accessed October 1, 2004).

Corporations Act 2001. (Cth). s. 180–84.

Dang, J. 2000. *The Governance of Corporate Groups*. London: Cambridge University Press.

Duncan, K., S. Gale, J. Tofflemore, and R. Yaksick. 1992. "Conceptualizing a Value-Added Approach to Security Management: The Atkinson Security Project I." *Security Journal* 3 (1): 4–13.

Dunk, A. S., and A. Kilgore. 1998. Financial markets, corporate governance and short-term pressures in Australia. In Corporate Governance, Accountability and Pressures to Perform: An International Study edited by I. S. Demira, and M. J. Epstein. Stamford: JAI Press, Inc., pp. 141–161.

Hansell, C. 2003. *What Directors Need to Know: Corporate Governance*. Toronto: Carswell.

Hayes, J., and J. Truscott. 2004. "The Integration of Risk, Safety and Security." *Security Oz Magazine* 29, 36–39.

Kaen, F. R. 2000. "Risk Management, Corporate Governance and the Modern Corporation." *Risk Management: Challenge and Opportunity*, edited by M. Frenkel, U. Hommel, and M. Rudolf, 423–436. Berlin: Springer-Verlag.

Lawson, M. 2004. "Be Serious, You Can't Take Risks." *Australian Financial Review*, April 7. http://afr.com/articles/2004/04/06/1081222459146.html (accessed September 19, 2004).

Leischen, S. 2011. Report finds workplace violence still a high risk. *Security Directors News*. Retrieved April 29, 2011 from www.security-world.blogspot.com.au.

McWilliams, J. 2011. Necessity or needless? CSO's fly privately for business pleasure. The Atlanta Journal-Constitution. Retrieved April 19, 2011, from www.ajc.com/bussiness/ necessity or needless? CSO's fly privately for business pleasure.

Nadler, D. A. 2004). "Increasing Director Performance." *Company Director* 20 (8): 8–14. Sydney: Australian Institute of Company Directors.

Pausenberger, E., and F. Nassauer. 2000. "Governing the Corporate Risk Management Function: Regulatory Issues." In *Risk Management: Challenge and Opportunity*, edited by M. Frenkel, U. Hommel, and M. Rudolf, 263–276. Berlin: Springer-Verlag.

Pownall, M. 2004. "Boards under the Microscope." *Western Australian Business News*, September 9–15, 14–15.

Rohde, L. 2004. "Gartner Analysts Point Out the Security You Don't Need." IDG News Service. http://www.csoonline.com.au/index.php?id=2113312780&eid=-302 (accessed September 21, 2004).

Walter, I. 2000. "The Relevance and Management of Reputation Risk in the Global Securities Industry." In *Risk Management: Challenge and Opportunity*, edited by M. Frenkel, U. Hommel, and M. Rudolf, 24–38. Berlin: Springer-Verlag.

White, A. 2001. "Flow On Effects of Recent Collapses." In *Collapse Incorporated: Tales, Safeguards and Responsibilities of Corporate Australia*, 41–70. Sydney: CCH.

# 3  Security Risk Management

## INTRODUCTION

During the two decades preceding 2010, the concept of risk management, as a formal discipline, emerged throughout the private and public sectors (Aven 2008; Power 2007). Risk management has become a well-established discipline, with its own body of knowledge and domain practitioners. Some of the Asia-Pacific nation-states have their own risk management standards, and some of the company directors and executives have the ultimate responsibility of ensuring that appropriate risk management practices meet internal and external compliance requirements (Brooks 2009). At an international level, the International Standards Organization propagates the ISO 31000:2009 risk management standard, which puts forward a philosophy, process, and framework for risk management.

Corporations have a significant responsibility, with social expectations, that they take all reasonable precautions to protect themselves, their costumers, the community, and the environment they operate within. A method to achieve this is risk management, and within corporate security, security risk management.

This chapter considers corporate obligation and compliance in risk management, with alignment to the ISO 31000:2009 risk management framework. Nevertheless, many of these standards and compliance requirements consider only risk management, not security risk management. Such an approach allows reasonable security to be implemented, using a recognized international risk framework.

Security risk management may be considered unique from other forms of risk management, as many of the more generic risk models lack key process and functions necessary for effective design, application, and mitigation of security risks. Such implementation may be used to enhance corporate governance and enterprise-wide security risk management, driven from a robust business case. Finally, an important outcome for security risk management is gaining consensus in risk mitigation strategies that meet the need of the corporation and its stakeholders.

## LACK OF RISK MANAGEMENT IN THE ASIA PACIFIC

There are a number of national and international risk management standards, but how are these used within the Asia-Pacific region, in particular in corporate security? As discussed, all parts of an organization will use risk management to some degree, and security is no different. International standards, such as ISO 31000:2009, act as the benchmark; however, this standard is currently being evaluated by a global survey (Dali 2011), using many different risk groups. Furthermore, the security use of ISO 31000:2009 may be flawed, as it neglects to raise and integrate specific security risk concepts such as threat, vulnerability, and criticality (Brooks 2011), unlike security risk management (see the later section titled Security Risk Management), which incorporates these concepts into an integrated framework.

A majority of Asia-Pacific nation-states do not have a defined risk management standard. Security managers use their own internal frameworks, followed in parity with the ISO 31000:2009 and the (now) old Australian Standard 4360:2004. ISO 28000 Supply Chain Security Management is a popular standard, driven from Singapore and with restricted use elsewhere. Nevertheless, the use of these standards should raise concern over the lack of a directed security risk management framework that incorporates threat, vulnerability, and criticality (Brooks and Cotton 2011) to manage security risks within the region.

## RISK

All activities carry some form of risk and thus there must be a decision as to whether to conduct an activity based on weighing the risk of the activity against the benefit of the activity. Demands for ever-greater reductions in risk exposure—on a cultural, social, community, corporate, and individual basis—can proceed beyond the point of overall benefit and become counterproductive. Risk management and mitigation strategies must be cost effective, unless imposed by law, in which case compliance is an organization's only option. Managers must be cautious about trying to provide a risk-free environment. The actions taken to reduce one risk can increase the organization's exposure to other more serious risks. For example, fail-secure locking systems may prevent looting and theft by staff, but may also result in the loss of life in case of fire.

There are three significant points about how people determine the acceptability of risk:

1. Risk is generally less accepted and particularly unwelcome when imposed by external factors over which people have little or no control. People demand high safety standards at work, and risks in the workplace are not as well accepted because people cannot control whether they are exposed to workplace risks if they wish to work.
2. Risk stemming from the activities of an identifiable scapegoat is not easily accepted. Accidents such as the *Exxon Valdez* oil spill are not accepted because there is clearly someone at fault. If this were not the case, the risk would be more acceptable.
3. Simple numbers and probabilities are inadequate to represent reaction to incidents of different magnitude. Catastrophes are given more attention than more frequently occurring risk where the consequence is smaller. As an example, more people die on the road than in terrorist incidents. Yet more attention is given to dealing with a catastrophe than driving a car, which leads to skew in risk management.

The way people perceive risk will also depend on their background, experience, and knowledge. Many risk managers place the emphasis on the provision of facts, which should be objective and rational to aid in the process of decision making. However, risk management should also consider perception, social issues, and how emotion affects risk, how people react to risk and why. Risk management is not always logical, in particular when dealing with risks that some believe they are not gaining any benefit from or cannot sense control over.

## SECURITY OBLIGATIONS AND COMPLIANCE IN RISK MANAGEMENT

Corporations and their directors are being advised to review their security; however, despite these warnings from government and industry associations, what is the obligation on corporations to have reasonable and sufficient security in place? What is often not provided in these warnings is the level of security that should be implemented and what degree of security will conform to what may be considered *reasonable* by an independent party—in principle, the courts.

Following a security-related event that causes loss, injury, or death and results in any form of dispute, claim, or legal proceeding, one of the primary areas to be reviewed and comparisons drawn is the relevant nation-state's standards that provide *expected* practice guidance. For any profession or activity where such well-established security standards exist, courts are likely to interpret what constitutes *reasonable* steps in light of such standards. Many business owners remain unaware and noncompliant with security-related standards, which are being regularly released. Perhaps important, no one is taken to court and ultimately imprisoned over a security standard, whereas they are punished for not providing a safe and healthy work environment. Ultimately, the board, directors, and staff could be charged with corporate manslaughter if reasonable action had not been taken.

> **Public companies are failing to adequately prepare for risk exposures:** An analysis by Reputex of the S&P/ASX 300, using more than 100 risk and performance indicators, identified that smaller cap companies are less prepared to manage risk than larger companies; companies which rated poorly against the risk indicators showed a 15 percent greater share price volatility; industries with lower risk exposures are under-prepared to deal with risks; and companies that performed well against the risk indicators in 2006 outperformed the S&P/ASX 300 by more than 6 percent (*Business Review Weekly* June, 2007).

If a corporation is exposed to numerous and commonly known security risks and is spending thousands of dollars on existing security measures, such as alarm monitoring, patrols, CCTV, and computer security, it can still be noncompliant with what may be considered reasonable security steps. The most common and obvious lack of compliance is that there are no formal and documented risk management and assessment steps conducted. Such documented process clearly communicates why the security risk has been identified and how it will be treated. Without formal risk management that documents the security strategy and functions, the issue of *reasonable steps* is otherwise open to conjecture, misinterpretation, and legal exploitation.

Standards in risk management and security design provide clear obligations for a formal risk management process to be followed and outline what is considered reasonable. This approach provides sound and sufficient protection for the organization and will minimize liability exposures as well as significantly enhance its strategy for business protection and longevity. Regretfully, it is all too common for action to be taken only after the event. Such a reactive response effectively doubles the cost associated with security management and demonstrates a lack of risk management and planning.

For example, in Singapore the Ministry of Manpower (2006, 2–7) has set out the Workplace Safety and Health (WSH) Act. The WSH Act aims to reduce risks at the source by making stakeholders accountable for managing the risks they create. Such an act attempts to ensure workplace safety in almost all aspects of business, including commercial, public, private, and heavy and light industries environments. Failure to comply could place the management liable to a fine or jail, with punitive penalties of up to S$20,000, six months in jail, or both. With such severity in penalties for noncompliance, organizations will need to adhere to this regulation and take the necessary steps to ensure workplace safety, primarily based on a risk management hazards approach. This risk management process will demonstrate that formal and reasonable care has been applied, providing a degree of protection for the business.

Organizations operating in, or servicing, a variety of sectors and industries are also exposed to more specific security guidelines and regulations, such as:

- Health and food industries (hospitals, biohazards, pathology, record keeping)
- Supply chain (customs, immigration, holding companies, distributors)
- Transport (aviation, maritime)
- Pharmaceutical and chemical-related industries (dangerous substances, explosives)
- Education (child safety, duty of care, school education acts)
- Finance and e-commerce (banking, merchant payment facilities)
- Security-related enterprises (firearms, data storage)
- Mining and resources (precious metals, explosive storage, industry acts)

In Australia, corporations are required to remain compliant to the Australian Privacy Act 1988 and state-based Occupational Health and Safety Act. These Commonwealth acts form the basic requirements on all government and industry to maintain secure management of confidential and personal information, and to maintain a secure workplace for the safety of staff and visitors. Nevertheless, as with most failures in security, an organization or person will not be taken to court for noncompliance to a security regulation or law; rather prosecution will be based on not providing a safe working environment by violating a safety regulation.

## WHAT IS REASONABLE SECURITY?

Privacy case law in several jurisdictions is gradually throwing some light on what constitutes the required "reasonable security measures." As the body of case law builds up and is summarized, corporations can expect to obtain a clearer view of their obligations, both generally and in a variety of specific circumstances. Nevertheless, across the Asia-Pacific region there are many issues specific to nation-states that need to be considered in-country.

Security principles under some nation-state privacy laws may read: "A record-keeper ... shall ensure that the record is protected, by such security safeguards as it is *reasonable in the circumstances* to take, against loss, against unauthorised access, use, modification or disclosure, and against other misuse." The main feature is that security principles in privacy laws place the obligation to take *reasonable* or *reasonably practicable* steps, either expressly or implicitly related to the particular circumstances. There is some past guidance material issued by nation-state regulators that has offered advice on how to assess the reasonable or practicable level of security.

There are also a handful of decisions available that provide some understanding on what security measures might be considered necessary. Examples of specific compliance measures considered by the regulators to be appropriate can also be found in the reports of conciliated cases published by some privacy commissioners, and in the reports of special investigations and audits conducted by those commissioners who have those functions.

No one expects or should expect risk to be totally removed, as no one expects security to be absolute. While it is understandable that there must be a practical limit on the amount a business can be expected to pay for security, it cannot be satisfactory to allow the decision to be made without any reference to contemporary standards or social expectations. Even the best precautions are likely to be vulnerable to both human error and deliberate circumvention. Unlike safety hazards, security risks are driven by the human threat, where an intelligent person uses his or her knowledge, capability, and motivation to try to defeat protection strategies. As an example, computer security is known to be a constant battleground between hackers on the one hand and the cyber security experts on the other. A hacker may have breached computer crime laws, which were inadequate means to sustain a claim for compensation. But the organization that has been hacked may have breached reasonable security principles and is likely to be viewed by a plaintiff as a much better target for a compensation claim.

Neither can an organization be expected to guarantee compliance with instructions given to staff. Individual employees will occasionally act willfully and recklessly in contravention of clear instructions; however, this may still result in the business being vicariously liable for any loss. Where this happens, organizations should expect to have to reinforce training and, where appropriate, to take disciplinary action in order to maintain a reasonable culture of security. Inaction will only reinforce the corporate culture of taking such risks and exercising noncompliance, effectively having middle-level supervisors condone such action.

**Failure to Encrypt Portable Devices Inexcusable:** BP recently revealed this week that an employee lost a laptop containing the personal information of roughly 13,000 people who had submitted claims associated with the last year's oil spill in the Gulf of Mexico. The data on the laptop, which included names, Social Security numbers and dates of birth was unencrypted. The fact that such data was not stored on an encrypted laptop has floored analysts, who said that it is inexcusable that many companies are still not using encryption to protect information stored on mobile devices. Many companies have chosen not to encrypt laptops and other mobile devices because of the costs involved, though analysts suggest that cost should not be an issue given the fact that a laptop can be encrypted for as little as US$15.00. Analysts also noted that the rising cost of data breaches should convince companies to use encryption, with a data breach costing a company an average of $214 per compromised record. (Vijayan 2011)

Nevertheless, it is clear that it is not sufficient to have security measures in place if they are not being appropriately implemented nor informed by a "live" risk management process. Most systems administrators would be aware of the need for regular password changes and for revocation or change to access privileges for staff who leave or have changed function, but audits commonly find that these disciplines are not enforced. Similar obligations apply to management of physical access, for example the need to supervise after-hours access by contractors, change keypad combinations, retrieve keys from departing staff, and ensure CCTV cameras and sensing devices are maintained and operating.

There must be security recognition at the corporation's board offering senior management support in order to maintain security. Independent security consultants need to demonstrate to business executives how to take better advantage of the systems already in place by raising awareness and recognition of the security functions. Often new or expensive security systems are not required, if existing systems are used appropriately. The most useful skill is how to communicate the security message within the business so it is understood and supported by all end users.

Reputation, uninterrupted reliability of critical and technical infrastructures, normal business processes, protection of physical and financial assets, employee safety, and shareholder confidence all rely, in some measure, upon the effectiveness of security functions. These measures have to be driven from a sound and reliable risk management process. When these systems or even small parts of these systems fail, and a loss or injury results, the organization should expect to defend a claim as well as manage a crisis. Current examples range from workplace murders and armed robberies to misconduct, theft and fraud, computer breaches, and lost data. These cases resulted in loss of life, damaged reputations, interrupted business processes, loss of productive staff hours, data loss, and legal proceedings, which would have been avoided or mitigated had security been sufficient, operated effectively, and was driven by sound risk management.

Security is a broad and recognized discipline with a wide range of component and technology applications. The provision of sound security risk management, policy, analysis, and proposals allows for a considered and balanced security management plan. Such balance promotes efficient spending to reduce under- or over-investment in security systems and provides *reasonable* security to treat known risks. This approach protects asset value, minimizes liability exposures, reinforces insurance requirements, and strengthens the ability to recover from crisis. The obligation on organizations is to have "reasonable" security risk management systems, and this will require the same degree of application and documentation as all other business management systems.

## AN INTERNATIONAL APPROACH TO RISK MANAGEMENT

The International Standards Organization propagates the ISO 31000:2009 risk management standard, which puts forward a risk philosophy, process, and framework. The standard, developed from the Australian Standard AS/NZS4360:2004, was first published in 1995, revised in 1999, and provides a generic structure to design, apply, management, and audit risk.

ISO 31000:2009 aims to provide a generic framework for the identification, analysis, evaluation, treatment, and monitoring of risk. The standard does not aim to enforce uniformity of risk management systems but rather to specify elements of the risk management process. The standard is generic and independent of any given sector or industry, including security (where dedicated security risk management should be used). Design and implementation of a risk management system will be dependent upon the organization's needs, objectives, products, services, processes, and practices employed.

ISO 31000:2009 provides a relatively uncomplicated approach to risk management principles, framework, and process, identifying the generic steps required of a risk management program. While in most jurisdictions, such standards are not legally binding, they are, nevertheless, persuasive. For this reason, any risk management system and therefore security risk management system should consider complying with ISO 31000:2009.

From a corporate perspective, it is suggested that the ISO principles provide little value to the security risk management process. These principles are ideal outcomes and if taken without critique, lead only to the failure of risk management. Reverse these risk management principles and one highlights the limitations of risk management. For example, decision making becomes a predetermined outcome through risk gaming (see the Risk Gaming or Gaining Consensus section). Risk management becomes an administration burden driven by process rather than adding value. The ISO 31000 process is cut and pasted for a corporate activity that is either under-engineered or over-engineered, far from tailored. There are many other examples for each principle, with some discussed in later sections.

Nevertheless, the ISO framework allows a clear and concise corporate iteration process to be applied across many nation-states and is a reasonable approach. If the users are aware of the benefits of a robust and consensual risk process, risk management is a useful tool in communicating risk across all stakeholders. In addition, it becomes and provides a degree of insurance against potential incidents, both positive and negative.

A typical iteration process, for example the ISO 31000 process, commences with *defining the context* where the scope is set. This step is followed by *consult*, where stakeholders are identified. The initial stages are perhaps the more important aspects and are often overlooked or not given the importance they deserve. As with any task, these are the planning stages that define what type of risk is to be considered, how risk is to be assessed, who will make up the team and team logistics, and whom will the process likely affect. Next the risks are *assessed*, integrating risk *identification*, *analyses*, and *evaluation*. This stage is perhaps the most creative part, where a suitable group of individual are gathered, the process is explained, and *brainstorming* commences. All risks should be considered and documented.

Risk assessment requires a competent facilitator—perhaps the risk manager or a professional consultant, someone who allows some debate and everyone to have an equal say. During this stage and once a broad list of risks have been identified, analysis needs to commence, where some measure of likelihood and consequence is assigned to each risk or clusters of risks (source risk). The completion of this stage should be a ranked list of analyzed risks with the most extreme first, followed by high, moderate, and, finally, low risks.

Once risks have been assessed, they can be *treated*. Such treatment should consider only the risks that are ranked *extreme* and *high*, where people, process, or assets can be used to treat the risk, depending on the most cost effective, corporate, and/or socially acceptable mitigation method. There are five traditional methods for treating risks:

*Reduce the risk.* Reduce the likelihood of the risk being realized. According to ISO 31000:2009, this can be accomplished through reduction in either likelihood or consequence. Appropriate security policies, procedures, and practices coupled with situational and social crime prevention strategies can be used to reduce risk.

*Transfer the risk.* Outsource the function exposing the organization to risk. An example is a bank, which contracts to handle cash transportation. Insurance is one of the better known methods of transferring risk to another party.

*Avoid the risk.* Eliminate the activity causing the risk exposure. Paying employees via electronic banking rather than cash avoids the risk of armed robbery.

*Redistribute the risk.* Where possible, distribute business functions that expose the organization to risk over a range of locations or time. Keeping off-site backup copies could be an example or not flying the corporation's whole board on the same flight.

**Mine Executives Die in Plane Crash:** Six mining executives were killed when their chartered aircraft, a twin turboprop, crashed in a dense forest in the West African nation of Congo. The aircraft was carrying board members of Australian based mining company Sundance Resources, a listed iron ore group that is developing a project in Cameroon. Executives who died in the plane crash were the Chairman, Chief Executive Officer, Company Secretary and three Non-executive Directors. Also onboard were two British, two French citizens and an American (*Australian Post* 2010).

*Accept the risk.* Sometimes there is no option but to accept a risk. Banks can limit the risk of armed robberies, but they have to accept a level of risk if they are to continue trading. An international corporation has to operate across a diverse and wide geographical location to remain profitable over time.

After risk treatment, any remaining risk can be considered *residual risk*. Such residual risk needs to be monitored to ensure that changing threat, environmental conditions, and business practice do not elevate the risk to a higher, more unacceptable level. Concurrently with the risk assessment stages, the risk process has to be *monitored and reviewed* and stakeholders *consulted* (Standards Australia 2004). These can be difficult tasks that result in misinterpretations due to many issues, such as perceived ownership of the risk benefit, financial stake, victimization of some, poor communication, or misaligned social understanding or, more correctly, concern; however, many of these issues are discussed in later sections.

## SECURITY RISK MANAGEMENT

ISO 31000:2009 provides a generic framework for a corporation; however, it lacks a number of significant process and functions that allow it to be effective in managing security risks. Security risk, as discussed, is a unique subset of risk management, and it introduces ideas such as *threat, criticality,* and *vulnerabilities*. None of these ideas is discussed in the ISO 31000 standard, greatly limiting its suitability for corporate security. Nevertheless, ISO 31000 should be the corporate risk management framework that security risk management resides within.

### THREAT

Threat may be considered a significant component of security risk management. As Brooks (2007) found, threat is a central theme within the understanding, management, and application of security risk. Nevertheless, many risk management standards, for example the International Standard ISO 31000:2009, do not mention the concept of threat.

Threat may be defined as the sum of *intent* and *capability,* and has to be clearly articulated within a security risk management process. However, threat is a difficult and often misunderstood concept within a corporate environment, in particular when dealing with security risks. An underlying method to better understand and articulate threat is through the *intelligence cycle.*

### CRITICALITY

What does the organization need to maintain—whether people, information, or assets—to ensure that its primary objectives are met to be able to continue to trade? For example, is there a particular person, a piece of equipment within the production line, or even a supplier that if lost for a predefined period of time has a significant effect on the organization? An organization that sells spare parts may believe that its headquarters is the most important part of their business, but in reality the online central ordering system is how staff place orders and goods get dispatched, via postal contractors. On the road, company representatives could still order from their cars or homes if headquarters burned down, so how critical is the headquarters? Answers will naturally be reliant on understanding each aspect of the business and organizational structure.

Criticality should be documented to aid both risk management and inform business continuity management. Both functions can benefit from a comprehensive and organization-wide criticality listing. Noncritical items need little consideration, if criticality is well understood.

## VULNERABILITY

What is weak or lacks resilience? Understanding vulnerabilities provides a benchmark for the current state of affairs. Risk management should be completed in the present, with a clear understanding of current vulnerabilities.

## INTEGRATING THREAT, VULNERABILITY, AND CRITICALITY

Once a clear understanding of threat, vulnerability, and criticality is achieved, these can be integrated to inform and direct security risk management. Threat and criticality can be mapped to articulate vulnerability. Nevertheless, vulnerability should not always be produced from this method. As with any risk management modeling, the complexity of the assessment should align with the expected reliability and validity of the outcome. Some vulnerability assessments can and should be completed with a more traditional site survey.

Security risk management process reflects the generic risk management process (Figure 3.1) inasmuch as the process commences with *defining the context*, where the scope is set. This stage is followed by *communicate*, to identify and list stakeholders. Next the risks are *assessed*, integrating risk *identification*, *analyses*, and *evaluation*; however, at this stage threat and criticality assessments inform the risk identification stage (Figure 3.2). From there, risk analysis gives a measure of likelihood and consequence to each risk or cluster of risks (source risk). The completion of this stage should be a ranked list of risks.

## SECURITY RISK MANAGEMENT TO ENHANCE CORPORATE GOVERNANCE

Corporate security managers must have a sound understanding of corporate governance principles to ensure the security function is integrated into the corporate governance framework. Primarily, corporate security should be ingrained into the company's risk management and, preferably, there should be a seat for the security champion on all risk management committees.

The region has had some prominent corporate crises in recent years. For example, in Australia the number of 2001–2 complaints to the Australian Securities and Investment Commission (ASIC) grew almost 13 percent from the public and 42 percent from external administrators. Matthews (cited in Elliott 2003) of the Australian Shareholders Association stated that "boards and their CEO's have a long way to go to restore shareholder faith and trust." The United States introduced legislation, the Sarbanes-Oxley Act of 2002, that requires extra oversight of auditing processes, elimination of conflicts of interest, and greater corporate transparency.

In 2003, a Connect 4 survey (cited by Fenton-Jones 2004) determined that in Australia the top 200 listed companies increased spending on audits by 10 percent to A$175 million. The increase was attributed to dealing with corporate governance compliance issues and revenue of board advisory services. Risk management, in particular, was seen as the main compliance issue.

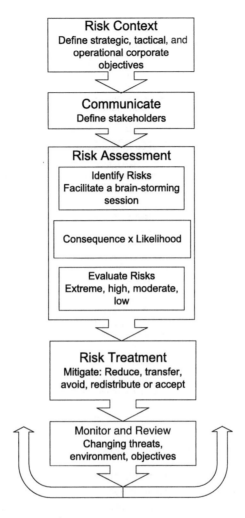

**FIGURE 3.1**   Risk management process.

Companies with operations in the Asia-Pacific region need to have enhanced risk management cultures, as poor corporate governance was identified as one of the root causes of the Asian financial crisis. It has been found that illegal practices of breach of trust, expropriations, embezzlement, and company theft appear to continue in many East Asian countries, but the punishment of such abuses remains largely weak.

**Tax evasion and money laundering:** In one of the biggest joint operations involving several law enforcement agencies in Malaysia, customs offices and more than 100 businesses nationwide have been raised in connection with tax evasion and money laundering activities. The syndicate had siphoned away billions of (Singapore) dollars. Two senior customs officers, 84 forwarding agents, a holding company and 24 of its related companies, and 25 customs offices were raided. The customs officers were detained under offences relating to the Customs Act, Income Tax Act, the Anti-Money

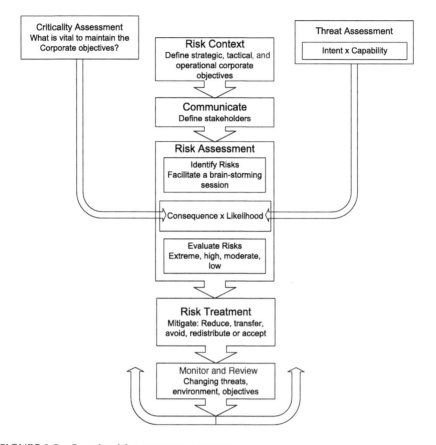

**FIGURE 3.2**    Security risk management process.

Laundering Act and Anti-Terrorism Act. Some 150 bank accounts have been frozen, including overseas accounts. This investigation was one of the biggest in Malaysia's history (The Star/Asia News Network, April 4, 2011).

While most corporations voluntarily comply, there is evidence of a lack of conformity and uniformity, and a suggestion that requirements are simply used as a means of maintaining legitimacy and control, to avoid litigation. This compliance approach highlights that the introduction of security policy and guidelines will make little difference if the corporate ethics culture is not right. Corporate governance is reliant on the basic principles of *acting in good faith*, viewing issues from other stakeholders' points of view, and taking responsibility for actions and decisions. Corporate security is equally reliant on these factors.

## IMPLEMENTING SECURITY RISK MANAGEMENT SYSTEMS

Effective implementation is perhaps the more difficult aspect when considering the subjective and dynamic environment of security mitigation. Hindsight is always a benefit after an incident and in particular when being prosecuted over an incident; however, as long as there was a clear and documented process that considered and provided a reasonable response that resulted in a degree of protection, the organization should prevail. But "security vulnerabilities are like the Florida fire ant—you can't kill them, all you can do is maintain your garden better than your neighbor so they choose to infest his yard instead of yours. Organizations without clear and effective security strategies will draw security incidents to themselves and away from the companies doing a better job," stated James Whittaker, chief security strategist.

Yet according to *The Global State of Information Security 2005*, a worldwide study by *CIO* magazine (Australia) and PricewaterhouseCoopers, most organizations are just holding their ground, although the third annual edition of the survey reports incremental improvement in the tactical battle to react to and protect against security incidents. *CSO* magazine stated that the data indicates a notable lack of focus on actions and strategies that could prevent these incidents in the first place—a "remarkable ambivalence" among respondents about compliance with government regulations, a clear lack of risk management discipline, and a continuing inability to create actionable security intelligence out of mountains of security data. For example, just 37 percent of respondents reported that they had an information security strategy and only 24 percent of the remainder stated that creating one is in the plans for next year. With increasingly serious, complex, targeted, and damaging threats continuously emerging, a noted lack of action is not the best defense.

Directed security risk management is often not effective when completed by other risk managers such as health and safety or financial staff as they do not take an "attacker" or threat perspective. Many medium- to large-size organizations that are without dedicated security advisors are likely to be unaware of many of their security vulnerabilities and related legal liabilities. Indeed, nor are they likely to be using existing security measures to their full potential, primarily due to a lack of clear direction, standards, and, in particular, a lack of awareness of what should be done.

Major changes are occurring in the field of security management, with continued improvement in professionalism and expertise, as well as the introduction of state standards and guidelines. Guidelines now exist for specific security risk management, security management systems, security technology, workplace surveillance, and business continuity, to name just a few. There are also industry-specific security guidelines for health, transport, and manufacturing, in addition, to current risk management and corporate governance guidelines.

Without a specific, well-conceived, and documented management system, security is unlikely to be fully and effectively integrated across the governance and risk management framework. There are simply too many other risk distractions, such as health, safety, and environmental risks, market risks, credit risks, and a plethora of financial risks. Security risks are often insufficiently assessed by managers who assess risk based only on their own perceptions and experiences. Without formal security experience and expertise, assessment and identified of risks could be very different and detrimental to those risks that the organization may actually face. Ignorance and a lack of clear responsibilities provided for security management at the executive and board level may allow poor or misdirected risk management to occur, thereby increasing the chance occurrence of incidents and surprise events. Ignorance is little protection for the executive and board.

To implement an effective security risk management strategy requires a formal systems approach, with strategic, tactical, and operational business goals being supported by risk management. Such a risk-directed security management systems approach should be no different from any other of the corporation's business or cost centers. Clear goals should be developed and approved by the CEO. These goals are fed down and developed into operational performance indicators, where performance can be gauged by the board. Nevertheless, to achieve such an effective security management system without constant reactive knee jerks to incidents requires a business-directed security manager who takes the following role:

- The security manager reports directly to the executive and/or board level.
- Full board and executive support is explicit.
- The security manager is an "internal consultant" rather than an operational position.
- A security manager is a true leader, operating at a strategic or tactical level.
- A clear and concise security risk management framework is provided.
- There is a degree of an intelligence function in defining corporate threats to inform the risk process.
- Like health and safety, every employee is responsible for security.

In support of such a security risk management system, include the following:

- Formulate a security policy that is supportive of and consistent with other policy documents.
- Establish security objectives and targets with the development of security management plans.
- Security administration should be formally established and implemented.
- The management structures and responsibilities that are implemented should reflect security management or reporting procedures.
- Conduct security risk identification, analysis, and evaluation of the effectiveness of existing security controls.
- All security issues and events should be formally monitored and recorded.
- Service agreements should ensure contractor and employee security compliance, including background checks and confidentiality agreements in employee selection procedures.
- Physical security should be closely monitored and integrated with computer and information security management.
- Security management systems should comply with state standards, if any.
- Business continuity management (crisis, disaster, and recovery plans) should be in place and testing procedures carried out.
- Security incident and investigation processes should be formally integrated with health, safety and environmental (HSE) information management systems.

Medium- to large-size organizations should give attention to the following five major areas in relation to their security strategy:

- User awareness
- Policy and procedures
- Information technologies
- Physical security
- Business continuity

Managing corporate and operational security is becoming increasingly critical as the very nature of corporate security is changing in response to significant business risks. Increasingly, the "inner-market," incorporating those working in and comprising the organization, become "knowledge workers" and independent professionals, whose behavior cannot be directly monitored or evaluated. This situation creates a security risk, such as fraud, theft, and intellectual property breaches, as well as many constant external threats. These risks are a challenge for any medium- to large-size organization to control over time and increasingly so in highly competitive and global markets.

## GENERATING A SECURITY BUSINESS CASE

There are two levels of risk within the realm of security risk management that need the consideration of the security manager, namely corporate and competitive risk. An understanding of both corporate and competitive risk is essential if the security manager is going to be able to manage the security risk to which the organization is exposed. A manager cannot protect that which they do not understand. Failure to understand the risk exposure will result in a failure to manage the organization's security risk exposure

Corporate risk relates to what the organization does or "What business are we in?" For example, the oil industry has different risks, both operationally and in a security sense, from the manufacture of perfumes and cosmetics. If an organization moves from one industry to the other, the security manager must be aware of the shifting security implications. If the organization changes what it does, then the security manager must be aware of the potential shift in risk exposure and how to manage the new risk exposure.

Competitive risk relates to how an organization does business. Security managers must understand and be involved in the competitive activities of the organization. Failure to understand these activities or the dynamic and applied environment will result in failure to be able to protect against them. One of the standard analytical tools for analyzing the competitive environment is the PEST analysis (political, environmental, social, and technological environment). Each of these factors is examined prior to making decisions as to the course of action that will best serve the greater organization. The message for the security manager is that any change, particularly creeping change, is a warning that risk exposure may have changed.

There are regular media reports of serious and significant security risks occurring against Asia Pacific corporations. One may even argue that in some sectors, security risks occur more frequently than other forms of risk. Yet in most cases when events have occurred, they either were preventable, could have been better mitigated, or were responded to inefficiently. Security is one of those areas that either is under-represented or lacks consideration at a senior management level, due primarily to a low perception of exposure to security risks. Security risk perceptions of senior managers are based on personal experience or influenced by the media reports of the day. In most cases, security measures are implemented only following an event, demonstrating that the organization either consciously assumed the risk or was simply ignorant to its existence. If this occurred in health and safety management, given current legislation, the organization may be prosecuted following a hazard event.

Time and again, large organizations that have conducted security audits and risk assessments are the victims of numerous security-related events. These events included burglaries, vandalism, major fire, petty arson, power failure, internal theft, and unauthorized entry to offices. But that is not necessarily the issue here, rather the fact that limited consideration is given to other risks, such as workplace violence, competitor intelligence, corporate espionage, and extortion. For example, information security and physical security were managed as two separate portfolios with no integration or communication strategy for each to support the other. Does this produce inefficacies with both groups repeating task or do they believe the other group is managing that risk?

For medium- to large-size organizations without formal security management in place, there is likely to be significant opportunity for them to reduce and mitigate risk by establishing and implementing an enterprise-wide security risk management system. The alternative is for the organization to continue operating without documented and coherent security risk management strategies, policies, practices, and procedures, and thereby being exposed to variable security risks and civil law liabilities. In the event of an injury or claim resulting from a security event, such as a major fraud, armed robbery, or data breach, an organization would benefit from its ability to demonstrate industry compliance and the fulfillment of "duty of care" and "fiduciary duty." Without a formal security risk management system as a starting point, this may prove difficult.

The most common and significant problems medium- and large-size organizations experience in their security management is a lack of direction (policy); they just do it their own way because "that's the way we've always done it here" (lack of procedures); and "oh, it wouldn't happen here, would it?" (lack of awareness and risk management). A security risk management system, like other management systems such as safety, finance, and human resources, enables a strategy and process to be in place that is suitable, practical, and consistent across corporate and business operations. Without a formally documented system and strategy, the effect is most often an ad hoc approach involving conflicting objectives among senior and mid-level managers. This approach results in dispersed accountability and contributes to a decentralized and uncoordinated approach, often operating in response mode only. In relation to security risks, this approach can potentially be catastrophic, in the form of preventable loss, injuries, or crisis.

With the introduction of security-related national and international guidelines, there is significant scope for any medium- to large-size organization to establish compliance. These standards could be an international ISO standard, or a standard taken from their own place of company registration or primary headquarters. However, it would be expected that from a compliance perspective, the perceived "best" framework is used in-country. Without a security management system that matches the standard of the organizations with other management systems, compliance with security standards is likely to fall short, or if met initially, will not be maintained over the longer term.

## EFFECTIVE RISK COMMUNICATION

Security risk management, as a core competency, has to have the ability to communicate the appropriate risk message. Studies (Larichev, Brown, and Flanders 1998) have summarized that risk communication must improve and that cultural differences must be taken into account, a core responsibility for the corporation and its board members.

> The American playwright Arthur Miller once said a good newspaper was a nation talking to itself. His definition implies a close relationship between a good newspaper and its community of readers (Kovacs, *West Australian*, April 22, 2000, 19).

A number of authors (Paton, Smith, and Johnson 2000; Yosie and Herbst 1998) have concluded that there is a need to involve lay people and stakeholders in some degree of the risk management process. To be effective, there has to be an inevitable and continual expansion of stakeholder involvement in risk decision making, resulting in stakeholders having a greater acceptance and understanding of the risk when they have been involved. Some of the major reasons behind the need to involve stakeholders include identifying "key issues, challenges associated with managing them, and analyz[ing] factors shaping their future use" (Yosie and Herbst 1998, 1). The following stakeholder observations were highlighted:

- Social interests were becoming more interactive.
- Current stakeholder processes are generally not well managed.
- There was a need to achieve a better match between stakeholder and the solution.
- There was no specific agreement on the definition of a stakeholder.
- The stakeholders challenge the effectiveness of experts in the decision-making process.

There is a need to have effective risk communication, otherwise the risk management process becomes a waste of time and resources, useful only for internal consummation. However, such internal consumption may be biased due to groupthink, a "yes" culture and little empathy for stakeholders. At this point, it should be noted that stakeholders are not always external community members but could for instance be board members, directors, or other department heads—anyone who may have to make some degree of decision based on the risk management outcome. Therefore effective risk communication attempts to do the following:

- Reduce public outrage.
- Inform and educate the public.
- Reduce public suffering, both perceived and actual.
- Develop empathy with the public and related stakeholders.
- Reduce the likelihood of social attention being focused not on the less significant issues or problems but on the important and significant issues and problems.
- Develop and utilize media communication.
- Make better informed decisions and policies.
- Increase the effectiveness and efficiency of risk management.

Effective risk communication can be achieved by following a simple model:

- Take a holistic approach to integrate risk communication into corporate plans so that they are culturally accepted within the organization.
- Gain and maintain the trust of the public so that your message is heard, accepted, and understood.
- Inform the public of issues in an open and transparent manner. Place the risk in a fair and understandable context, without complex, unrelated, or irrelevant exposure comparisons.
- Have a known and credible spokesperson. Credibility is "determined by the perceived expertise and trustworthiness of the source" (Cox 1999, 87).
- Be aware of cultural and perceptual issues.
- Develop support and use the media. The media reflects society's perceptions, although these may be positively amplified.
- Be timely and act in a proactive manner.
- Plan, prepare. and practice.
- Be open and maintain transparency.

Risk communication is a complex process that has many facets; however, without effective risk communication risk management cannot be used to its full potential. The level and nature of risk communication primarily depend on the intended audience and the delivery of the message. This message delivery is a prime skill and requires the executive or board to take this role. The greater and more diverse the audience, the more difficult effective risk communication becomes and the better the message giver needs to be. The nature of the risk also plays a significant part.

## RISK GAMING OR GAINING CONSENSUS

The risk management process must produce as reliable and valid outcome as possible, cognizant of its subjective nature. A security risk management model may be designed at a corporate or international level, but applied at the operational or in-country level. A typical scenario may be a commercial development, where diverse and geographically spread divisions use a corporate risk management model to assess the variability of their proposed projects. Projects are given the approval to proceed at an international level, with a criterion being the risk assessment outcome.

After the risk process has been used for a while, it does not take users long to begin to understand what they need to achieve from the risk process to reach an outcome they want. Due to the subjective nature of the inputs, in particular with security risk management, they begin to *game* the system using inputs that produce their desired outcome. They quickly learn what inputs have the greatest impact on the outcome.

A solution may be to lock the model, giving the users access only to input data and review the outcomes. A better approach is to educate users in the importance of risk management and the benefits to them. Nevertheless, both these methods effectiveness can be reduced to gain an output wanted by the users. Koller (1999, 32–33) states that the only effective solution to this problem is to use *risk police*, a group of experts who do the following:

- Review the effectiveness and appropriateness of the inputs.
- Come to a consensus as to the validity of the input values.
- Become a historical reference.
- Enforce consistency in the risk assessment process across all projects.

Nevertheless, the staff members who review such process have to have a certain skill set. The review members should:

- Be experts in their field.
- Be impartial.
- Have tenure on the panel for an appropriate period.
- Have a high level of interpersonal skills.
- Be empowered.

Consider Koller (1999, 33) when he stated that "establishment of such review boards for each risk-model can be an expensive and time-consuming task. However, establishment of responsible, impartial and empowered boards of review is the only risk-process technique I can recommend that will result in realistic and consistent risk-model results."

## DRIVE FOR A SECURITY RISK CONSENSUS

There is a need to gain common understanding or clear definition of risk within the group. Such common understanding should include not only decision makers—often seen as the corporate executives—but also other stakeholders that may be affected by the risk activity without due benefit. In risk management, an individual's assessment is driven by his or her own perceptions. In conducting security risk management, the process must clearly define the scope and identification stages. In addition, the risk scope should be carefully controlled in order to give appropriate results toward the risk assessment task.

Security risk management is increasingly used to direct limited resources in the mitigation of threat; however, risk management can result in these limited resources directed in an inappropriate or less effective manner. Risk management should include a number of discrete steps, with risk assessment embedded within these steps and incorporating risk identification, analysis, and evaluation. It is at this assessment stage that many factors may result in the risk management process being less than effective including individuals' perceptions of risk, parochial attitudes, invested interests, undefined risks, bias, or a limited understanding of a risk. To overcome these issues, some form of group consensus should be achieved.

An individual approach to risk analysis produces varying results in risk rankings or defined mitigation strategies. While this would be expected, due to individual opinions, there are few patterns in the differences between individuals or, at a more strategic level, departments. In fact, there are limited differences between organizational employees, and individuals do not in general adopt a parochial attitude toward their risks. Such a view is seen to contradict others, which purport that people skew risks to favor their own interests (Beard and Brooks 2006). Empirical evidence would suggest so, but within an organization this does not appear to be the case, although external stakeholders could and do hold diverse views and these are more significant.

There is a need to gain common understanding or clear definition of risks within the group. For example, what is considered *serious assault* will vary between a single group based on aspects such as gender, experience, and knowledge. An individual's assessment is driven by his or her own perceptions, and less important perceived risk had a more common view, whereas higher risk had a greater diversity of views. All risk management tasks should consider the situation, using such approaches as group interviews, Delphi method, and nominal group techniques. In addition, the results gathered from such group approaches can be used to ascertain accuracy and, importantly, can confidently be used to allocate resources to minimize security threats.

## CONCLUSION

Risk management and security risk management are a core function for the corporation, led by the board, directors, executives, and security manager. Risk management, whether general risks or security risks, provides a formal, documented, and consensual approach to decision making, risk mitigation, and security strategies. As a best-case scenario, risk management provides informed decision making, allowing limited resources to be used effectively to protect against a diverse range of corporate risk, and protects the organization and its board against prosecution when things go wrong. As a worst-case scenario, risk management is an administrative and resource-extensive burden that leads to a risk-averse organization. However, to provide such informed decision-making or, at worst, protection, risk management has to follow a defined and formal method.

We are all exposed to risk, and to be a success in business there is a need to partake in risky activities. However, there are international standards that provide a reasonable approach to risk management, and to undertake such activity is a corporation's responsibility. One such standard is the International Standards Organization (ISO) 31000:2009 Risk Management, which can be applied within the Asia-Pacific region effectively. There has been and will continue to be examples of where corporations are not applying appropriate risk management, and they are exposing themselves not only within the nation-states they operate within but also within their home country.

Security risk management is unique from the ISO 31000 view of risk management. Security risk management has to take an intelligence-driven threat stance, considering the corporation's criticalities and vulnerabilities. Such an approach ensures that where possible a reasonable level of security is applied, based on an informed view. This informed view has a clear and documented audit trail that justifies why such mitigation strategies were applied. As long as these strategies are reasonable, the organization and its employees are protected.

The implementation of security risk management is difficult, considering the dynamic and subjective nature of security risks. As long as the security manager reports directly to the CEO, has board or executive support, is a leader, and develops and propagates a clear risk framework that links into the culture of the organization, then security risk management can succeed. From that point, it is a matter of developing robust security business cases, based on informed risk strategies. A sound security risk management process supports and enhances corporate governance.

## REFERENCES

Aven, T. 2008. *Risk Analysis: Assessing Uncertainties Beyond Expected Values and Probabilities*. West Sussex: Wiley.

Beard, B., and D. J. Brooks. 2006. *Security Risk Assessment: Group Approach to a Consensual Outcome*. Paper presented at the 2006 Information Warfare and Security Conference, Perth, Western Australia.

Brooks, D. J. (2007). *Defining Security through the Presentation of Security Knowledge Categories*. Paper presented at the 7th Australian Security Research Symposium, Perth, Western Australia.

———. 2009. *Key Concepts in Security Risk Management: A Psychometric Concept Map Approach to Understanding*. Saarbrucken: VDM Verlag.

———. 2011. "Security Risk Management: A Psychometric Map of Expert Knowledge Structure." *International Journal of Risk Management* 13 (1/2): 17–41.

Brooks, D. J., and H. Cotton. 2011. "Security Risk Management in the Asia-Pacific Region: What Are Security Professionals Using?" In *Proceedings of the 4th Australian Security and Intelligence Conference*, 27–37. Perth: Edith Cowan University.

Cox, E. P. 1999. "Warnings and Risk Communication." In *Warnings and Risk Communication*, edited by M. S. Wogalter, D. M. DeJoy, and K. R. Laughery, 85–97. Boca Raton, FL: Taylor and Francis.

Dali, A. 2011. "Global Survey on ISO 31000 Risk Management Standard." http://www.linkedin.com/groups?mostPopular=&gid=1834592 (accessed October 18, 2011).

Elliott, G. 2003. "Gloves Off in Board War: Shareholders Attack Executives over Pay Disclosure." *The Australian*, October 8, 33.

Fenton-Jones, M. 2004. "Finance Collapses around the Work Force Change." *Australian Financial Review*, March 11. http://afr.com/articles/2004/03/09/1078594355732.html (accessed September 10, 2004).

Koller, G. 1999. *Risk Assessment and Decision Making in Business and Industry: A Practical Guide*. Boca Raton, FL: CRC Press.

Larichev, O. I., R. V. Brown, and N. E. Flanders. 1998. *Numerical and Verbal Decision Analysis as Practical Tools—Part II: General Comparison*. Retrieved April 15, 2012 from www.fisher.osu.edu/~buther_267/.

Ministry of Manpower. 2006. *Guide to the Workplace Safety and Health (Risk Management) Regulations*. Ministry of Manpower—Occupational Safety and Health Division. http://www.mom.gov.sg (accessed July 12, 2011).

Paton, D., L. Smith, and D. M. Johnson. 2000. "Volcanic Hazards: Risk Perception and Preparedness." *New Zealand Journal of Psychology* 29 (2), 86–91.

Power, M. 2007. *Organized Uncertainty: Designing a World of Risk Management*. Oxford: Oxford University Press.

Standards Australia. 2004. *HB 436:2004 Risk Management Guidelines: Companion to AS/NZS4360:2004*. Sydney: Standards Australia.

Vijayan, J. 2011. "What a Cyberwar with China Might Look Like: Former U.S. Diplomat Describes Hypothetical Scenario." *Computerworld*, March 31. http://www.computerworld.com/s/article/9215370/What_a_cyberwar_with_China_might_look_like.

Yosie, T. F., and T. D. Herbst. 1998. "Using Stakeholders Processes in Environmental Decision Making: An Evaluation of Lessons Learned, Key Issues and Future Challenges." http://www.riskworld.com.Nreport (accessed May 25, 2009).

# 4 Security Threats

## INTRODUCTION

This chapter introduces specific security threats that may exist against organizations. These are many and varied, making them difficult to counter if some thought is not preapplied. However, all threats have been experienced either by the corporation itself, by close partners, or within the industrial group. Threats to corporate security may also be influenced by the business activities of the company. Most corporations and their staffs have short memories when considering threats, and the past can predict what is likely to occur in the future. Sources of threats are likely to be dynamic and may be financially, politically, emotionally, or environmentally motivated. Although threats may be difficult to articulate in some formal sense, corporate security has a duty to be aware of such issues, mitigate the risk, and in general otherwise be prepared.

From a corporate perspective, threats may be difficult to articulate and define, as threats have to consider a person's or group's intent and capability. In a corporate world, this is well understood in the competitive environment, but poorly understood from a security perspective. This limitation is perhaps because threats are dynamic, situational, and often influenced by a range of macro and micro environmental factors. In addition, to truly understand a threat requires time, resources, and effort, to proficiently understand intent and capability. Therefore this chapter presents many past and present threats that a corporate security manager should consider and commence preparation to provide some degree of mitigation against.

## REALIZED THREAT

Crisis plans should be developed to cater for the *most credible* worst-case scenarios, without scaremongering. Companies do not necessarily need to plan for every scenario; but what is needed is a plan that encompasses the worst, then it can be adapted as lesser situations arise. What is required are processes that are already established to deal with crises in general, including environmental events, extortion, kidnapping, serious infection, or health issues and workplace deaths. You need preagreed, clearly defined lines of responsibility and delegation. There are also simple operational issues of ensuring you have adequate communications, with enough phones, e-mail, operators, and 24-hour access. This should not be worked out in the heat of a crisis, and if it is, then it's probably already too late.

A crisis can be more like a marathon than a sprint, so do not expect a crisis to last a few days or a week; some may take months or even years, particularly before full recovery is realized. Planning is crucial as a crisis situation will demand that you do things that you might not otherwise ever consider, so it's important not to get locked into paradigms. Most importantly, organizations should get outside help when needed and actually have consultants or experts within their corporate network before they are required. Do not expect that you or your own team will have all of the expertise in-house (Holloway and Betts 2005). Nor should you expect to easily engage your most preferred expertise at short notice and without a preestablished relationship.

A failure to act promptly will almost certainly be damaging to an organization's ability to control public and legal exposure and minimize damage to operations and reputation. Should litigation arise from resulting losses, such as a product defect, a slow reaction will draw criticism from the courts and may exacerbate any subsequent damages claim or sanction against the organization. At the very least, confidential notification of the existence of a threat to other organizations in the supply chain, even when the threat is not considered credible, will increase the level of trust and goodwill in the commercial relationship between suppliers that will be critical in the recovery process (Holloway and Betts 2005).

## SOPHISTICATED TRANSNATIONAL ORGANIZED CRIME

The *Internet Security Threat Report*, released by Symantec (2010), has determined that cybercriminals are becoming more professional and commercial in the development, distribution, and use of malicious code and services. In the pursuit of making money, organized cybercriminals are searching for vulnerabilities or holes in existing software, particularly applications like Microsoft Office and web browsers, in order to compromise financial and identity access. They have moved from hunting gambling and pornography websites to traditionally trusted websites, such as music download, shopping, financial, social networking, and career recruitment websites.

## FOOD AND PRODUCT CONTAMINATION

The 2006 food contamination cases in Queensland, Australia, involving Sizzler Restaurants and George Weston Foods highlight the need for well-prepared crisis response plans. Extortion attempts were also made the previous year in 2005, against Mars and Snickers chocolate bars in New South Wales. Australian product extortion threats over the last decade have cost manufacturers millions of dollars and present significant crisis response challenges that include maintaining public safety and consumer confidence in the product as well as minimizing negative publicity and legal liabilities.

For example, in 2006 George Weston Foods recalled its Top Taste and Fine Fare Products, following contamination cases in Queensland, Victoria, and Tasmania. In January, a razor blade was found in a Top Taste cake; in March, a metal rod was found in another cake; and in May, a sewing needle was discovered in a third Top Taste product. The company was required to formulate and execute an action plan, which included a full product recall and an advertising campaign to tell customers what to do. However, the company was severely criticized by the Australian Consumer Association for delaying the recall by a reported five months.

In February 2006, two separate incidents of deliberate food contamination occurred at Sizzler Restaurants in Brisbane. Patrons had discovered green pellets in food, which were later confirmed to be rat poison. Sizzler also implemented food security procedures and conducted a national advertising campaign to restore consumer confidence.

In 2006 in response to these cases, the Australian Queensland State Government introduced mandatory reporting of suspected food tampering that covers both retailers and manufacturers. Restaurants, takeaways, and food factories face fines of up to A$15,000 for not reporting suspected or confirmed food tampering under the laws. The Queensland Health Minister said, "Incidents involving both Sizzler and Top Taste cakes this year could have been handled a lot better if those businesses were legally obligated to immediately inform Queensland Health when they first suspected that someone had tampered with their food."

Product extortion cases in the past have included Colgate-Palmolive, which received a potassium cyanide-laced tube of toothpaste at its head office in 1991. In 1997, the Arnotts company recalled biscuits across 3,000 supermarkets and service stations after it was informed that its products would be poisoned if an extortion demand was not met. Nestlé received a similar threat that year. In 1998, Sanitarium Health Foods received a threat of contaminants in its soy milk and conducted a product recall. In 2000, Herron Pharmaceutical capsules received threats that its products had been poisoned with strychnine, requiring the withdrawal from sale of millions of dollars worth of stock and the implementation of new antitamper wrapping. In addition to the Mars extortion in 2005, Multiplex disclosed a threat to shoot one of its crane drivers unless A$50 million was paid to the extortionist.

These trends within Asia-Pacific region and globally suggest that food and pharmaceutical industries are particularly at risk, although there have also been a number of cases across a range of industries. In the last decade, extortion cases have emerged in e-commerce industries, particularly online betting and casinos.

## KIDNAPPING AND EXTORTION

One of the largest current dangers while traveling is kidnapping, with between 12,500 and 30,000 foreigners kidnapped around the world each year. Kidnaps are carried out by drug and criminal gangs and often go unreported. The police may be helpless to intervene or corrupt, organizations do not want negative publicity, and insurance firms want to avoid copycat crimes. The practice of paying ransoms is common. Similarly, many companies do not wish to admit that their staff should be learning how to deal with these types of events, as accepting that they are exposed to this level of risk may result in negative publicity affecting stakeholder relationships. Litigation and increased insurance costs could also be considered a danger. A common causation is that people by nature can be extraordinarily naïve and collectively, and most shockingly, complacent or corrupt.

**Cost no issue in security needs:** In a world of significant and unpredictable risks, large companies try to maintain safe perimeters around their executives. "I don't think risks have changed a whole lot," said Bob Hayes, managing director of the Security

Executive Council, a Washington-based research and services group. "But risk awareness on the part of executives has changed a great deal. Corporations are much, much
more aware of risks." Last year, Walt Disney spent US$562,034 for security regard-
ing chief executive Robert Iger, and American Express has spent US$330,000 over
the last three years on home security systems for chief executive Kenneth Chenault
(McWilliams, April 16, 2011, cited in *Security Management*, April 19, 2011).

The manner in which a company will react to a threat of extortion will depend on
the particular circumstances, including the nature and credibility of the threat presented, the risk of harm to consumers, and the likely effect on the reputation of the
company. Due consideration of these matters will dictate the nature of the response,
which may range from a simple warning to consumers to a full-scale product recall
supported by an intensive media campaign.

Where possible, an extortion response decision should be taken after a timely
and rigorous investigation of the threat or tampering. All stages of the investigation should be underscored by a consideration of the likelihood of injury to consumers and the severity of that injury. Where investigations reveal that a threat
is credible, the response taken by the company, in particular in the first 24 to 72
hours, will be crucial to its chance of successfully dealing with the event. Prior
planning will clearly demonstrate its value at this stage. Needed immediately are
factual and liability-based investigations to guide decision making and assist continuing legal advice.

Where an immediate threat to public and consumer safety is posed by extortion, a
company will rarely have time to gather all available information relevant to the credibility of the event. With a situation of product tampering, the first decision—even
before a product recall is implemented—is the necessity and timing of contact with
authorities. Obtaining input at an early stage from police or other relevant authorities
(such as the Therapeutic Goods Administration in Australia) will also be critical,
particularly if inquiries can be made within an acceptable range of publicity risk.

**Computer expert arrested over extortion:** Actor Tom Cruise was the target of a
US$1M extortion attempt in exchange for returning photographs of his wedding to
Katie Holmes. The photographs were obtained by the 33-year-old computer technician
after having access to the photographer's computer.

Some level of police involvement is inevitable where a credible extortion threat
has been received and public notification is necessary. Even where an extortion
threat is suspected to be a hoax, it would be prudent to notify police in order to create a record and an audit trail that can later be pointed to as a demonstration of the
organization's proactiveness. This action will also build a line of communication
and trust that can be beneficial should a credible threat emerge. The police should be
familiar with the commercial implications of major product extortion, and when a
line of communication exists, authorities are not insensitive to the need for discretion
and confidentiality, particularly where organizations are making notification decisions prior to a determination of whether or not a threat is credible (Holloway and
Betts 2005). Such practice is applicable to many crisis events.

One message that emerges from the experience of companies faced with product extortions is that an up-front approach to the media and a proactive stance in dealing with the crisis will for the most part attract praise from both the public and the authorities. Conversely, organizations that avoid media attention at all costs frequently attract the most attention and also lose the ability to manage whatever "spin" the media wish to place on the crisis. More importantly, organizations will begin to lose trust in the eyes of the media, authorities, and public, making them a larger (perceived) target. One way for an organization to ensure accurate reporting of its response to a crisis is to involve itself in media liaising, which should include engaging with social media to maximize positive media opportunities.

Research conducted by organizations in the food and manufacturing industries suggests that, as soon as a product is recalled from the marketplace, consumers want to know what steps are being taken to address the extortion issue and an estimate of when the product will likely be returned to shelves. Communication with consumers at this point is critical to avoid consumers moving to a competitor's products. Successful organizations should advertise throughout the course of the crisis and provide information as to what is being done "behind the scenes," from manufacturing to packing and shipping. Such an approach demonstrates that the organization is working to return the product to the market (Holloway and Betts 2005). The message is that increased communication enhances reputation.

Organizations that prioritize the concerns of their customers and their key stakeholders are ultimately rewarded by the process. The rewards are not short term, especially in cases where a product must be recalled from the market. Yet experience indicates that consumers remember organizations that promote consumer safety, and the result is reputation protection and a longer-term viability of brand and profitability. Organizations should work with their legal and other advisors, that is, public relations and risk consultants, to ensure that at the forefront of every decision associated with an extortion is a focus on the public concern that everything has been done by the company to appropriately manage a potential crisis (Holloway and Betts 2005).

**Ransomware emerged as a new online threat:** A form of computer virus which accesses data and then encrypts it, effectively holding it hostage until payment is made to get the data back. This type of attack is an extension of phishing, whereby the victim is tricked into providing information. Larger corporations, particularly online merchants, have been subject to cyber-extortion in the past; however, this type of attack is now beginning to target home users and small businesses, primarily as they present a much smaller risk of being caught. Ransomware first appeared in the US in May 2005.

## TIGER KIDNAPPINGS: PREVENTION THE BEST POLICY

The tiger is a skilled predator that will stalk its prey before pouncing and making a surprise kill. Likewise, this approach is also used to circumvent the highest or thickest walls, most complex security technologies, and best-made vaults by using the weakest link in the chain, human beings. The methodology, referred to in the security industry as "tiger kidnapping," is so called to distinguish this crime from conventional kidnapping and to reflect the fast-moving nature of events conceivably prompting an immediate and decisive police response.

Tiger kidnapping involves short-term hostage taking in order to take control of personnel who have immediate or high-level access to cash or valuables. Captives are frequently held overnight, and the aim of the criminals is to frighten their victims to such a degree that they will follow their instructions and not contact the police, even when they have an opportunity to do so. The characteristics of a conventional kidnapping are entirely different from those of a tiger kidnapping and the two should not be confused. Conventional kidnapping remains an international traveler's risk and an extremely dangerous situation. Kidnappings usually involve the taking of an individual or small group who have personal or family wealth or who work for an apparently wealthy employer. The kidnappers abduct and hold the prisoner(s) while they make demands for ransom, usually money. These offenses are particularly dangerous for the hostage because most kidnappers underestimate the difficulties involved in holding a prisoner for extended periods. Personal profiles, media management, negotiation, and crisis management are more relevant to traditional kidnappings.

In contrast, tiger kidnapping is carried out in a much shorter period of time and therefore most efforts should be toward prevention, as responses will most often be after the event. The threat to life is significant and the modus operandi may manifest itself in many different forms. Incidents fall into a range of categories, which include the following:

- The victim and hostages have been taken at their home.
- The victim has been approached on the way to or from the workplace.
- The victim receives a text message or e-mail.
- The victim has received or been handed a threatening letter or note.
- The victim is threatened by a relative, friend, or associate.

In the first category it is immediately obvious to the victim that hostages have been taken, but in the remainder there can be a claim of having taken hostages when in fact none have been taken. In each case there is a target, victim, potential hostages, and finally a robbery or acquisition of ransom. Invariably, inside information leads to a victim being singled out. It is known that criminals or their associates will gain employment for that very purpose, hence the predatory nature of the crime. This risk is one of many reasons to ensure that employee selection and vetting are thoroughly conducted. Friendships may also be initiated at the workplace and extend into private time.

**Home invasion, kidnap and hostage drama in the US turned tragic**: Two men broke into a prominent doctor's home and kidnapped a female member of the family to withdraw money from the bank under duress. The family were held hostage for hours. After leaving the bank, suspicious bank employees called the police who surrounded the house. In their escape the two offenders shot dead the doctor's wife and two daughters and set the house on fire. The two men were captured after ramming police vehicles (*West Australian*).

A person's way of life (gambling, drug habit, infidelity) may mark him or her as a potential target. Inadvertent loose talk outside the work environment and/or non-compliance will also attract attention in the wrong quarters. Nor is it only company executives and families that could be targeted. Consider that in many workplaces the receptionist is tasked with controlling access to cash, securing banking information, and issuing security passes.

Security planning should consider the offense categories and associated scenarios, including:

1. There is forced entry, family members are separated and bound, and threats are made. The victim is forced to go to the workplace, accompanied by gang member(s), where valuables are stolen. In this case, the victim has sole access to the premises and safe/strong room.
2. A telephone call is made to the victim during business hours stating that his or her spouse and/or children are being held, which may or may not be true. The victim is instructed to liberate a specified amount of cash/valuables and take it to a rendezvous, which may be the first of several to avoid police surveillance. Again, the victim will have or be able to engineer sole access to the safe or vault.
3. Threats are made to an employee of the target company in terms of serious harm being meted out to a friend, relative, or victim him or herself if he or she fails to follow certain instructions in respect of the facilitation of a theft or robbery. No actual kidnapping is involved in this case, simply a demand by menace.
4. A senior employee is coerced into accompanying a criminal gang to the workplace. Members of the victim's family may also be present to exert maximum duress and force occupants of the premises to allow entry. Once inside, the coercion continues with a view to obtaining valuables in process and/or storage. The storage area (vault) would probably not be secured/locked at the time of attack.

Two notable case histories that reflect the extent of losses resulting from tiger kidnapping events are in Belfast, Ireland, December 2004 where GBP$21 million was stolen, and in Tunbridge, UK, February 2006 where GBP$53 million was stolen. Recorded figures have shown that since 2003, there has been a yearly increase in this type of offense within the United Kingdom culminating in a substantial increase in 2006. The most at risk are those businesses operating in the financial sector.

In May 2009 in Belfast, Ireland, four people were rescued by police after being held overnight at a house while a man was ordered to go to his place of work, collect cash, and leave it at a designated drop location. Dublin police made seven arrests in the wake of the E$7.6 million robbery. The kidnappers had taken photographs of the family members bound and gagged. Bank representatives had agreed to conduct an industry-wide investigation into making their bank safes less vulnerable to their own employees.

The increase in the rate of tiger kidnappings within recent years has been attributed to the hardening of physical security, while overlooking the most important element, the human factor. The offense does not apply to just managers of

banks and cash depots. Tiger kidnappings have also targeted jewelers, supermarket managers, and even McDonald's staff. All workplaces containing cash and/or
valuables should consider the risk of becoming prey to an extreme, surprise, and
high-loss event.

Security planning should naturally focus on the most important phase of a tiger
kidnapping operation, the preoffense stage, where offenders engage in lengthy target
selection and planning. It is at this stage where a number of procedural and physical
security measures can be applied in an attempt to offset the risk to a business. The
strategy for the second phase, during the offense, will focus on the personal safety
of the employees involved and the early warning of the incident to others. Finally,
the strategy for the postevent phase should ensure that measures are developed to
significantly reduce the secondary impacts, including harm mitigation, by executing
a considered response and recovery plan.

An effective training program of interactive briefings for employees has been
shown to provide the most effective method of raising awareness of tiger kidnapping
and ensuring that employees understand the response required. This training is more
effective when updated regularly or used to supplement wider personal security
briefings to ensure that policies and procedures introduced are relevant, understood,
and able to be trusted and performed under severe duress.

Ensuring that a crisis and communications response plan is compiled and able
to be invoked effectively is a further crucial element for companies once an incident is taking place. When notified of an incident, organizations that do not have
clear response procedures can increase the impact of the incident, endanger the
personnel involved, and cause additional secondary problems that affect reputation and possibly lead to avoidable legal ramifications. Many within the banking
sector are using external consultants to both provide immediate incident response
and support, and act as long-term crisis and communication advisors following
the event.

Current treatment strategies offer no single solution; however, there are more
often lessons learned from previous incidents and case study information. The most
critical and effective approach is to be proactive during the planning stage of the
offense and recognize the importance of the human key in the commissioning of
the crime. Organizations within the banking sector that lead best practice in the
area have been recognized as those with a risk management approach that combines
focused training and support for at-risk personnel with effective policies and procedures, separation of responsibilities and duties with supportive physical security
measures, liaison with police and other agencies with sector information sharing,
and an effective crisis and communication plan with a tested business continuity
plan. By implementing a proactive approach, companies will not only minimize the
risk of a tiger kidnapping being planned against them but most importantly provide
a safer working environment for employees.

## COMBATING TRANSNATIONAL HIGH-SEA PIRACY

The world's maritime and shipping industries are becoming increasingly concerned
with the proliferation of high-sea piracy occurring in such places as the Malacca

Straits, Gulf of Aden, Somali Basin, and Suez Canal. Piracy spiked to 409 attacks in 2009, up from 293 in 2008. The number of attacks where seafarers were fired upon increased threefold to 120 attacks. As of January 2010, the last paid ransom totaled US$7M, with 14 ships holding 247 crew, highjacked and to be released. Of the 35,000 vessels navigating the Gulf of Aden including 15 percent of the world's oil, the U.S. Navy fleet commanders estimate that 75 percent of vessels are not following security best management practice against piracy, with second- and third-tier shipping operators appearing most complacent.

> **India plans new law to deal with piracy:** Faced with repeated instances of piracy in the high seas with Indians' wellbeing at stake, New Delhi is putting together a robust mechanism to deal with the menace, contemplating and working on not just a new domestic law against piracy but also negotiating with the littoral states of Somalia and some independent ones within it to ensure that acts of piracy do not go unpunished because of logistical, legal or diplomatic issues. The legislation will put together some of the vital points of international laws against piracy, provisions of the IPC and the admiralty laws. It will not be of any help in the negotiation process after Indians aboard a ship have been taken hostage which, according to experts in the field, often proves to be a major hurdle when the liners belong to smaller shipping companies. "It will be a comprehensive piece against piracy. For example, now our domestic laws do not even define piracy. This has made it difficult to try the 120-odd pirates who are at present in our custody" (Abantika, *Times of India*, April 28, 2011).

Indonesia has had significant success in reducing piracy in the Malacca Straits through tri-nation agreements and capacity building, settlement and return to peace of the Aceh separatist conflict, and an arms decommissioning. Despite infrequent attacks occurring in the region, the risk of piracy has been reduced to a treatable degree. The impact of piracy has been felt throughout international shipping. As an example, Australian-flagged ships, Masters, and Royal Australian Navy have all had direct contact with pirates in the Gulf of Aden. Australian shipping began avoiding the area and navigating via the Cape of Good Hope, some 5,000 nautical miles (nm) farther than via the Gulf of Aden and Suez Canal. Research has shown that taking this route results in significantly greater costs. For an ultra large crude carrier the cost is an additional US$7.2 million, and for a 100,000 tonne container ship the additional transit costs would be US$2.84 million.

Piracy is a form of transnational organized crime and involves clans of pirates operating predominantly off the coast of Somalia and Nigeria. The Malacca Straits and other waters in Southeast Asia have also been at high risk of piracy in the recent past. Piracy has been a maritime risk for centuries. It was therefore somewhat surprising that the international shipping industry appeared to treat the 2009 spike in attacks as a new phenomenon, as if taking the industry by surprise.

International naval forces, operating under a range of UN (United Nations), EU (European Union), and NATO (North Atlantic Treaty Organization) task forces are managing a maritime security patrol area in the Gulf of Aden, an area the size of Australia. Naval forces have been tasked to protect World Food Program shipping, protect other vulnerable shipping, establish surveillance, and deter and disrupt piracy activities. There is a continued need for optimizing the coordination of naval assets and rules of engagement. The military is overcoming many obstacles. There are more than 30 nation-states involved, making communication and coordination a huge challenge. China introduced three vessels to the theater, creating a unique collaboration between the United States, UK, Russia, China, and India. Despite this collaboration, it is estimated that 60 naval vessels would be required to effectively patrol the area. As of 2010, the highest number of U.S. frigates and destroyers in theater has been 13, with 5 or 6 more common. Of the 57 interceptions in 2009 to January 2010, 35 occurred between October 2009 and January 24, 2010, resulting in 38 arrests and 171 suspected pirates released.

In the Indian Ocean, piracy is influenced by the monsoon seasons, between the periods of March to May and October to December, to provide suitable conditions. In 2005, pirates were operating within a range of 165 nm off the Somali coast. In 2009, the pirates were operating at ranges exceeding 1,000 nm off the coastland. Using dhows as mother ships to launch high-speed skiffs, some attacks have been known to be as fast as 11 minutes from the time of initial visual contact to boarding a vessel. They will often target low-speed vessels, traveling at around 12 knots with low freeboards allowing easier boarding. The illegitimate activities will also facilitate smuggling, arms dealing, and drug trafficking.

The navy has advised industry to take immediate actions for self-defense. The presence of war ships has been resolved as of the end of 2011 and the disruption by boarding, searching, confiscation, and destruction of arms and equipment (ladders, hooks, and ropes) will continue. UN Resolutions 1816, 1838, 1846, and 1851 refer to the rules of engagement and the use of necessary means; however, UN Resolution 1851 has made a shift from a military and use-of-force focus to a law enforcement focus. This change of focus has created jurisdictional issues, and engaging military in a law enforcement role is often problematic.

The major issues facing the international community include capacity building in Somalia, monitoring unregulated fishing in the region, integration of China into the Internationally Recommended Transit Corridor (IRTC), international legal frameworks, naval force flow via intelligence, surveillance, target acquisition, and reconnaissance (ISTAR), and use of multistate maritime patrol and reconnaissance aircraft (MPRA). Hampering efforts further, naval assets are restricted from entering Yemeni territorial waters or airspace.

Ship owners will continue to seek greater protection from naval forces and UN intervention to address onshore piracy clans. The problem of piracy starts on-shore. There remains an urgent need for reinstatement of political capabilities in such places as Somalia before piracy in the Gulf of Aden can be appropriately dealt with. Ship owners need to evaluate the security and training options for masters, officers, and crew. Self-protective measures onboard include using armed or unarmed guards, target hardening and ship readiness against boarding, and maritime reporting protocols with naval control and navigation through a designated IRTC such as the Suez Canal.

Vulnerability assessments need to be based on the planned shipping route, international intelligence, and assigned threat. Measures such as the speed, freeboard height, cargo, self-protective measures deployed, transit time, and area and distance from closest port all have to be considered. This approach is just common security sense, but also ensures a degree of compliance to international shipping codes such as the International Shipping and Port Facility Security (ISPS) Code.

Maritime security guidelines have been released collaboratively by government and industry. The security framework is established in accordance with the ISPS Code, which requires the implementation of a ship security plan, containing policy, risk assessment procedures, and self-protection practices. Measures that ship owners and operators can take as part of the ship security plan include:

- Implement security policy and practical measures in accordance with ISPS.
- Implement an evaluation process for crew selection, including psychoanalysis, and ensure that joining the crew is voluntary.
- Provide training and testing to ship masters and senior officers in piracy avoidance and self-protection practices.
- Provide training and drilling to the crew in antipiracy ship readiness procedures and techniques. Training may need to be realistic and could involve psychological assessments due to the risk of a hostage situation being encountered.
- Plan appropriate shipping routes to avoid hot spots.
- Brief the company crisis management team and make ready or have available a help desk, family and media management plan, and counselors.
- On board the ship, various physical security measures can be deployed before entering high-risk areas, such as:
  - 24/7 lookout, with binoculars, night vision, and satellite tracking in addition to navigation watch.
  - Razor wire on railings, with electric charge.
  - Use of long-range acoustics weapons.
  - Slippery foams on deck and overboard.
  - Deploying nets and ropes alongside to interfere with outboard motor propellers.
  - Use of on-board fire hoses and bilge releases overboard.
- Traveling at full speed and being proficient to maneuver the vessel while under attack.

The industry is seeking continued escorts through high-risk areas, placing a large drain on military resources. The gathering of intelligence has been hampered by the size of the maritime theater and the limited number of human intelligence sources as the pirate clans are notoriously difficult to infiltrate. There is limited electronic intelligence due to the isolated culture and use of antisurveillance methods, including the use of onshore trip wires that are cleverly deployed and difficult to detect. The military is still developing its understanding of the piracy pattern of life. What has been learned is that so long as piracy is profitable, it will continue.

Piracy will be a high risk for some time. The spike in attacks is expected to occur in line with the clearing of the monsoon season in the Indian Ocean, starting around April through to June. During the spike of August to December 2009, there were eight highjackings from 10,000 ship transits. All eight vessels had deficiencies within the best management practices. All 14 ships highjacked between July and December 2009 were not reporting to UKMTO (UK Maritime Trade Operations) or registering with MSCHOA (Maritime Security Centre—Horn of Africa). It has been found that 80 percent of attacks are thwarted by self-protective measures.

## WORLD CONFLICT AND TERRORISM

World exposure to terrorist attacks in Mumbai (2009), Jakarta (2004, 2009), Glasgow (2007), London (2005, 2006, 2007), Russia (2004), Spain (2004), Bali (2002, 2005), and New York (2001) has raised social concern over the ability of governments to protect their citizens. The former Australian prime minister, John Howard, stated that the 2002 Bali attacks had touched all Australians, resulting in the federal government committing an additional A\$3.1 billion to deal with the terrorist threat. The financial impact of 9/11 cost the United States 0.75 percent of GDP or US\$75 billion. These issues have raised both national and corporate requirements for security that can effectively protect their citizens and staff at a reasonable cost.

In the Asia Pacific, those at particular risk are businesses and individuals operating actively in an economy that reaches various parts of the world for commercial activity. These include oil and gas workers; bank and insurance staff; aid workers; government and embassy officials; various NGOs; international associations and political groups; and sporting organizations and even sporting people.

> **Reliance Executive is killed in India:** A power company executive in India was killed in a shooting that was committed by leftist militants opposed to industrial development. The general manager of Reliance Power's operations was travelling with other Reliance executives to inspect land for a company project in Jharkhand's Chatra district when Maoist rebels opened fire on their convoy. In addition, several other Reliance employees were injured in the shooting. The shooting came at a time when Maoist rebels have become increasingly violent in protecting tribal lands from being encroached on by industry (*Wall Street Journal*, April 6, 2011).

## CONTINUED TERRORISM EVENTS

How will world security and terrorism issues impact Asia Pacific business and industry to 2020? World and regional affairs, involving military conflicts and terrorist activity, have a recognized and close association with market value, supply chain security, and development opportunities. This association and a number of direct threats, in their various forms and degrees, necessitate corporations being considered as at risk from an attack. Terrorism attacks within Asia Pacific are varied, but can be focused into a number of distinct geographical and event-prone areas. Typical and recent terrorism events include:

- Mumbai (2009): Pakistan's army continues to fund the terrorist group Lashkar-e-Taiba that was responsible for the 2008 attacks that killed 164 people.

- On March 9, 2011, 36 people were killed and 100 people wounded when a Taliban suicide bomber detonated his explosives at a funeral procession in the Khyber Pakhtunkhwa province of Pakistan.
- On April 3, 2011, 49 people were killed and 100 injured when three explosions occurred at three locations within the Sakhi Sarwar shrine located in Dera Ghazi Khan, Pakistan.
- On April 15, 2011, 28 people were injured including police officers, when a suicide bomber detonated his explosives during prayers at a mosque in a police compound in the city of Cirebon, West Java, Indonesia. This attack was the first suicide bombing within a mosque in Indonesia.
- Indonesian police were alerted on April 21, 2011, to a 330-pound explosive device that had been placed atop an underground gas pipeline about 100 yards from a Roman Catholic church outside Jakarta.
- On May 2, 2011, Osama bin Laden was killed at his compound in Abbottabad, Pakistan, as a result of a U.S. military strike conducted by a small team of Navy SEALs and the Central Intelligence Agency (CIA).
- On May 23, 2011, approximately six armed members of the Pakistani Taliban attacked a military base in Karachi, Pakistan, killing 16 people. Two militants were killed, a third detonated himself, another was buried under debris, and two escaped.

## SYNOPSIS OF TERRORISM EVENTS

The Pakistani and the U.S. counterterrorism partnership has been strained, as Pakistan is critical of the United States' current strategy in Afghanistan and promotes anti-American sentiments. Poor relationships were not helped by the U.S. release of CIA contractor Raymond Davis who shot two Pakistanis in what he reported was an attempted robbery. Pakistan objects not only to the presence of CIA operatives on its soil but also to the use of agency drones in tribal regions. Pakistan's senior army and intelligence officials say that they want a return to relationship rules between the CIA and Pakistan's ISI drafted in the 1980s.

At the time the United States took a "hands-off" approach, leaving fewer than 100 CIA officers with the rest being ISI. However, such a shift is unlikely, as even Pakistan's president Asif Ali Zardari accuses the ISI and the army of playing both sides in the war on terror. For example, Pakistan's army continues to fund the terrorist group Lashkar-e-Taiba, which was responsible for the 2008 attack in Mumbai that killed 164 people. Nevertheless, Pakistan faces a constant threat from terrorist groups, and it currently has more troops on the ground in its tribal regions than NATO has in Afghanistan. Despite these contradictions, observers say the United States must preserve its relationship with Pakistan if its continued pursuit of al-Qaida operatives in the area is to succeed (Riedel, *Newsweek*, April 17, 2011).

Indonesian police thwarted a major terror attack, when on April 21, 2011, they were tipped off that a 330-pound explosive device had been placed on top of an underground gas pipeline approximately 100 yards from a Jakarta Roman Catholic church. The church is capable of holding up to 3,000 people. Investigators suspected that the bomb was set to go off during Good Friday celebrations when the church would be filled with worshippers ("Good Friday Plot" 2011).

The Pakistani minorities minister was killed by a group of gunmen who ambushed his car in Islamabad, Pakistan. He had previously received death threats for wanting to reform the blasphemy laws, which carried a death sentence for anyone who insulted Islam. The minister, who was visiting his mother at the time, had been offered police assistance but had refused and therefore became an easy target. He was the only Christian in the federal cabinet and spoke in the defense of a Christian mother of five who was sentenced to death in 2010 for blaspheming Islam (VOA News 2011).

On May 26, 2011, 36 people were killed and 56 wounded, many critically, when a suicide car bomber attacked the office of the district coordination officer in Hangu, Pakistan. The attack caused a large crater and severe damage to the shops, police buildings, and courts. The majority of casualties were civilians. Officials said the bomb contained 400 kg of explosives, resulting in many of the injured being trapped in the rubble. The Pakistani Taliban claimed responsibility for the attack, which they said was in retaliation for Osama bin Laden's death, and in the statement, spokesman Ehsanullah Ehsan threatened that there would be even larger attacks in the future ( 2011).

On May 3, 2011, 11 policemen were killed and 25 injured as a result of a landmine attack by Maoist rebels in the state of Jharkhand, India. Paramilitary and state police were sent to the Sendha area after receiving intelligence that Maoists had set up camp there. Upon arrival, the Indian servicemen's vehicle exploded as it drove over a landmine. A firefight broke out between the police and the rebels, resulting in the death of eight rebels (PTI, May 3, 2011, cited in International Institute for Counter-terrorism).

The 26 suspects arrested by Pakistan and British authorities in connection with the plot to blow up nine transatlantic airlines included a biochemistry student, a British Conservative Party member's son, and a Heathrow Airport security guard, who had an all-areas access card and was wearing his airport uniform when arrested. Media reports claimed that neighbors described some of the suspects as devout family men with a strong interest in Islam, although some were described as being insular and withdrawn from their local communities.

It is no secret that Britain has experienced a homegrown terrorism problem. There is anecdotal evidence that British Muslims were increasingly radicalized. A poll conducted in 2006 by a British television station found that a quarter of Muslims surveyed felt that the July7 bombings were justifiable, almost half thought that 9/11 was a U.S. and Israeli conspiracy, and a third said they would rather live under Sharia law.

Like the July 7 London bombers, radicals can be motivated by an anger toward their own foreign policy toward such areas as Iraq, Afghanistan, and other Muslim countries. British intelligence monitors formal and informal groups opposed to military activities, and young Muslims who travel to Pakistan. The plot in 2006 became the biggest antiterror surveillance operation in British history, with more than 1,500 people involved. It is alleged that up to 50 people were under surveillance before focusing on the 24 British suspects. What is the capacity of authorities, federal or state, to monitor and mount such an operation? It is not beyond them, but it would be a significant drain on resources that could otherwise be directed at front-line law-and-order activities, including drug and organized-crime investigations, public order, and crime prevention.

British police alleged the suspects planned to use a peroxide-based compound to make a potent explosive that could be ignited with an MP3 player or mobile phone. The suspects are alleged to have studied timetables of three U.S. airlines. Similarly, in 1995 al-Qaida members planned to use liquid chemical explosives to destroy a dozen transatlantic planes. A test run had been carried out by planting a bomb, which killed a Japanese businessman on a flight from Manila to Tokyo. Arrests were made before the plan was executed, but it involved teams of two or three to board each plane, carrying components that would be harmless in isolation but when combined could be used as explosives. The liquid explosive would be detonated using a common electronic device.

The arrests resulted in the cancellation of 600 flights at Heathrow Airport, effectively disrupting the travel of more than 400,000 people. Restrictions introduced in Europe and the United States meant that laptop computers, mobile phones, iPods, MP3 players, containers of liquids and gels measuring more than 3 ounces in volume, and nonessential items have been banned on passenger flights. Airlines flying to the United States must also implement increased checks on services such as meals and baggage screening.

A year after the Wheeler report detailed security deficiencies at Australia's largest airports, all the Australian government did in response to the plot is say it would again review airline security regulations. Over A$1.2 billion has been spent in Australia on airport security since 9/11. Security upgrades have been carried out or are in the process of being carried out at 150 regional airports. Despite this, it is alleged that 384 aviation security identification cards are missing. There has also been illegal behavior detected involving Australian baggage handlers and security screeners, and customs officers were allegedly warned off cooperating with a parliamentary inquiry into aviation security.

In the United States, the Bush administration in 2006 raised for the first time the level of airport security to code red, and terrorism was virtually guaranteed to fuel a highly charged national security agenda leading up to congressional elections. The seriousness of the threats to American security has been claimed by some to be as severe as Nazism and Communism. It is worth noting that in 2011 the United States dropped the use of color-coded terror warnings.

In 2010 Australian officials claim to have prevented three attacks in Australia in the past 12 months. Eighteen men in Melbourne and Sydney, Australia, were arrested on terror-related charges, followed by three more later that year. The accused are alleged to be associated with an Islamic cleric who preached from his Melbourne home. Some Muslims are resentful of the new antiterrorism laws, which they view as being aimed at their community. The Internet is also used to influence local Islamic radicals. There are numerous sites preaching Islamic extremism. It is not so much the high-profile fundamentalist clerics who are of most concern; rather it is those who are too radical for any formal prayer hall and who hold private classes for their students. These are very difficult to detect and infiltrate.

## NATURAL CATASTROPHIC EVENTS AND
## RISK OF GLOBAL WARMING

Natural disasters such as earthquakes, floods, and droughts cause significant world-wide deaths and injuries, resulting each year in billions of dollars in economic losses. To mitigate these disasters, many billions of dollars in humanitarian assistance, emergency loans, and development aid are expended. Yet efforts to reduce the risks of natural hazards remain largely uncoordinated across different hazard types and do not necessarily focus on areas at highest risk of disaster. In addition, social expectation to control and manage such events is increasing. Society does not accept such disasters, even when they are natural.

Hurricane Katrina in the United States demonstrated that the world's leading super power was unprepared to deal with the aftermath of a large natural disaster. The hurricane destroyed the cradle of jazz, New Orleans. More than 1,200 people were killed and the hurricane was the most deadly to strike the United States since 1928. The World Meteorological Organization stated in its annual 2005 review that weather extremes reached new levels in view of the unprecedented severity of drought, flood, and hurricanes.

> **Pakistan food and water crisis:** Over the coming decades, Pakistan will face the real prospect of serious food and water storages if challenges posed by climate change and overexploitation of natural resources are not effectively and comprehensively managed. In 1947, at time of independence, nearly 25 percent of Pakistan was covered by forest, but today this figure is 5 percent. Water is becoming ever scarce, which supports 45 percent of the population through water, dependent agriculture such as rice and wheat. The challenges that face Pakistan require not only a concerted strategy and significant resources, but also international community support (DeSilva-Ranasinghe 2011).

Such water and food crises will lead to changing and unstable geopolitics, as Asian Pacific states drive to protect their own natural resources. Agriculture, both sea and land based, provides significant financial support to the nation-state, as well as feeding the populace. Furthermore, changing water patterns will increase this pressure. This threat is more significant than the past decade has been with the war on terrorism (DeSilva-Ranasinghe 2011), as such issues will affect and drive large populations.

> **"Human" milk from Cows: China pushes GM food:** China is creating a bumper crop of genetically modified (GM) produce to ensure food security and grab the global lead in the controversial but lucrative biotech sector. In 2008, Premier Wen Jiabao said "To solve the food problem, we have to rely on big science and technology measures, rely on biotechnology, and rely on GM." The following year, China launched a S$4.4 billion R&D effort to grow GM crops (*Straits Times*, April 2, 2011).

The World Bank published a report in 2006 entitled *Natural Disaster Hotspots: A Global Risk Analysis* that presents a global view of disaster risks associated with major natural hazards, namely earthquakes, volcanoes, landslides, floods, drought, and cyclones. Natural disaster hotspots (Independent Evaluation Group 2006)

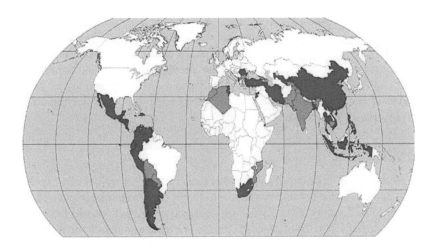

**FIGURE 4.1**    **(See color insert.)** World states vulnerable to two or more hazards. Note: Red = high threat; orange = medium threat. From Independent Evaluation Group, 2006. With permission.

present a global view of major natural disasters (Figure 4.1), which are areas at relatively high risk of loss from one or more natural hazards.

Hotspot nation-states are World Bank client-countries (borrowers) that have significant levels of vulnerability to two or more natural hazards, and vulnerability is expressed as "high" when 50 percent or more of GDP is at risk or "medium" when 30 to 50 percent of GDP is at risk. The map summarizes the results of an interdisciplinary analysis of the location and characteristics of hotspots for six natural hazards. Data on these hazards are combined with distribution of population, economic output, and past disaster losses to identify areas at relatively high risk from one or more hazards.

With increasing population and infrastructures, the world's exposure to natural hazards is inevitably growing. The strongest population growth is located in coastal areas that have a greater exposure to floods, cyclones, and tsunamis. In addition, remaining land available for urban growth is generally risk-prone and located on flood plains or steep slopes subject to landslides. Statistics indicate an exponential increase in disasters and this raises several trending questions: Is the increase due to a significant improvement in access to information? What part do population growth and infrastructure development play? Finally, is climate change behind the increasing frequency of natural hazards? (UNEP/GRID, 2005).

## MARKET RESPONSE TO TERRORIST AND DISASTER EVENTS

The European markets plunged initially on hearing about the transatlantic terrorist plot but recovered relatively quickly. Airlines were buffered somewhat by lower oil prices that offset fears of reduced international travel. Shares in Qantas, which spent A$260 million on security in 2005 and employs 1,500 security personnel, fell 3 cents while the Australian share market remained steady. However, QR Sciences, which developed explosive detection scanners for hand luggage, jumped 18 percent. Security consultants also reported a surge in inquiries from companies doing business in Europe and the Middle East, amid strong concerns about international travel. Those businesses most affected include the international travel and accommodation sector and transport and export logistic companies. Most companies are beginning to review their crisis management and contingency plans for protecting employees and preserving transnational operations.

## CONCLUSION

The world may be considered a dangerous place, and organizations often operate in a global market. These organizations have a duty of care to their staff and stakeholders to ensure that security-related risks are managed effectively to enhance confidence and productivity. The list of potential threats is broad, as much as the Asia Pacific is large and diverse. Threats are difficult to articulate and therefore define, as threats have to consider a person or group's intent and capability and also the dynamic environment. In addition, to truly understand a threat requires time, resources, and effort, because how can you truly understand intent and capability in a diverse geographical and cultural group?

Therefore this chapter has presented past and present threats that a corporate security manager should consider to provide some degree of mitigation. Threats that have been considered include kidnapping, both traditional and tiger, food and product tampering, piracy, natural catastrophic events and global warming, transnational and organized crime, world conflict, and terrorism.

## REFERENCES

DeSilva-Ranasinghe, S. 2011. *Pakistan's Food and Water Crisis: More Detrimental to Security Than Extremism*. Perth: Future Directions International.
"Good Friday Plot Feared after 330-lbs Bomb Is Found Near Gas-Line by Catholic Church in Indonesia." 2011. *New York Daily News*, April 21, cited in ICT Incident Database Report, International Institute for Counter-terrorism.
Holloway, P., and J. Betts. 2005. A Forethought for Malice. *Lawyers Weekly* 264:20–21.
Independent Evaluation Group. 2006. *Hazards of Nature, Risks to Development: An IEG Evaluation of World Bank Assistance for Natural Disasters*. Washington, DC: World Bank.
Luo, X. and Liao, X. 2009. Ransomware: A New Cyber Hijacking Threat to Enterprises. IGI Global. Retrieved May 5, 2012 http://www.irma-international.org/viewtitle/20635/.
"36 Killed in Northwest Pakistan Suicide Bomb Attack." 2011. *Times of India*, May 27, cited in ICT Incident Database Report, International Institute for Counter-terrorism.
Symantec. 2010. Symantec global internet security threat report: Trends for 2009. Mountain View, CA: Symantec Corporation.
UNEP/GRID. 2005. *Trends in Natural Disasters 2005*. Retrieved May 25, 2011 from http://maps.grida.no/go/graphic/trends-in-natural-disasters (accessed May 25, 2011).
VOA News. 2011. "Pakistanis, World Leaders Protest Minister's Assassination." March.

# 5 Security Trends

## INTRODUCTION

Examining what the future holds is always fraught with danger, but remains the essence of identifying opportunities as well as managing threats and risks. This chapter examines existing trends indicative of changes within the security profession, technology, and contemporary issues relating to the short- to medium-term security risk environment. At a geopolitical level, an examination of trends in terrorism, civil unrest, privacy, workplace surveillance, and crime prevention is provided. Furthermore, analysis of the digitalization of CCTV surveillance and biometric systems, societal change resulting from the convergence of media and device technology, and trends in corporate security standards and practices, legislation, and industry regulation have been considered.

## BEYOND 2020: OVERVIEW OF REGIONAL SECURITY TRENDS AND TECHNOLOGY

The Asia-Pacific region has troubling and unresolved security issues, including continuing fragility on the Thai–Cambodian border, the internal situations in southern Thailand, the southern Philippines, Myanmar, India, and Nepal, as well as the ever-fragile environments in a number of the Pacific islands. Nevertheless, are the crucial subregions of Northeast and Southeast Asia going to remain areas of continuing peace and stability for the foreseeable future, or are we in for some quite nasty shocks? (Evans 2011).

Security management will continue to be considered a profession offering a large service range for business, from education and training services to strategic planning, risk management, and technology applications. The main challenge is in raising awareness about the threats and risks, and overcoming apathy toward security risks. Countries that have grown up under the various shadows of war, terrorism, and violence will have an enhanced security awareness and understanding. Even without scare tactics, confidence can be improved with direct results seen in productivity while under stress, with a typical example being a well-planned and executed business continuity program. Is it not better to consider and become accustomed to a risk, rather than discover that you could not cope if the risk eventuated?

For the sake of enhancing global competitiveness, regional organizations should be formally managing their security responsibilities and planning for their response to a diverse range of security-related risks, both physical and electronic. Nevertheless, to effectively manage threats and risks there has to be some degree of future trending. Being aware and trying to understand such trends across the Asia-Pacific region is complex. Such trends to consider may include the dynamic nature of the region, changing focus on the terrorist threat, issues of civil unrest, street violence, and riots, privacy in Asia Pacific, corporate security as a cost center, the need to raise the corporate security culture and ethics, increasing externally imposed standards, keeping up with the changing fraud methodologies, ever-increasing deployment of mobile technology, the complexity of nation-state legislation and governance, and the expectation that the profession will become more professional.

## THE CHANGING ASIA-PACIFIC REGION

There needs to be recognition that the Asia Pacific is gradually becoming the Indo Pacific. The rise of India is becoming as visibly important a phenomenon as the China expansion, but this has so far been insufficiently noticed by global corporations or policy makers. Trade volumes between East Asia and South and West Asia now far outweigh those across the Pacific, and such trade is growing dramatically. Much of it is Gulf oil to fuel China's growth, but a lot of it is also burgeoning bilateral trade between the two nation-states, and the overall trend is unmistakable. In addition, much discussion has been raised regarding military buildup occurring in India and China, reflecting the growing extent of their maritime interests in particular (Evans 2011).

## TERRORISM

Terrorism in many parts of the world is a changing threat, highlighted by the reduced media attention many incidents now gain. In addition, the significant resources that Western nation-states have used to combat this threat have begun to have a significant result. Nevertheless, some Asia-Pacific nation-states still suffer from the terrorism threat and this is unlikely to reduce for decades. These states often have a lesser profile in the Western world, although depending on the success of the groups this could change. Such change could have a significant effect in some of these more exposed Asia-Pacific nation-states.

### TERRORISM: WHERE HAS ALL THE HYPE GONE?

Despite terrorism issues falling from the news agenda in many parts of the Western world, reports from certain parts of Asia Pacific continue. Nevertheless, the type of focus and its international quality may remain minimal but the problem will, for decades to come, be a concern.

> **Top JI operative in custody in Pakistan:** Pakistan arrested a top Indonesian Jemaah Islamiah (JI) terrorist Umar Patek, one of Indonesia's most wanted and involved in the 2002 Bali bombing which killed 202 people. The arrest followed a tip off from the US Central Intelligence Agency (CIA). Patek would be eventually returned to Indonesia. Paket is a skilled explosive expert and senior member of JI network, having escaped Indonesia in 2003 (*Straits Times*, April 2, 2011).

**Pakistani militant group a global terror threat:** There are fears that the Pakistani terrorist organization Lashkar-e-Taiba could attack Western targets. Current and former members of Lashkar-e-Taiba, which is believed to have been responsible for carrying out the 2008 terrorist attacks in Mumbai, have said that the group's only goal is to reunite Kashmir, the territory whose control is disputed between India and Pakistan. However, experts have said that Lashkar-e-Taiba could be on the verge of broadening its reach beyond the South Asia region (Gannon, *Kuwait Times*, May 4, 2011).

Any corporation operating in the Asia Pacific would be wise to understand the political, social, and environmental situation that may drive the terrorism threat. Without an effective intelligence function, many corporations could be exposed when moving or expanding into what could turn quickly into dangerous and highly exposed markets. For example, the Australian terrorism insurance scheme may be expanded beyond the mandated A$300 million after a three-year review. The funds have been established to act as a first line of protection against the financial cost of a major Australian terrorist attack. Under the direction of the Australian Reinsurance Pool Corporation, Australia has a three-tier approach with the initial insurance cover provided by the A$300 million insurance scheme. The next layer is a A$1 billion line of credit underwritten by the federal government, and the third is a A$9 billion government funded indemnity. The review proposed that as of 2009, large insurers would have to pay A$10 million from their own reserves for a major terrorist attack, which may be increased to A$100 million.

## CIVIL UNREST: STREET VIOLENCE AND RIOTS

Civil unrest will be an issue in some Asia-Pacific nation-states as they move from subsidence economies to industrialized economies or environmental change takes effect. In addition, changing social expectations from citizens who seek to gain greater political and social freedom as they become more financially secure may also engender civil unrest. The Asia-Pacific region has a diverse range of political and social nation-states, from dictators to democracies.

**Thailand "Red Shirts" protest in Bangkok:** Twenty-thousand Red Shirt protesters descended on the streets of Thailand's capital, taking over the Bangkok Democracy Monument as they held a peaceful but noisy rally. Marching from the central business district, the anti-government demonstrators arrived at the monument in the afternoon local time and were planning to stay on until midnight. The gathering was called to mourn those killed during 2010s violence to demand the release of Red Shirt leaders who were detained on "terrorism" charges. "Because we don't know and don't have an answer as to when the leaders will be granted bail, people outside must show their power through peaceful means to show that those who are behind bars do have friends," a Red Shirt leader and a member of parliament stated (NDTV, January 24, 2011, Associated Press).

The Democracy Monument was one of two locations where clashes between the protesters and the Thai military took place during the nine-week 2010 protests. About 90 people were killed and more than 1400 were wounded in the unrest, as the protesters tried to force Prime Minister Vejjajiva to call early elections. This demonstration marked the group's second big gathering after the Thai government lifted a state of emergency in Bangkok on December. The law technically barred gatherings of more than five people but was widely ignored by the Red Shirt movement. The group continues to be active and is treated as a major threat by the government. Hundreds of police turned out to provide security for the demonstration (NDTV, January 24, 2011, Associated Press).

Civil unrest can and does erupt with little international notice; however, for most there are many signals that should raise the alert awareness of those operating in-country. Such local awareness can be gained from open-source media and, importantly, local operators. Local operators will understand the underlying feeling that nation-state citizens may have and what the day-to-day in-country issues are.

## FRAUD AND PREVENTION: KEEPING UP

Fraud and fraud prevention will have to be improved as fraudsters are becoming smarter and more "tech savvy" in terms of cyber security. The risk of fraud should not have just an external focus, rather an internal and external trending concern often exists. The internal threat is perhaps the greater issue, but this is generally due to decay with security mitigation or just poor accountability or a lack of any accountability whatsoever. The outsider threat is where perpetrators are becoming increasingly clever in their ability to find and exploit vulnerabilities—in general, the human component of system vulnerability.

### INTERNAL THREAT

An 2006 Ernst and Young global fraud survey found that 90 percent of companies believed their controls were tough enough to prevent and detect fraud, yet fewer than half had a documented antifraud policy and had not communicated whatever antifraud policies they did have to their agents or partners. The study also highlighted problems with dealing with whistle blowers. Another study from the University of Melbourne found that organizations without auditing systems were missing significant levels of corporate fraud.

Organizations are well advised to conduct thorough background checks and screening of all executives and directors, despite perceived reputations, detailed resumes, and outstanding qualifications. Furthermore, this should not be confined to the senior management group; even a simple police check can show the integrity of the prospective employee.

All companies should have an **employment screening standard**, which is designed to reduce the risk of potential security breaches and to ensure the integrity, identity, and credentials of staff and contractors. The standard should provide guidance on:

- When security checks should take place such as at the start of employment, before completion of probation periods, and before promotion

- Verifying identity, and checking resumes, education credentials and police records
- Privacy issues such as parties to whom the information can be released
- Training and probity checks on staff employed to do screening

## SMARTER EXTERNAL AND ONLINE THREAT

**ID Fraud costing billions—Surprised?** The Australian Institute of Criminology estimates the cost of fraud, predominantly identity theft, is more than A$5 billion a year, or a third of the total cost of crime in Australia (Lozusic, R. 2003).

The trend in external fraud would appear to be in one distinct area, the electronic world. Continued international security breaches of personal data protection may be through identity theft using stolen credit card information, scamming with e-mails, and the hacking of online financial transactions. Such data is traded on the black market and this trend is highly likely to continue into the foreseeable future. However, this is also likely to expand into the on-line social media arena, using the many specialized social media systems that are smaller and less able to protect their data, unlike Facebook. Theft of personal information is motivated by the subsequent purchase of this information for end users to commit identity crimes, mainly identity fraud, but it can also include a range of crimes, including people smuggling, drug trafficking, money laundering, pedophilia, and terrorism.

**The act of manipulating pay-per-click advertising:** Perpetrators inflate the number of people who have legitimately clicked an on-line advertisement, either to make money for themselves or to bleed a competitor's advertising budget. Click fraud is following a trajectory that will be familiar to any CSO, and it's a telling example of how sophisticated and profitable electronic crime has become. First, the good guys started looking at server logs to find IP addresses in patterns that indicated fraud. The bad guys responded by creating automated bots that simulated different IP addresses and had varying time stamps. Then, the good guys improved their click-fraud detection tools, with a cottage industry sprouting up that specializes in helping on-line advertisers monitor for fraud. Queue up "click farms", where the bad guys hire people in other countries to do the clicking in a way that looks more realistic. "It's a cat-and-mouse game" (Sherman, 2002).

**40 million credit card users exposed:** US transaction processing company CardSystems Solutions exposed private details of 40 million credit card users worldwide after being hacked in 2005. Driver's licence, passport numbers and birth certificate details were compromised (Crawford, M. 2005).

**In April 2011 Sony's Playstation Service was hacked** forcing it to be shut down. Account information was compromised across the 77 million users (Colville 2011).

*Computerworld* recently reported that "Australia will not follow the lead of the US by introducing stiffer data protection laws to safeguard sensitive information held by companies despite compelling recent evidence of a thriving black market trade in the personal data of Australians."

An estimated 25 percent of reported frauds to the Australian Federal Police involve the assumption of false identities. A survey by KPMG of over 1,800 businesses found that almost 12 percent of fraud committed by outsiders involved the use of false documents. The survey of small businesses found that one-third of online traders have been victims of online fraud; over half of those businesses hit became repeat targets of fraudsters; and average losses for small business ranged from A$100 to A$3,500. The types of identify fraud activity include counterfeiting and "skimming" of credit cards; use of stolen credit cards or numbers; "phishing" scams using false or "ghosted" websites; people fraudulently obtaining money, loans, or credit; people fraudulently obtaining benefits or entitlements; and tax evasion scams.

Businesses are advised to appropriately secure and manage all sensitive information, shred unwanted documents, use a locked mailbox, have accounts monitored and validated, not divulge financial information to unknown third parties, ensure business premises are physically secured, and use computer security policy and systems. They should also have a culture of reporting suspicions and asking for further information should staff suspect incidents of identity fraud, such as when individuals are unable to provide identifying information or have a lot of reasons why normal procedures should not be followed.

## PRIVACY

Even through the threat of terrorism has, in general, reduced across the region, the issue of privacy is growing. Opposed to this increasing privacy concern and driven, in part, from the last highly visible terrorism environment, nation-states have allowed their security services to have greater access to private information to ensure better protection against terrorism. The view of many is that the war on terror has led to an erosion of privacy. Many nation-states now have a greater understanding of their own citizens and also those visiting their territories. There is also an increase in states sharing information, such as the transfer of funds, and movement of people and assets.

> **Automated targeting system** is reportedly being used by the US government to give all 356 million travellers leaving and arriving in the US a secret, computer generated security score which rates the risk they pose of being terrorists or criminals. The risk assessments are not allowed to be seen or directly challenged and can be kept for 40 years. The program apparently considers each person's travel record, where they are from, how they paid for tickets, motor vehicle records, seating preference and type of meals eaten (*West Australian*, December 2006).

### WORKPLACE SURVEILLANCE—WHAT YOU CAN'T DO OR IS IT STILL WORTH IT?

In Australia, a legal trial involving an unfair dismissal claim against Primelife Corporation included the secret videotaping and bugging of board meetings, and the tapping of employees' telephone calls without their knowledge. Up to 64,000 employee telephone calls were recorded. Under the Australian Telecommunications

(Interception) Act 1979, it is illegal to make recordings of telephone calls without the party's knowledge or a warrant, which must be obtained by a law enforcement agency. Under workplace surveillance legislation in New South Wales, employees must be advised in writing prior to surveillance being introduced.

The Australian Victorian Law Reform Commission report tackled a range of workplace privacy issues including e-mail monitoring, video surveillance, drug and alcohol testing, and genetic testing. Under the commission's proposals, employers would need authority from a regulator for such testing or to track workers. Some workplace surveillance legislation allows hidden cameras to be used to visually monitor the workplace provided they do not record private conversations or activities and are installed only to detect theft or unlawful conduct. Otherwise, employees should be advised in writing and signs posted for visitors advising them that security cameras are in use. Nevertheless, this issue when extrapolated across the Asia Pacific is not clearly defined by any means, as many states have quite different and dynamic legislation. The most appropriate approach when considering such workplace surveillance is to obtain local legal advice.

The images captured by CCTV or other camera systems are also subject to many privacy acts. For example, in Australia, state and federal surveillance acts provide protection for the employee against the inappropriate disclosure of information obtained in the workplace, whether by electronic surveillance or otherwise. Any complaints to the privacy commissioner may result in an investigation. Furthermore, the Telecommunications (Interception) Act strictly prohibits the interception and recording of telephone calls unless under special circumstances, which are not related to workplace surveillance needs (Rossi 2005).

**Barrister charged over listening devices:** Accused Barrister Lloyd Rayney and an associate were charged over the use of electronic devices used to record telephone conversations in the home of his estranged wife, Corryn Rayney, a Supreme Court registrar found murdered in August 2007. Her husband, a prominent Perth lawyer was named by police as a suspect and charged with her murder (*West Australian* 2008).

Privacy is a fundamental right recognized by international law; however, state legislation "at the moment does not have very much to say about the balance which should be struck between employers' legitimate needs and workers' rights to privacy … Technology has surged ahead with new ways to monitor, test and, [*sic*] track workers, but our laws have lagged behind" (Kerstein 2005). However, there is a general corporate view that this is not a significant issue and that the corporation itself can manage these issues. For example, Australia's Victorian Employers' Chamber of Commerce and Industry government relations manager David Gregory rejected mandatory regulations, stating that employers would accept "guidance material" but that's where it ends (Kerstein 2005). Business lobby group Australian Business Limited (McBride 2005) has recommended that all businesses undergo an audit of current surveillance activities and devise an Internet and computer usage policy.

A corporate security manager should clearly have an understanding of the local legislation pertaining to privacy and such issues as workplace and external surveillance. They need to ensure that they have in place clear and concise policy and local procedures that are legally sound, and that they carry out regular surveillance audits, on such systems as their investigators, CCTV systems (including operators), and other audio and video systems. Nevertheless, the issue of privacy is likely to be more significant as time goes by, including the capture and storage of CCTV images.

## UNEXPECTED DIFFERENCES IN PRIVACY REGULATIONS

"Despite having similar political systems and using new technology in similar ways, the use of regulations will vary significantly" (Busch 2011). In Europe, "which would appear to have a common perspective on 'privacy policies' ... in reality regulations change both the amount and type of personal data that is kept" (Busch 2011). "Privacy regulation is highly dependent on local context and the particular institutional arrangements in each nation-state. For example, British citizens are resistant to identity cards but largely unconcerned about CCTV, while German citizens worry about CCTV but have been carrying machine-readable identity cards for decades without problems" (Busch 2011). Nevertheless, the UK may have some of the most stringent privacy legislation in CCTV images than any other nation-state.

Overall, the political debates on different areas of privacy regulation were found to vary substantially between nation-states, with biometric identity documents generating the highest levels of controversy. The extent of political discussions seems to depend on citizens' varying levels of trust in the state, a point to note when considering the many government approaches across Asia-Pacific states. However, it has been found that differences between political parties had little impact on regulatory policy, and variations in political institutions played a decisive role in determining outcomes.

In highly centralized nation-states, there is less influence on policy making, whereas regulators who operate in a more fragmented federal structure give perpetrators more points for access. In addition, the early institutionalization of data protection commissioners and agencies has led to regulators long making a significant contribution to public debate. Events such as the terrorist attacks of 9/11 have had a significant impact on privacy regulation. Heightened security measures were a direct result of these attacks and the responses from politicians in a number of policy areas, "resulting in common solutions which were then implemented at a national level (Busch 2011). 'Regulations often come about as a result of a political agenda and not from technological advancements'" (Busch 2011).

## CHANGING TECHNOLOGY: GREATER
## CONVERGENCE AND COMPLEXITY

New technologies can offer immense benefits, but we need stronger protections in place (Office of the Australian Information Commissioner 2007).

Security technology, once a domain of older stand-alone technological systems, is now catching up with other, more progressive, industries. Gone are the days when each security system had its own network or cables laid to each camera or door. Security systems are now becoming integrated and system convergence is occurring. Such convergence will increase wherein security systems are operated alongside building management, building plant control systems, lighting systems, IT networks, and telecommunications. There are many technology advantages with such an approach, but this approach will expose the organizations to a more complex and difficult system to understand. As the systems become more complex, so do hidden vulnerabilities that are prone to "Trojan horse" attacks and "major" failures, rather than minor loss of functions.

There is likely to be an increasing reliance on technology, as it becomes "intelligent" and more integrated. Again, there are significant organizational benefits in taking such a route, but how secure is the system? A simple issue is the intruder alarm system, which in the past always had an uninterrupted power supply. How many building intelligence systems operate with such power redundancy, when all the detectors, alarm signals, CCTV, and access control operate via separate devices?

## CCTV to Detect People, Weapons, Drugs, and Explosives

CCTV is one of the most difficult security technologies to use effectively; however, it is becoming more effective with the emergence of intelligent CCTV systems that assist in things such as detecting illegitimate movement against the normal people flow, or noticing when a bag is left unattended for a period of time, facial recognition, and many more such claimed developments. For example, CCTV will be enhanced by the capacity to scan for weapons, drugs, and explosives hidden under people's clothes from up to 25 meters away. A British company, ThruVision, has developed a powerful camera that identifies objects by the natural electromagnetic rays (terahertz). The camera can detect objects when hidden and when people are moving, does not reveal body details, and is harmless. Terahertz lie between infrared and microwaves on the electromagnetic spectrum (*West Australian* 2008). Such claims have to be questioned, as simple screening will block such detection. Nevertheless, we begin to rely on such technology without truly questioning its resilience or validity.

Decades from now such CCTV functionality will be fully digital and integrated, but in the current and next decades, such systems have to be used in select and controlled environments. For example, zone CCTV detection works well with light-controlled environments and should be used, but as an aid to the operator, not necessarily as the detector. CCTV will become more integrated onto IT networks, with the use of IP-based systems to control and monitor such systems anywhere in the world, and the ability to install many more cameras as they become progressively and significantly cheaper. However, this will not make CCTV any more or less effective than it is in its current format, which is rather ineffective as a crime prevention tool.

## Biometrics

Like CCTV, biometrics has over the last two decades been hailed as the next great panacea for security and in particular access control. For example, fingerprint scanners may be introduced for all airline passengers with discussions occurring between the British government and the airline industry for the introduction of tightened border controls and preventing forged travel documents. The British High Commission has commenced issuing biometric visas that store the applicant's fingerprint. All visitors to the United States are already subjected to iris and fingerprint checks on their arrival (*West Australian* 2006) and Australia, Indonesia, Malaysia, Japan, and other Asia-Pacific nation-states are currently using forms of biometric in their border security validation process.

> **Fingerprint and eye scans for motorists and smartcard privacy:** Roadside fingerprint scanners will check a person's identity on the spot. Though the scheme is voluntary, those who decline are conveyed to the nearest police station to have their identity verified. Studies suggest that only 60 percent of offending motorists provide their real identity and the machines claim to be 95 percent accurate.

Combined with biometrics are Smartcards. Such cards will include a digital photograph, the holder's name, and other relevant data, depending on where and who issues the card. Such a card will be used to access government services, ensuring that the more liberal nation-states use the introduction of such a card as a benefit to the user, rather than greater perceived government control. Nevertheless, such a card will not be used for identification (as yet) with legislation being introduced to deny police, nation-state governments, and banks from demanding access (*West Australian* 2006).

> **Big Brother Stuff for International Travellers:** A single credit card sized driver's license will be rolled out across 25 nations in the European Union, which will be linked to a database to ensure drivers who have their license revoked in one country cannot get a new one in another. Micro-chips can also be inserted for increase anti-theft protection (*West Australian* 2006).

Although the use and propagation of biometrics and smartcards are likely to increase, there is going to be far slower uptake than many people suggest. Slow uptake is due, in part, to slow portal rate, the extra cost, and the ability to easily spoof such systems (Brooks 2010), just to name a few limitations of biometrics.

## Online Corporate Security Vulnerabilities: Changing Use or Abuse of the Web

As discussed, there is likely to be an increasing use of the online environment to carry out complex fraud and other criminal activities from any part of the world. The proliferation of traditional threats to the expanding online arena creates new opportunities for organized crime, activist groups, competitors, and foreign governments. The corporate security professional must remain highly proficient in ICT advancements, including social media, online gaming, covert communication tactics, and mobile technology.

> **Defending against global information war:** Recent attacks on the Internet's root servers was more than just a few hackers having fits and giggles with the DNS. In fact, the incident could be the first volley in global information warfare between the private sector of the US and the government of China. The story as the unclassified media has played it: Three of the world's 13 root servers that manage the DNS, translating URLs into IP octets, were victims of intense distributed denial-of-service (DoS) attacks with malformed packets. The US Department of Defense and ICANN servers were the hardest hit, although there was no major damage (Schwartau, *Network World*, February 21, 2007).

It is timely considering corporations are at the center of a digital revolution. A report by the analyst firm IDC predicts digital information will rise sixfold by 2010, reaching 988 exabytes. Even in 2006, the amount of digital information created and copied worldwide was equal to 161 billion gigabytes or 161 exabytes. That is equivalent to 3 million times the information in all the books ever written, or the equivalent of 12 stacks of books, each extending more than 93 million miles from the earth to the sun.

Presently, 80 to 90 percent of external computer and network attacks are opportunistic—the work of someone who finds the site by chance—and the remainder are targeted at a specific facility (such as industrial espionage). Organized crime has moved into computer crime in a significant way, setting up high-tech sweatshops in undeveloped nations where legions of cheap, skilled computer-heads search cyberspace seeking easy-to-penetrate systems. Most hackers, once in, will simply go looking for financial data that can be stolen, packaged, and sold. But attackers who know what they are doing can and have seized control of central and critical systems.

The issue, for example, is that computer users cope with 10 new application vulnerabilities every day, with no immediate relief in sight. In a six-month period there was a 31 percent increase of vulnerabilities, with the Firefox browser faring worse than Internet Explorer, with 25 critical vulnerabilities discovered compared with Explorer's 8 (Symantec's 2010). There was also an alarming rise in the number of bot networks available worldwide. When ordered by hackers, bots use the network to send out spam or invalid data, disabling other computers and targeted websites.

Customers should be notified if personal details are collected indirectly or through third parties. The amount and range of data sharing and the degree of risk would determine the level of obligation applied to organizations. "'Harness emerging technologies such as portable digital signatures and other forms of digital identity to allow consumers to manage their own portfolio of data collection consents. This is particularly important in the case of bundled consents,' the submission said. 'Strengthen guidelines for assisting and monitoring trans-border data flows including the monitoring of compliance'" (Rossi 2007).

## BETTER AND DIRECTED SECURITY RISK MANAGEMENT

Over the past two decades, the concept of risk management as a formal discipline has emerged throughout the private and public sectors (Aven 2008; Power 2007). Risk management has now become a well-established discipline, with its own body of knowledge and domain practitioners. Some Asia-Pacific nation-states have their own risk management standards, and in many it is the senior company executives who have responsibility to ensure that appropriate risk management practices meet internal and external compliance requirements (Brooks 2011). Nevertheless, many of these standards and compliance requirements consider only risk management, not security risk management. Security risk management may be considered unique from other forms of risk management, as many of the more generic risk models lack key concepts necessary for effective design, application, and mitigation of security risks.

The current practice of risk management and security risk management in the Asia-Pacific region is diverse, with many corporate security managers using other nation-states' standards. For example, a large number of risk managers use Australian Standard 4360:2006, a standard that was outdated in 2009 by the current ISO 31000:2009 risk management standard. Nevertheless, internal standards are almost in equal use; however, the extent to which the corporations within each country use no risk management standard or ISO 31000 reduces significantly. One standard that comes to the fore is the ISO 28000, which is widely used and is primarily focused toward supply chain management. The current use of risk management standard and framework is still nation-state specific, although some international standards are becoming more widespread.

There will be increasing social and community expectations that effective risk management is applied and that when applied is robust. It is likely that validation of the effectiveness—or otherwise—of risk management will be demonstrated through the courts. If risk management proves to be ineffective, nation-state governments are likely to impose greater legislation and standards in an attempt to control such social risks.

**Lack of Risk Management** may have led to federal court legal proceedings being instigated by a software company, AG Software, against an Australian state following their decision to create a copy of the software for an off-site disaster recovery operation. Following the copy of the data management platform and storing it off-site (a central issue to the dispute), AG Software has claimed A$1 million in license fees for the extra copy. In relation to the case, the defence claims that making a disaster recovery copy of IT systems was such "standard practice" that even if a license agreement did not provide that right, copyright legislation stepped in and allowed licensees to do so (West Australian, November 2006). We have not found any existing case law in direct relation to this issue and the outcome of this case may have a significant bearing on wider disaster recovery practices.

Beyond the next decade, there will be a drive to define and practice specific security risk management standards and frameworks, not just generic risk management. As discussed in previous sections, security risk management has to take a threat-led risk management approach. The degree by which progress is made into formal propagated frameworks or nation-state standards will be directly related to the ability of the security industry to become professional and demonstrate a common approach. It is expected that this is unlikely, due to the nature of security and its many competing interests.

As a trend, the use of ISO standards will become more commonplace, leading to these standards being the benchmark for the security manager. There are many standards that relate to security; however, these are not all explicit. For example, standards may be within what many may consider an allied discipline such as business continuity, IT systems, and supply chain management. Nevertheless, it is likely that for the next decade risk and security risk management will still remain nation-state specific, so it is important that the corporate security manager gains an understanding of what standard or framework is most used in his or her country of operation.

Finally, if risk management does demonstrate it is ineffective from a legal perspective, the drive by some nation-states to maintain such a risk focus will wane. If this is the case, other philosophies or frameworks will be developed as future generations of risk management. One such contender is resilience. Nation-state government focus will change from risk management to embedded corporate resilience that will oversee security, business continuity, IT and computing, and the other implicit functions such as leadership and values.

## BUSINESS CONTINUITY MANAGEMENT

The threat of and the focus on terrorism is dissipating but will still require a degree of corporate protection. Terrorism does occur in Asia-Pacific region, unannounced and with much dismay, and this threat is highly likely to be around for many decades to come. It would be wonderful to know how many organizations have assessed their risk exposure or response to these probable events. Those who have not may simply be hoping nothing bad happens at all, as the general case is that catastrophe always happens to someone else.

Many medium- to large-size organizations will have developed and tested an emergency evacuation plan; however, organizations should continue developing plans in order to operate the business after a major event or emergency. There should be a crisis management team that immediately comes together if something goes seriously wrong, as well as an approved policy that provides clear direction as to what is expected of the team, particularly for public relations and ethical decision making. There should be a business continuity plan that details exactly what needs to be done to get the business back to maximum productivity following interruption. There also needs to be a disaster recovery plan that can *kick-start* the business if all or major parts of the business are stopped, seriously disrupted, or destroyed. Plans must be practiced and tested at least biannually for best results and for strong team cohesiveness during a real crisis. Companies should realize that these exercises provide opportunities for them to critique the business, often creating value through enhanced business protection.

The modus operandi used in Southeast Asian, European, and Middle East terrorist attacks should be integrated into crisis management and business continuity plans by organizations. The London and Bali bombings demonstrate that should a terrorist attack occur in a regional city, similar scenarios are likely to unfold. Nevertheless, such a plan can and is ideally suited to manage many other consequences, such as a major power outage, a natural disaster, loss of facilities, staff, and other resources, and another local industry suffering a significant incident.

## SHORT-TERM PLANS: A SUREFIRE WAY TO CRIPPLE BUSINESS

Disaster recovery plans are floundering in the small and medium enterprise (SME) and enterprise sectors, because many businesses fail to look at the short-, medium-, and long-term objectives of a complete disaster recovery plan. This lack of foresight is what will eventually kill the business, not just the actual disaster. An organization's failure to keep regular (at times biannual) procedures and schedule real-life testing often blindsides its plan, according to users and vendors (Crawford 2006).

## CRISIS COUNSELING VERSUS SELF-ASSESSMENT AND LEARNING

There has to be a greater understanding of duty-of-care responsibilities that the employer has for the employee. An area that will become more significant over the next decade is the mental health of employees that like physical health has to be protected in the workplace. For example, nonsmoking is now the norm in many Asia Pacific facilities to ensure a healthy and safe workplace.

The Australian Centre for Post-traumatic Mental Health released guidelines on post-traumatic mental health, which have been endorsed by the National Health and Medical Research Council. These are the first guidelines that state that psychological debriefing should not be offered on a routine basis. These new guidelines follow evidence that venting inner turmoil immediately following a traumatic incident is not only unhelpful but can sometimes make stressful responses worse. The guidelines recommend the provision of psychological first aid where those subjected to potentially traumatic events are supported, their immediate needs met, and are monitored over time to see if problems develop. Most people will recover on their own with the help of family and friends. Longer-term problems may develop over the following weeks and include sleeping difficulties, anxiety, increased alcohol and drug use, and relationship problems.

There is an important message here for organizations to change what may be an automatic response and postscript to media releases following a major event, in that all survivors are receiving counseling. Available scientific evidence now indicates that psychological debriefing after a traumatic event does not assist victims, and in most cases the involvement of trained counselors appears to increase the risk of post-traumatic stress disorder. The assumption is often made that "everyone" must get professional counseling. Talking to a counselor can interrupt natural recovery processes, can cause retraumatization, and describing to victims the symptoms they are likely to suffer may actually induce those symptoms through suggestion (*West Australian*, October 2006).

For example, following the London terrorist attacks only 1 percent of people surveyed wanted counseling, whereas 75 percent wanted to speak to family and friends. This figure demonstrates that employers have a moral obligation to make friends and family available to members following a trauma. The responsibility is not to try to offer "professional" help but rather to provide sympathetic and empathetic listening, encouraging employees to talk if they want to or just being with them while they remain silent and think things through (*West Australian*, October 2006). This type of thinking is critical if crisis management is to be effective and reduce the impact of traumatic events.

Directors, senior executives, and security managers will do their organization and staff a disservice by not planning for a crisis management response, maintaining attention to what developments are being made and what other organizations are doing to avoid and control disasters. Your organization does not exist in a vacuum and crisis plans should continually stay abreast of new findings, developments, and learning opportunities.

## GREATER PROFESSIONALISM

If the industry does not develop a consensual and common front, nation-state governments will try to control the social risk of not having a professional security industry with legislation, regulation, and standards. Such state controls will stifle any chance that the industry will have of becoming a true profession. In addition, such legislation and standards further reduce the ability of the industry to provide some degree of self-control and develop into a profession. What is the future likely to hold for the security industry and people working within it? And what does the security industry need to do to ensure that it does develop into a profession and not be stifled?

### DEFINING THE MANY PARTS OF SECURITY

What is corporate security and what does it do? Ask 10 people, either inside or outside of the corporate security apparatus, and you will get 10 different responses. The reason is that security as a concept lacks definition (Tate 1997) and is diffuse, yet is a distinct field of practice and study (ASIS International 2003: Brooks 2009b). Nevertheless, the security industry is both a diverse and specialty industry that has a requirement for both generic and domain-specific skills (Hesse and Smith 2001) and, being a relatively young and emerging discipline, continues to expand. Therefore, corporate security has to have a clear understanding of its operating boundaries, from which further understanding of a body of knowledge could be achieved. There are many overlapping and diffuse parts of security that interact, interrelate, and have interdependencies with corporate security, such as policing, national security, military security, and private security, to name just a few.

There is still further work required in gaining common understanding in defining security and a corporate security body of knowledge; however, it could be suggested that both are required. Nevertheless, there is increasing research by tertiary institutions, and national and international professional groups are responding to these issues. It is expected that clearer demarcation will be achieved and that will result in the ability to better define corporate security. The only issue is that it is likely to be at least a decade away, as terms such as *homeland security* have further confused the debate and understanding.

## CORPORATE SECURITY AS A COST CENTER

Over the next decade there needs to be a focus toward raising the strategic value a corporate security manager should bring an organization. To ensure that security moves beyond the belief by the executive group that security is "guns and guards" requires corporate security managers to operate at the C-Suite level, as discussed in previous chapters. But how is this achieved and what are future drivers likely to look like? For many current security managers, this will take a significant cultural and operational change in how they see themselves and the security function.

There is an evolving trend toward corporations having no full-time corporate security manager and relying on contractors for such advice. Many organizations believe that they cannot justify full-time security management, using contract security services and on-site security supervisor as part of the total package being provided by the contracting guard company. However, the extent to which this site manager is qualified to take on the role beyond that of supervising contract security officers is questionable and may present a conflict of interest. Yet, when on site and one asks "who is in charge of security?" the on-site supervisor is often named.

A corporate option may be to use an industry-certified corporate security professional who assumes the role of security management support and advisor. These professionals operate under contract to oversee and monitor many aspects of the security strategic operations including security risk management, security management review, oversight of guard force operations, and physical plant and technology security vendors. The expertise provided by these professionals is at least equal to that of a full-time security manager minus the expense of payroll, taxes, and fringe benefits. Such contracted services may provide a degree of "troubleshooting" and represent an option. Nevertheless, corporate security has to move away from being reactive, which mimics policing (public security). There has to be a strategic focus aligned to the corporate goals, driven by a focused, educated, and performance-driven executive security manager. Such an approach will yield significant benefits, both tangible and intangible.

## RAISING CORPORATE SECURITY CULTURE AND ETHICS

Ensuring appropriate nation-state and regional ethics and compliance is a critical goal for a corporation, some would suggest even surpassing risk management, although specific risks such as conflicts of interest, corruption, and breaches of electronic data and privacy remain concerns. Embedding core values and strengthening ethical leadership are the critical priorities for a corporate security manager. Such focus toward culture and ethics is likely to gain greater focus for many Asia-Pacific nation-states and corporations. Culture can be used as a strategy, as many Asia-Pacific nation-states move toward attracting overseas corporations to their shores. Nation-state culture and ethics can demonstrate a robust and resilient regional base for many companies.

In a 2011 survey, ethics and compliance managers saw themselves as the champions for creating ethical, values-based cultures, with 58 percent stating that their primary mandate is to ensure ethical behaviors and alignment with core values.

However, only 42 percent believe their core mandate is compliance with law and regulation, and 68 percent indicated that creating long-term value for the business is a principal benefit of an ethical culture. Yet the survey suggests that the ability of ethics and compliance managers to inspire and sustain ethical cultures at their companies may be limited. Some would argue that culture as a strategy, fuelled by values that are translated into tangible behaviors and embedded in the gears of a business, can create sustained competitive advantages. So what do ethics and compliance managers need to overcome and what innovations should they consider in their role as "culture builders"? Strategies that will assist include:

1. *Make ethics and compliance a core management mind-set.* Rather than considering ethics and compliance to protect against law and avoid damage to the company's reputation, make ethics and compliance a core management discipline and mind set. Such an approach was taken with the adoption of safety and environmental management during the 1980s and 1990s.
2. *Seek partners beyond your traditional domain.* Ethics and compliance managers should extend their influence and better fulfill their "culture" mandate by building deeper partnerships with nontraditional partners.
3. *Move outside the executive suite.* Only 22 percent of ethics and compliance leaders worry about whether executive management supports and promotes an ethical culture within their companies; however, 45 percent have concerns about the commitment of middle managers. The concept is to get middle managers with values-based leadership embedded in leadership development programs and on-the-job training.
4. *Target your microcultures.* Half of ethics and compliance leaders see potentially poisonous microcultures in sales and emerging markets operations. Those cultures, whether present in remote locations or specific business units, expose companies to the risk of significant ethics and compliance breakdowns. Targeted interventions can significantly reduce these risks.
5. *Do not put all your eggs in the online education basket.* Diversify ethics and compliance education beyond online compliance training and awareness. Local nation-state managers can act as role models and often translate lessons from the theoretical to the practical.
6. *Bring the code of conduct to life.* The corporation ethics and compliance policy is the guide for ethical behavior, which should extend beyond the narrow definition of legal requirements. Avoid legalese and make the policy relevant and engaging for employees, enlist managers to make the code part of regular business conversations and staff meetings, and make sure that it is translated for and speaks to employees all over the globe (Greenberg 2011).

## INCREASING STANDARDS

If the security industry and its members as a whole do not increase their professionalism (see the later section on this matter), nation-state governments will have to manage this social risk, which will result in greater government control. Such control will require greater and more rigorous regulations and legislation to control the industry. Greater regulation will further restrict the industry to be truly effective and to develop into a true independent profession. In addition, such regulation, from corporations' perspective, will increase their compliance requirements and reduce the ability of corporate security managers to operate at the executive level.

In many parts of the Asia Pacific, standards are being developed, accepted, and propagated, including those ISO standards from the International Organization for Standardization (ISO). However, the Asia Pacific is diverse and many of these standards are nation-state specific and considered the benchmark for operations. For example, Australian standards, as with most nation-state standards, are "published documents setting out specifications and procedures designed to ensure products, services and systems are safe, reliable and consistently perform" (Standards Australia n.d., 2). Such an approach ensures that a common *language* is achieved within an industry, driven by the more progressive parts of industry, legislation, and community expectations.

There are now standards for many parts of the security industry, from CCTV to security screen, and from risk management to IT business continuity. For example, Australia has released a set of security standards designed to help government and business protect the community and key infrastructure against a major disaster or terrorist attack. These Australian standards are also designed to help businesses recover from catastrophic events such as storms, earthquakes, or criminal activity including computer hacking or information theft.

In Singapore, the Ministry of Home Affairs produces many standards and handbooks. For example, the *Guidelines for Enhancing Building Security in Singapore* (Homefront Security Division 2010) is a compilation of international best practices in building security. It provides the building and construction community with practical information and guidelines on how they can take personal action to enhance the security of their buildings. In addition, other relevant security standards include, but are far from limited to, the 2010 Code of Practice for Construction, Installation, Operation and Maintenance of Intruder Alarm Systems (Singapore Standards 2010), and the 2009 Private Security Industry Act to govern the central alarm monitoring station operator (Ministry of Home Affairs 2009).

Nevertheless, do standards improve the security industry or are they just another compliance issue that corporations have to address? Unfortunately, it is the latter. For example, Australia has had a national Standard AS2201.1 that defines prescriptive requirements for intruder alarm systems. However, in practice a significant number of installed intruder alarms do not comply with this standard. Seventeen percent of alarm panels were located outside an alarmed area, 15 percent of panels were located in the entry/exit point, 46 percent of the panels were not capable of dual end-of-line supervision, and 59 percent of the systems were configured in single end-of-line supervision. These items contravene sections of the Australian Standard AS2201.1 and would appear to demonstrate systemic failure within this sector of the security industry (Brooks 2009a).

Standards, in this case, did not improve the security industry but rather allowed systemic noncompliance across all parts of the industry. This issue was considered to be due to a lack of industry-focused vocational training and education, limited industry self-regulation and supervision, restricted licensing regime, and inappropriate or ineffective legislation (Brooks 2009a).

## LEGISLATION AND GOVERNANCE

It is generally considered that nation-states will develop and apply legislation to control social risk if they feel that the industry responsible cannot. Such increased legislation will stifle professional development of the security industry. Such an issue will affect the security industry in many ways, not least increasing the need to ensure compliance across the diverse environment of the Asia Pacific and restrict more innovative approaches to threat and risk mitigation.

Some nation-states have called for tougher standards to force organizations to notify customers of security breaches that expose customer information. Curtis said forcing organizations "to notify customers of a breach is a strong market incentive that will encourage organizations to adequately secure databases and increase customer trust" (cited in Workshare 2007, 3). Many submissions to the various government groups have called for a tougher regulatory climate as a result of a huge increase in high-profile data breaches in recent years, which have made many privacy acts outdated and almost redundant. For example, the U.S. Congress has introduced a data breach notification bill and more than 30 U.S. states have passed similar laws since 2005.

There has been a strong push by industry for tougher data governance standards. For example, the largest custodian of credit information in Australia, Veda Advantage (formerly Baycorp Advantage), claimed there is an "urgent need" for stronger data governance standards and that there should be greater obligations on companies that aggregate data. Many want biometric information to be classified as sensitive under such privacy acts to ensure a higher level of protection than that for other forms of personal data. "In addition, all organizations including small businesses that are generally exempt under the Privacy Act and handle biometric information, should also be covered under the legislation" (Rossi 2007).

### PROFESSIONAL ASSOCIATIONS

As highlighted in Chapter 1, the Asia Pacific has many professional bodies that represent parts of the security industry, for example, ASIS International, which is one of the more supported organizations and has greater membership than many others. Many of these associations cross-represent many parts of the security industry, which reduces their true effectiveness to develop and support such diverse membership. Until a single group takes control or there is clear demarcation across the industry, the security industry will for many decades be inappropriately represented.

Industry bodies are stovepiped groups that have their own agenda for generally one part of the industry, but they want to represent all parts. A single overarching association—the most preferred option for the greater good and development of the security industry—is highly unlikely due to the diversity of the industry itself and competing associations. Nevertheless, if associations can define clear boundaries as to whom they represent, as some have, there is hope that such associations will provide a significant benefit in developing the industry.

### INCREASING HIGHER EDUCATION

At the tertiary level, many corporate security courses have been developed from related disciplines—police, justice, or criminology studies (Smith 2001). In addition, many relevant courses in corporate security are offered only at the vocational level, restricting the industry professionalism and informed research. Nevertheless, according to Smith, security knowledge is being established though the development of appropriate domain concepts (2001, 32), a view supported by Simonsen (1996 230) who stated that the "body of knowledge of security has grown rapidly in the past decade."

By developing such defined knowledge and supporting this with vigorous research inquiry, corporate security could develop its own distinct scholarly area of study. Research studies are required to feed into tertiary educational institutes, inform pedagogy, and develop curriculum. If this is achieved, increasing tertiary educational institutes will offer relevant courses, applied practicing boundaries will be better understood, and the industry will drive toward understanding and, later, professionalism.

In the past decade, there has been a significant increase in higher educational security courses, but these are still diffused and questionable in regard to how they support the relevant part of the security industry. Such courses as counterterrorism, homeland security, critical infrastructure security, and many others maintain the past confusion on what constitutes corporate security. There is no easy solution to this issue and that is unlikely to change for the next decade.

The industry needs the ability to better understand and define itself with clear operating boundaries. The relevant professional bodies need to support and propagate these boundaries, which will allow tertiary institutions to link with the industry and their professional bodies. Such convergence will increase *focused* tertiary educational offers, increasing convergence to knowledge and skill sets, and further defining boundaries. Such convergence will go a significant way in resolving this complex and difficult issue.

## CONCLUSION

To enhance global competitiveness, corporations should formally manage their security responsibilities and plan for their response to a diverse range of security-related risks. Nevertheless, to effectively manage threats and risks there has to be some degree of future trending. The future of the Asia-Pacific region is likely to be one of great success, with increasing wealth and social stability. However, there will be nation-states that will have significant problems, as the region itself is large and very diverse. Or, as suggested, are we in for some quite nasty shocks (Evans 2011)?

It is likely that any changing security issues will have clear indicators, and most corporations should be able to track these in time to protect their interests and, more importantly, their in-country employees. Nevertheless, this is unlikely to extend to the nations-state's citizens. Being aware of in-country threats and risks to maintain appropriate vigilance is vital in overcoming apathy toward security.

Being aware of and trying to understanding such security trends across the Asia-Pacific region is complex. Such trends to consider may include the dynamic nature of the region, changing focus on the terrorist threat, issues of civil unrest, street violence and riots, privacy in Asia Pacific, corporate security as a cost center, the need to raise the corporate security culture and ethics, increasing externally imposed standards, ever-changing technology, the complexity of nation-state legislation and governance, and the expectation that the profession will become more professional.

## REFERENCES

ASIS International. 2003. *Proceedings of the 2003 Academic/Practitioner Symposium.* University of Maryland. College Park, MD: ASIS International.

Aven, T. 2008. *Risk Analysis: Assessing Uncertainties beyond Expected Values and Probabilities.* West Sussex, UK: Wiley.

Brooks, D. J. 2009a. Intruder Alarm Systems: Is the Security Industry Installing and Maintaining Alarm Systems in Compliance to Australian Standard AS2201? *Security Journal* 1–17. doi: 10.1057/sj.2009.12.

———. 2009b. What Is Security: Definition through Knowledge Categorisation. *Security Journal* 1–15. doi: 101057/sj.2008.18.

———. 2010. *Assessing Vulnerabilities of Biometric Readers Using an Applied Defeat Evaluation Methodology.* Paper presented at the Proceedings of the 3rd Australian Security and Intelligence Conference, Perth.

———. 2011. "Security Risk Management: A Psychometric Map of Expert Knowledge Structure." *International Journal of Risk Management* 13 (1/2): 17–41.

Busch, A. 2011, June 22. Research reveals unexpected differences in privacy regulations. Retrieved April 19, 2012, from http://www.esrc.ac.uk/news-and-events/press-releases/15896/research-reveals-unexpected-differences-in-privacy-regulations.aspx

Colville, R. 2011. Sony PlayStation hack: a glimpse into the world of online crime. Retrieved May 2, 2011, from http://www.telegraph.co.uk/technology/sony/8478949/Sony-PlayStation-hack-a-glimpse-into-the-world-of-online-crime.html

Crawford, M. 2005. Data protection laws on ice. Retrieved April 15, 2012, from http://www.computerworld.com.au/article/139534/data_protection_laws_ice/

Crawford, M. 2006. Short-term plans a sure fire way to cripple business: Many companies below par on DR readiness. Retrieved April 16, 2012, from http://www.computerworld.com.au/article/165552/short-term_plans_sure_fire_way_cripple_business/

Evans, G. 2011. *The Asian Region in 2011: Trends and Tensions.* Presentation to Asia Link, Melbourne, February 21.

Greenberg, D. May 9, 2011. Culture as a Strategy: Why Companies Should Innovate in Ethics and Compliance. Insights Corporate Compliance. Retrieved May 25, 2011 from http://www.corporatecomplianceinsights.com/culture-as-a-strategy-why-companies-should-innovate-in-ethics-and-compliance/.

Hesse, L., and C. L. Smith. 2001. *Core Curriculum in Security Science.* Paper presented at the the 5th Australian Security Research Symposium, Perth.

Homefront Security Division, Ministry of Home Affairs. 2010. *Guidelines for Enhancing Building Security in Singapore.* Singapore: Ministry of Home Affairs.

Kerstein, P. 2005. Australian State Calls for Workplace Surveillance Legislation. CSO. Retrieved April 15, 2012, from http://www.csoonline.com/article/214431/australian-state-calls-for-workplace-surveillance-legislation.

Kerstein, R. 2005. "Australian State Calls for Workplace Surveillance Legislation." http://www.csoonline.com/article/214431/australian-state-calls-for-workplace-surveillance-legislation (accessed January 17, 2012).

Lozusic, R. 2003. *Fraud and Identity Theft.* Briefing Paper No. 8/03. NSW Parliamentary Library Research Service. ISBN 0-7313-1733-5.

McBride, S 2005. Australian workplace spying law takes force in October. Retreived April 15, 2012, from http://computerworld.co.nz/news.nsf/news/AEEAC7567AEFB3FFCC 25706E0019F1FC.

Ministry of Home Affairs. 2009. Private Security Industry Act (Chapter 250A) No. S 169. Singapore: The Minister for Home Affairs.

Office of the Australian Information Commissioner. 2007. Media Release: Amend Privacy Act to address security breaches, biometrics and data-matching, says Privacy Commissioner. Retrieved April 22, 2012, from http://www.privacy.gov.au/materials/types/media/ view/6198

Power, M. 2007. *Organised Uncertainty: Designing a World of Risk Management*. Oxford: Oxford University Press.

"Research Reveals Unexpected Differences in Privacy Regulations." 2011. http://www.esrc. ac.uk/news-and-events/press-releases/15896/research-reveals-unexpected-differences-in-privacy-regulations.aspx (accessed June 24, 2011).

Rossi, S. 2007, September 17. Government steps up electronic surveillance without a warrant. Computerworld. Retrieved May 5, 2012 from http://www.computerworld.com.au/ article/185605/government_steps_up_electronic_surveillance_without_warrant/.

Rossi, S. 2007. Review of Privacy Act reveals push for tougher data protection standards. Computerworld. Retrieved April 16, 2012, from http://www.computerworld.com.au/ article/175902/review_privacy_act_reveals_push_tougher_data_protection_standards/.

Sherman, C. 2002. Coping with Fraudulent Pay-Per-Click Traffic. Retrieved April 15, 2012, from http://searchenginewatch.com/article/2049120/Ask-the-Search-Engine-Coping-with -Fraudulent-Pay-Per-Click-Traffic.

Simonsen, C. E. 1996. "The Case For: Security Management Is a Profession." *International Journal of Risk, Security and Crime Prevention* 1 (3): 229–32.

Singapore Standards. 2010. *SS558:2010 Code of Practice for Construction, Installation, Operation and Maintenance of Intruder Alarm Systems*. Singapore: Singapore Standards.

Smith, C. L. 2001. "Security Science: An Emerging Applied Science." *Journal of the Science Teachers Association of Western Australia* 37 (2): 8–10.

Standards Australia. n.d. *Image a World without Standards*. Brochure. Sydney: Standards Australia.

Symantec. 2010. Symantec global internet security threat report: Trends for 2009. Mountain View, CA: Symantec Corporation.

Tate, P. W. 1997. *Report on the Security Industry Training: Case Study of an Emerging Industry*. Perth: Western Australian Department of Training, Western Australian Government Publishing.

Workshare Global Security Threat Report. 2007. Retrieved April 16, 2012, from http://www. workshare.com/go/research/07aprilthreats.pdf.

# 6 Internal Corporate Crime
## *Crime, Fraud, and Misconduct*

## INTRODUCTION

The following chapter presents a selection of recent internal-security vignettes, sorted by case type and circumstances (Table 6.1). These vignettes will provide corporate security managers with a breadth of events that have occurred and therefore have a likelihood of occurring in their own corporations. It is apparent from the cases included herein that organizations must be forever vigilant in preventing and minimizing internal risks, with the most prevalent vulnerability being the nature of human beings, regardless of corporate position or social standing. The objective of raising these cases in the context of corporate security is to initiate awareness and acknowledgment of the fact that security risks will emerge in any large or transnational organization at some point in time, and have a similarly diverse range of consequences.

## CORPORATE CRIME

**Executive deception:** Australian Wheat Board (AWB) has been denied legal professional privilege over documents relating to its Iraq transactions. The Australian Federal Court ruled this week that AWB intentionally tricked the United Nations by deliberately and dishonestly structuring AWB to "misrepresent the true nature and purpose of the trucking fees and to work a trickery on the United Nations. Privilege does not attach to these documents as they were brought into existence in furtherance of a fraud or other impropriety," Judge Neil Young said in his preliminary findings (*Lawyers Weekly* 2006).

AWB is still facing mounting legal and recovery costs from the Iraq bribery scandal. The company has accumulated A$9 million in costs associated with the Cole inquiry and this is forecast to increase to A$20 million. There have also been investigations by the Australian Tax Office, Australian Federal Police and class action law suits from growers and shareholders. Potential liabilities have been reserved at A$250 million and net profit may drop by 9 percent over the next three years (Australian Financial Review 2006). At least 16 executives, directors and advising lawyers may now be charged with Commonwealth and Victorian state offences, involving dishonesty and deception. Other possible offences include breaches of the terrorism financing laws and money laundering provisions of the Reserve Bank regulations.

AWB Directors who knowingly or unwittingly paid A$300 million in kickbacks in the Iraq Food for Oil scandal have effectively cost the company's shareholders A$900 million in reduced company value. These figures need to be raised at any board table when directors are dealing with any perceived or directly related facilitation, bribery

### TABLE 6.1
### Internal Crime

**Internal Corporate Incident**

| | |
|---|---|
| Corporate crime | Political misconduct and scandal |
| Fraud | Corruption and bribery |
| Internal theft | Supply chain and resilience breakdown |
| Insider trading | Workplace violence |
| Director ethical breaches | Food and product contamination |
| Governance and compliance | Failings and breaches of technology |
| Privacy | Loss and misuse of information |

or money laundering issues. Dealing with corrupt companies or as part of accepted business practice in corrupt countries might be considered necessary for short term gains, but has been proven that it is not only bad for long term business but it can be catastrophic to the company (Rowley and Tomkin 2006).

**A\$200m lawsuit against airlines over price-fixing:** Qantas and six other airlines have recently received a A\$200 million federal class action suit on behalf of freight users for an alleged cartel to fix fuel, security and war-risk surcharges. It relates to another claim against 15 other airlines worth A\$1 billion (Gettler 2007).

**James Hardie directors receive lawsuit:** Australian Securities and Investments Commission (ASIC) appears to be making an example of James Hardie directors who were on the Board when the CEO allegedly lied in public statements about the adequacy of funding arrangements for claims by asbestos victims. This includes lawsuits against non-executive directors. The business judgment rule will provide the directors a defence, but they will need to prove they made their decisions in good faith, without conflict of interest, for a proper purpose and that they fully informed themselves, including the entitlement to rely on executives and advisors. ASIC alleges that the directors had sufficient information to know that the statements were false and that they were not simply relying on assurances from the CEO (Kohler, *West Australian* 2007).

**Intel charged with monopoly abuse:** European regulators have charged Intel with monopoly abuse for blocking rival computer chip maker Advanced Micro Devices access to customers. The case is based on complaints from a direct competitor rather than customers or consumers (White, A. n.d.).

**ACCC action against Google and a client:** The Australian Consumer and Competition Commission (ACCC) has initiated legal action against Google, its Australian subsidiary and one of its clients, the Trading Post for deceiving users between paid and unpaid search results on the search engine. The ACCC claims that the companies engaged in conduct that was misleading or deceptive or likely to mislead or deceive, in breach of the Trade Practices Act (*West Australian* 2011).

**Corporate war crimes:** Three **former employees of Australian based company,** Anvil Mining have been recommended for prosecution for complicity of **war crimes**

following a massacre of villagers, two years ago, in Kilwa, Congo. Anvil's deputy general manager, a subsidiary's general manager and two others were charged with having knowingly facilitated the commission of war crimes (*West Australian* 2006).

# FRAUD

**Fraud doubles in two years:** KPMG has released their latest fraud survey that indicates that the **incidence of fraud has doubled in the two years.** In eight cases, the fraud was worth more than A$4 million. The most common frauds were false invoicing and stealing cash. Those who defrauded companies for the highest amounts were senior executives and directors, who fabricated loans and pilfered cash. Organised crime and identity theft were also rising. 14 percent of employees who stole from their employer had done it before at a previous job. Employers should check references and conduct thorough background and criminal history checks (KPMG 2004).

**Trade secrets:** Pepsi received a letter from a person claiming to be a high-level Coca-Cola executive willing to sell trade secrets. To Pepsi's credit it reported the approach, which resulted in three people being charged with fraud and stealing trade secrets. One of the offenders was a Coca-Cola administrative assistant (Litterick 2006).

**PNG Police Commissioner under investigation:** Papua New Guinea Police Commissioner is being investigated over allegations he blocked a police inquiry into a A$1.84 million fraud (Mission and Justice 2006).

**Middle Eastern Prince:** An Australian has been arrested in Malaysia after to trying to cheat his Canadian business partner out of more than A$1.77 million in a fraudulent oil deal. The Australian allegedly claimed that he was a Middle Eastern prince and was leading an extravagant lifestyle, including driving expensive sports cars (*The Age*, August 2006).

**Fake expert jailed:** A British man has been jailed for five years after giving evidence at hundreds of criminal trials, tricking judges, lawyers and police into believing he was a forensics expert, even though he held no qualifications and copied many of his reports from the internet. Over a three year period he was paid more than A$600,000 for his "expertise" (*Daily Mail Reporter* 2009).

**Oxfam aid fraud:** International aid agency, Oxfam, is considering what to do with 10 corrupt staff. After investigating amounts paid to suppliers for quantity of goods delivered, following aid to the tsunami-hit Aceh, a A$29,000 fraud was uncovered. Another 12 staff may be involved. This type of fraudulent activity can occur in any medium- to large-sized business if there are no fraud prevention measures (*The Age* 2006).

**Employees' misleading information:** Access Management Consultants have released research that indicates that 43 percent of resumes contain untrue or misleading information. The research also showed that only 59 percent of HR Managers verified the authenticity of candidate qualifications, only 78 percent verified experience and less than 50 percent checked for criminal history. Time constraints were the main causes for insufficient background checks and managers were also using their "own judgment". The costs of replacing a dishonest employee could be as high as 200 percent of the person's salary (*Sunday Times* 2006).

**Fraudsters exploit the World Cup:** When the South African World Cup kicked-off, so too did a wave of Internet security threats. Malicious e-mails and phishing scams were distributed that were deliberately designed to exploit sporting fans. The scams are designed to lure people after tickets, merchandise or other memorabilia. It is an example of the entrepreneurial change in on-line threats from the usual money-driven scams, run by highly organized criminals. A recent e-mail scam in Japan, allegedly run by the Russian Mafia, offered access to premium World Cup tickets for A$10 via a Web site. It was a hugely successful phishing scam that trapped a lot of people.

Another World Cup e-mail scam offered a wall chart of the event which, when executed, infects the user with a Trojan. To minimize risk, businesses and individuals should ensure they run the latest anti-virus signatures, update firewalls, anti-spyware programs, install recent operating system patches and also connect filtering software on Web gateways to block non-reputable sites. But most important is education; ensure you and your employees are aware of malicious threats and preventative measures and see to it that they report anything they see as a risk.

**Fraudulent inspectors:** Inspectors, posing as government safety representatives, are approaching and inspecting businesses, threatening owners they are liable for A$20,000 fines and trying to force them to pay A$750 for safety instruction books. At least three Australian businesses have been targeted. Impersonating an inspector is an offence under the Safety Act, and Business owners and managers should remain astute and check the credentials of any person offering advice or services (Bowler, J. n.d.).

**Biggest trader fraud in history:** Surpassing and dwarfing Nick Leeson's Barings Bank fraud of US$1.6 billion in the 1990s, a French trader has fraudulently accumulated US$8.3 billion in fake account losses at France's second biggest bank, Societe Generale. A Wall Street stock-broking firm described it as "everyone's worst nightmare" (*West Australian* 2008).

**Private investigator working for Hewlett-Packard charged with identity fraud:** A San Francisco private investigator was charged with identity fraud and conspiracy for his role in Hewlett-Packard's ill-fated boardroom spying probe. He has agreed to plead guilty and will now potentially testify against others in HP's chain of command. He is alleged to have secretly obtaining a journalist's social security number, using it to create an on-line account with a telephone company in the reporter's name and then accessing detailed phone logs. In addition, the investigators was accused of illegally obtaining and transmitting personal information on HP directors and employees during HP's attempts to find the source of boardroom leaks to the media (*West Australian* 2006).

## INTERNAL THEFT

**The true scale of the insider threat:** A LogRhythm survey of 3,000 UK workers revealed that 37 percent of people have shared privileged company information with their friends and family, while 21 percent of laptop/desktop-owning respondents stated that they have transferred company data to their personal computer, even though more than half of these devices (58 percent) were shared with, or could at least be accessed by, other people. Smartphone users also present a risk, with 14 percent admitting that they transfer work data to their personal handsets. The research also indicated that many employees would leak company information to the media if they thought their employer was acting immorally or illegally, with 26 percent willing to become whistleblowers. A further 34 percent stated that they would report this activity to the police. When asked about the scale of the security risk posed by employees, 82 percent of respondents stated that they believed the insider threat to be equal to or greater than the threat posed to organizations by external attackers.

"This research shows that there are many ways in which security breaches can occur, regardless of the insider's intentions," stated Brewer. "In transferring information to a personal laptop or Smartphone, an insider is putting that information at risk of misuse. It need not be deliberate action, but simply carelessness that does the damage." The survey also suggests that the security risks posed by employees may worsen in the future, as workers between the ages of 18 and 24 were routinely the worst offenders. They are more likely to transfer confidential information to external devices; in particular to smart phones, where figures were 10 percent higher than average at 24 percent.

When asked about how easy it was to access company secrets, 19 percent reported that there was no policy restricting access to information on the company network, while a further 15 percent said that although there was a policy, it was still possible for unauthorised people to access privileged content. Support for more stringent security procedures was high, with 63 percent favouring strictly enforced policies to prevent unauthorised staff from accessing data, 60 percent advocating disciplinary action for staff in breach of the rules and 52 percent backing the use of technology to monitor access to restricted files (*Help Net Security*, April 7, 2011).

**Potter book leaked:** Despite what was intended to be strict security in the lead up to the release of the last Harry Potter book, a complete copy was released over the Internet days before the official release. Various sites posted the copy and were later taken down in efforts to suppress the leak (*West Australian* 2007).

**Business owner in credit card scam:** A liquor store owner has been charged with providing his customers credit card details to a third party, which then conducted illegal transactions to the value of A$25,000 (*West Australian* 2007).

**Accountant's fraud:** An Australian accountant has been charged with stealing nearly A$850,000 from an engineering company. It is alleged that he made 224 electronic transfers into six private accounts, including more than A$570,000 to a casino. The company is taking civil action in an attempt to retrieve some of the money (*West Australian* 2007).

**Lawyers charged with theft and fraud:** A lawyer was charged with stealing more than A$700,000 from his former firm and clients over a five-year period. Another Barrister was convicted of fraud for receiving more than A$22,000, after forging his deceased's father's signature on a Centrelink form to continue receiving his pension, paid into a private company account (*West Australian* 2008).

**Owner did not authorize $400k exec payment:** A company became aware of a series of unauthorized payments that have been made to a former executive, up to approximately A$414,000. The board had been advised by the individual concerned that the unauthorised payments would be repaid to the company in full; however, it is now no longer entirely confident as to the recovery of all of these funds nor as to the timing of the proposed repayments (WA Business News). The company is currently receiving appropriate professional advice in relation to this matter and its consequential effect upon the company. Once the board is in receipt of this advice, it will provide a further update to the market. It anticipates that such an announcement will be made and the suspension of the company's shares will remain in place until further notice (*West Australian* Business News 2008).

**Rs9m Robbed in Biggest Bank Heist of the Year:** Six armed men stole Rs9 million from the Muslim Commercial Bank in Karachi, Pakistan. According to the Special Investigation Unit (SIU), which is heading the investigation, one of the suspects is Anwer Ali, a private security guard working for the bank. Ali reportedly arrived for his shift as usual at 6:30 am, and then allegedly let in five other accomplices who captured and tied up bank staff as they arrived for work. The manager of operation for the branch was then forced to open the vault at gunpoint. Although the bank staff attempted to alert the private security company, it failed to respond to the situation. The company's manager did not arrive at the bank until 1:00 pm. The SIU confiscated the security company's records, but when they visited the address given for Ali it was found he only lived there for a week in February, when he was hired by the bank. The company had little other information on Ali and both of the security guard's guarantors were found to be fake. The police tracked down one of the guarantors, who said he had never met the suspect and that his CNIC number had been misused (ASIS International 2011).

**Department of Homeland Security Terror Report Warns of "Significant Insider Threat" to US Utility Facilities:** Sabotage by an insider at a major utility facility, including a chemical or oil refinery, could provide al Qaeda with its best opportunity for the kind of 9/11 anniversary attack Osama bin Laden was planning, according to US officials. The Department of Homeland Security has issued a report warning about a possible threat from al Qaeda operatives who could carry out attacks on major utility facilities on or around the 10 year anniversary of the 9/11 attacks. Such attacks could consist of sabotage perpetrated by an insider working at a utility facility, the report says. The report noted that violent extremists have already been able to obtain insider positions at chemical and oil refineries, and have tried to "solicit" employees in the utility sector. Former Homeland Security chief of staff Chad Sweet noted that an attack on a utility might be appealing to al Qaeda because it would be the only way that the group could kill large numbers of Americans as Osama bin Laden had been planning to do before he was killed in a Navy SEAL operation in May 2011. However, the Department of Homeland Security has said that it does not have any specific threats against US utilities. Nevertheless, DHS spokesman Matt Chandler said that the department plans to work with its partners in the utility sector and at the state and local levels to protect utility facilities (*Daily Mail*, July 21, 2011).

## INSIDER TRADING

**Director insider trading:** Directors are regularly and consistently tempted to commit insider trading offences by conducting share transactions whilst in possession of market sensitive information, which is not yet known by the market. How often are directors trading illegally through transactions that are conducted through affiliate, but unconnected entities? Insider trading is a criminal offence under most nation-state legislation and often punishable with five years imprisonment.

**Insider trading rampant in Asia:** *Finance Asia* asked readers how Asia rates as a hub for insider trading. They scored the region highly, confidently asserting that the level of market manipulation puts Galleon hedge fund founder Raj Rajaratnam to shame. The Rajaratnam trial exposed insider trading in a number of Asian companies' shares, including Taiwan Semiconductor Manufacturing Company and Singapore's Flextronics. Insider trading scandals are common throughout the region. At the end of February, regulators in Korea banned Deutsche Bank's securities unit from trading derivatives on its own account for six months and fined it a record amount after a two-month investigation into charges of market manipulation and tardy reporting.

In India, the Securities and Exchange Board of India's new chief regulator, U.K. Sinha, started work in February and is already busy with an insider-trading investigation into Reliance Industries. Hong Kong's departing regulator, Martin Wheatley, has earned respect for the job he has done during the past six years, but there is still plenty of work to do. Huang Guangyu, the corrupt founder of Gome, appears to remain in charge of the company even from his jail cell. The *Finance Asia* review found that 62 percent of readers believed that insider trading is rampant in Asia, while 36 percent said that it was no more or less a problem than in other markets. Only 2 percent claimed insider trading was less prevalent here than elsewhere (Ferguson, *Finance Asia*, March 15, 2011).

**Insider trading: Tiger Asia challenges the SFC's strategy in court:** A lawsuit between Hong Kong's Securities and Futures Commission (SFC) and Tiger Asia Management LLC could soon alter how the city's courtrooms deal with insider trading. Currently progressing through Hong Kong's court system, the dispute between the New York hedge fund and the SFC is expected to receive a ruling from the high court within weeks. Tiger Asia and three of its officers are challenging a court order sought by the SFC that bans the firm from trading in Hong Kong and requires it to disgorge alleged insider trading profits. As a part of its defence, Tiger Asia has argued that the civil proceedings initiated by the SFC are an error of law, as insider trading is a criminal offence in Hong Kong and should be dealt with through criminal proceedings.

In Hong Kong, most cases of insider trading are dealt with by the Market Misconduct Tribunal (MMT), an independent body established under the Securities and Futures Ordinance. The MMT typically conducts civil proceedings in public and is empowered to impose civil sanctions on wrongdoers; however, insider trading in Hong Kong is also a criminal offence, similar to the US and UK. Convicted offenders could be subject to a maximum penalty of HK$10 million and 10 years' imprisonment.

In contrast, the MMT is widely considered to have the most authority in dealing with insider trading in Hong Kong. Earlier this year the SFC, through proceedings conducted by the MMT, imposed a life-long ban on an individual in connection with insider dealing in the shares of Mirabell International Holdings Limited. The sanctions imposed are similar to those currently facing Tiger Asia. Zhang Bijia, a former employee of Access Capital Limited, was prohibited from dealing in securities for life. Liu Yan Yan, a former trainee solicitor of Norton Rose, was also sanctioned in the proceedings. Moreover, an order to disgorge notional profits from the insider trading was also imposed (Asia Editor, E-Discovery, June 8, 2011).

**SFC to appeal court's ruling on Tiger Asia:** The Court of First Instance handed down reasons for its decision that the court has no jurisdiction to determine whether or not New York-based asset management company, Tiger Asia Management LLC (Tiger Asia) and three of its officers, Bill Sung Kook Hwang, Raymond Park, and

William Tomita (collectively the Tiger Asia parties), have contravened Hong Kong's insider dealing and market manipulation laws. In the ruling, the Court of First Instance has ruled that only a court exercising criminal jurisdiction or the Market Misconduct Tribunal (MMT) has jurisdiction to determine whether a contravention of Hong Kong's insider dealing laws and market manipulation laws has occurred, with the result that the Securities and Futures Commission (SFC) cannot seek final orders under section 213 without such a prior determination. The SFC challenges the correctness of this court decision and intends to appeal the ruling. The SFC alleges the Tiger Asia parties contravened Hong Kong's laws prohibiting insider dealing and market manipulation. The allegations relate to trading by Tiger Asia in shares of China Construction Bank Corporation (CCB) and Bank of China Limited (BOC). The SFC is seeking remedial orders against the Tiger Asia parties and injunctions to protect the Hong Kong market. The Tiger Asia parties are not within the jurisdiction of Hong Kong's criminal courts nor, in the SFC's view, should they be entitled to receive immunity from prosecution, which would be the result if proceedings were commenced before the MMT (*Enforcement News*, June 21, 2011, Securities and Futures Commission).

**Couple amass fortune from insider trading:** Christian Littlewood was a London banker earning £400,000 (S$820,000) a year; however, he used information from his office to get his Singaporean wife Angie Lew Siew Yoon to make £590,000 from illegal insider trading. The profits helped the Littlewoods build a 3 million pound property portfolio in London. The most serious case of insider trading to come before a British court as the couple traded multiple shares over an eight-year period motivated by greed, a Crown Court judge found. Judge Leonard told Littlewood, 37, that although he lived a lifestyle well beyond most, your desire to amass yet more wealth meant you could not resist making use of the sensitive information you had. "No other case has matched this one in its scale, in the position you held or in the profits made," said the judge when sending Littlewood to jail for 40 months, the stiffest insider dealing sentence to date in Britain (Vijayan, *Straits Times*, February 5, 2011).

**US insider trading ring broken:** The US Securities & Exchange Commission has uncovered a US$19 million insider trading scandal that involved brokers for top financial firms and two lawyers. A USB executive used disposable mobile phones and coded messages to tip hedge fund traders of imminent changes to analyst ratings, and a Morgan Stanley compliance officer and former lawyer informed her husband about pending takeovers. Others of the 13 people involved included hedge fund portfolio managers, compliance personnel and registered representatives of Wall Street's "top tier" firms.

**US insider trading charges:** The vice-chairman of US based International Securities Exchange Holdings and two financial consultants have been charged with insider trading before ISE's merger with Eurex in 2007. Charges include conspiracy and ten counts of securities fraud. It is alleged that non-public information about the Eurex merger, a subsidiary of German stock market operator Duetsche Boerse was leaked to the consultants who subsequently traded in shares and options (Stoyeck n.d.).

**Restricted trading:** The **chief executive officer** of Energex, Queensland's state-owned energy company, was forced to resign after admitting that he traded in shares of two of the company's largest competitors, in breach of the company's restricted trading register. Energex was preparing to sell its A$1 billion retail segments, which had the interest to the competitors. The previous CEO had committed suicide and the former chairman is facing child sex charges. The activities of the company's executives and directors have ignited debate about the level of corporate governance in government owned corporations (*Australian Financial Review* 2006).

## DIRECTOR ETHICAL BREACHES

**Japanese entrepreneur jailed for securities fraud:** A Japanese businessman who guided Livedoor Co., from start-up to a household name in Japan has been found guilty of securities laws violations after masterminding a network of decoy investment funds for the purpose of manipulating his company's accounting and value. He was sentenced to two and half year's jail.

**Recruitment executives sacked over violating code of conduct:** Two top Australian executives of US owned Hudson Recruitment Agency have been sacked in violation of the company's code of conduct. The dismissals relate to breaches of fiduciary duties and employment obligations, and the deliberate nondisclosure of a conflict of interest. They were alleged to have been involved in a competing business. Hudson is one of the top three recruitment businesses in Australia, formerly trading as Morgan & Banks (*West Australian* 2006).

**Australian businessman ruled to be lying in Family Court:** A leading Perth businessman was forced to admit he deliberately lied to the Family Court during a bitter divorce dispute. He has been penalized A$1.5 million and faces the prospect of criminal charges (*West Australian* 2008).

**Whistleblower website launched:** Wikileaks is developing an uncensorable Wikipedia for untraceable mass document leaking and analysis and claims to have received over 1.2 million documents so far from dissident communities and anonymous sources. The Web site proposes the primary interests are oppressive regimes in Asia, the former Soviet bloc, Sub-Saharan Africa and the Middle East, but they also expect to be of assistance to those in the west who wish to reveal unethical behaviour in their own governments and corporations. They aim for maximum political impact; this means interface is identical to Wikipedia and usable by non-technical people (http://wikileaks.org/2012).

**Company directors jailed over share warehousing scheme:** Two accountants and former company directors of public companies Hallmark and Welcome Stranger Mining have been jailed for 3 years over their links to tax haven trust companies and involved in the purchase of Hallmark and Welcome Stranger Mining shares, using offshore trusts and agents. They were convicted of 29 charges, including providing misleading information, permitting voting on related party resolutions and breaching their director's duties in not acting dishonestly. Judge Fenbury stated at sentencing that the men's conduct had revealed a high degree of criminality (ASIC 2007).

**Mining company director guilty:** The former chairman of an Australian based mining exploration company, Eagle Bay Resources, has been sentenced to 16 months jail, suspended for two years. He was found guilty by a jury in the District Court of four charges of making materially misleading statements or statements that he ought reasonably to have known were materially misleading at the time they were made. In sentencing, Judge Mazza noted that the integrity of the market is put at risk by this type of conduct and that the chairman had escaped jail by the barest of margins. Judge Mazza stated that people in charge of companies must understand they must be scrupulous in the information they provide to the market. The charges relate to a number of false and misleading statements made in respect of Eagle Bay's "Myall Creek Gold Project" in a media release and an associated announcement made by Eagle Bay to the Australian Stock Exchange in late 2003 (ASIC 2007).

**CEO of Pan Pharmaceuticals to face trial:** Selim, the former chief executive officer and managing director of Pan Pharmaceuticals Limited, has been committed in court to face four charges brought by the Australian Securities and Investments Commission (ASIC). The charges relate to the provision of information by Selim to the directors of Pan Pharmaceuticals. It is alleged Selim gave information to the directors that he knew omitted certain details, which rendered the information misleading in a material respect. Information related to an investigation by the Therapeutic Goods Administration into Travacalm and Pan Pharmaceuticals (ASIC 2007).

**Australian lawyer ruled guilty of unprofessional conduct:** A barrister has stated he will appeal against a State Administrative Tribunal ruling against him for unprofessional conduct, following allegations he broke into the office of Lang Hancock to obtain a copy of his will, attempted to sell confidential information to the media and for disclosing scandalous information (*West Australian* 2008).

## GOVERNANCE AND COMPLIANCE

**ASIC fines insurance group $100,000 for non-disclosure:** Following takeover negotiations with Suncorp-Metway, insurance group Promina was fined A$100,000 for failing to disclose a A$7.9 billion bid until 38 hours after it was received, which allowed 10.76 million shares to be traded in that period. Shares closed 38 cents above the previous day. These circumstances are indicative of insider trading and market manipulation. The Australian Securities and Investments Commission (ASIC) has not indicated it will be investigating further (ASIC 2007).

**Businesses to be ready for anti-money laundering legislation:** AUSTRAC (Australian Transaction Reports and Analysis Centre) will receive sweeping new powers to search offices, seize information and demand the appointment of external auditors to ensure the financial sector and other businesses comply with new federal laws pertaining to counter terrorism financing and money laundering. Industry is concerned with the cost of compliance, which includes stringent requirements to produce reports on customer identification and the risk of links to clients involved in terrorism financing or money laundering.

AUSTRAC has called on company directors and executives to take responsibility to ensure their organizations have appropriate standards in place. The laws passed last year as the *Anti-Money Laundering and Counter Terrorism Financing Act 2006* brings Australia in line with international regulations and are aimed at the financial and gambling sectors, particularly banks, credit unions, financial planners and asset managers (*Australian Financial Review* 2007).

**Misconduct investigations double in the Health Department:** An Australian state Health Department's annual report revealed 121 misconduct investigations were conducted last year, compared to 64 in the previous period. Seven cases related to sexual assault, three to corruption, thirteen assaults, nine thefts and thirteen cases of misusing information technology (*West Australian*, April 2006).

**Sexual misconduct:** An Australian Education Department will establish a professional standards branch following a Crime and Corruption Commission (CCC) report into the department's handling of sexual misconduct complaints. The CCC found that the department had breached its own policy by placing greater weight on the welfare of employees than adhering to a safe learning environment for students. Too much responsibility was placed on local or district managers and insufficient attention was given to identifying and managing risks. Local managers were not held to account, there was poor record keeping and managers did not adhere to their own policies and procedures. The report resulted in significant political and reputation damage and the resignation of the department's director-general and the head of human resources (*West Australian*, November, 2007).

**Workplace bullying:** An email survey of 2000 people states it found that 40 percent of respondents claim to have been bullied and 73 percent nominated the boss as the perpetrator. The problem was worst in the legal sector. Bullying can range from threats of dismissal unless employees performed work outside their job description, to more subtle forms (*West Australian* 2006).

**Government Employees Superannuation Board scam:** The Government Employees Superannuation Board is alleged to have been covering up A$6.3 million trading rort involving 15 staff. The GESB staff and about 170 members allegedly exploited a "loophole", which maximised profits at the expense of other members by navigating market fluctuations. The trading reduced up to A$2,500 from member retirement savings, which has since been made up by GESB. The minister responsible for the State Superannuation Act that governs the GESB stated that it was "disappointing that some staff had behaved inappropriately and depending on the outcome of the investigation some staff could lose their jobs". GESB chief executive Michele Dolin said the rort would have been disclosed following a review (*West Australian* 2006).

## PRIVACY

**Illegal use of records:** Hundreds of Australian **Centrelink** staff have been caught inappropriately looking up the records of friends and ex-lovers. The privacy breaches were uncovered using specially designed spyware software. As a result of a two-year investigation, Centrelink has uncovered nearly 800 cases of what it has described as inappropriate access by staff to customer records. Nineteen staff have been sacked and nearly 100 resigned when they were confronted with the allegations. Five of the cases have also been referred by Centrelink to the Federal Police (ABC News 2006).

**British Government loses millions of personal civilian records:** Two compact discs, containing bank details and addresses of 9.5 million parents and the names, dates of birth and national insurance numbers of 15.5 million children have been lost. A junior employee at HM Reserve and Customs posted the discs, unrecorded and unregistered. The discs have not been located a month after going missing. The information may be hoarded for years and will assist in identity fraud and potentially by paedophile syndicates. British police subsequently searched buildings belonging to TNT, as it emerged that another six discs have also gone missing. The additional discs contained telephone recordings between individual tax credit claimants and the HMRC helpline. The following week, the British Government confirmed that the personal details of three million learner drivers have been lost. The information was reportedly lost by an American data holding company. The data was held on a hard disc drive and contained names, addresses and telephone numbers of teenagers and others taking learning driver exams. None of the discs have yet been recovered (The Telegraph, November 20, 2007).

**Criminal history is proposed grounds for discrimination:** Equal Opportunity Commissioner Yvonne Henderson has proposed that irrelevant criminal records would be not be grounds to deny equal opportunity to an applicant and would be unfair to employees. The Chamber of Commerce and Industry has rejected the proposal (*West Australian* 2007).

**Social Website beats lawsuit after claims they were open to online predators:** US based News Corporation, parent company of MySpace, has received a court ruling vindicating a suit for negligence, recklessness, fraud and misrepresentation after claims by five girls that they were lured into sex traps by predators on the popular teenage social website. A US Judge ruled that MySpace was not responsible for people's honesty online or their encounters (Channelnewsasia, 2007).

**Online identities:** The online web site Spideridentity allows you to purchase many state documents such as birth certificates, state identity cards, social security cards, and others (Identity Crawler n.d.).

**HSBC Australia exposes sensitive customer data:** More than 100 HSBC Australia customers had their banking details, names and home addresses, as well as other personal financial information exposed in a serious security breach by staff. The breach was exacerbated by the sheer volume of documents and sensitive nature of the information that was exposed. The documents, which were found on an early morning peak hour train in Sydney, left HSBC customers dangerously exposed as the paperwork listed customer names and addresses along with their banking details such as branch and account numbers.

Up to 50 letters of approval for mortgages, which included property values, repayment information, even deposits with six digit cheques that had been photocopied. In addition to personal customer information, there was training material that featured customer black lists. Notified of the incident, a spokesman for the Office of the Federal Privacy Commissioner, confirmed an official investigation is underway. "We will look into the matter and make sure procedures are in place to ensure it doesn't happen again," he said. Asked about penalties, the spokesman said the role of the privacy commissioner is to mediate and ensure the institution has taken steps to secure customer information.

A HSBC Australia spokeswoman confirmed the breach adding that the "incident had already been addressed. The employee concerned has been disciplined and the privacy commissioner has also been advised of the incident." The spokesperson did not disclose the disciplinary action taken, but did confirm there were no plans to notify customers affected by the breach. "It was extremely limited data relating to 24 separate accounts," the HSBC spokeswoman said. "It included no sensitive information as defined by the Privacy Act. All records have been retrieved and we're of the view no customers have been impacted. "HSBC takes its compliance and data security obligations extremely seriously and have standards in place to ensure ongoing compliance with all regulatory requirements, including our privacy obligations. "Unfortunately this isolated incident is simply a case of human error."

While HSBC does not believe the information is "sensitive", Hydrasight senior analyst, Michael Warrilow, thinks customers may feel differently. "Based on current laws there is no requirement for HSBC to disclose details of the breach. This breach is not an isolated incident, it happens a lot but we do not hear about it," Warrilow said. "Until disclosure laws are introduced in Australia it will continue to happen. "Even the privacy commissioner has no criminal jurisdiction, the commissioner can only mediate a settlement. In other words, the office can bark but not bite" (Rossi, *Computerworld*, March 21, 2007).

**University freely releasing confidential personal information***:* The University of Sydney staff willingly provided student information to various law enforcement agencies upon request and without first ensuring service of a warrant or subpoena. In some cases the university provided contact and course details, duration of study and payment methods. Crimes reported to be under investigation since 2004 included murder, assault, sex crimes and fraud (*West Australian* 2008).

## POLITICAL MISCONDUCT AND SCANDAL

**Election case study—Sri Lanka:** The Program for Protection of Public Resources (PPPR) of Transparency International Sri Lanka (TISL) monitored the use and abuse of public resources during the presidential and parliamentary elections in 2010. The results of the monitoring showed evidence of widespread abuse of state resources in both elections, which included the use of state vehicles and aircrafts by candidates, use of government buildings for election meetings and other propaganda work, excessive use of state media for the promotion of governing party politicians, use of state services for the support of the governing party, and the participation of public officers in active electioneering, including propaganda-related activities. The final report concluded that both the presidential and parliamentary elections were tainted by the abuse of state resources, which not only impacted negatively on the image of electoral integrity in Sri Lanka, but contributed to the erosion of public confidence in the electoral process.

Although Sri Lanka is known for its early introduction of universal franchise in the Commonwealth and regularly held elections as a flagship of democratic process, the programme showed that abuse of state resources is increasing. It not only compromises the integrity of the elections and the principles of equality and fair play but also ends up costing the general public. However, most people do not view such practices as an offence; it is tolerated and even accepted. By recording the instances of abuses, the program aimed to create public awareness and debate, as well as using the information to militate against the practice in the future (http://www.transparency.org/regional_pages/asia_pacific).

**Senior British government members caught in suspected cover-up:** Britain's director of government relations was arrested by police following allegations that political honours were being traded for cash and for perverting the course of justice (*West Australian* 2007).

**Minister misconduct: Minister misconduct, conflict of interest, corruption, drug and sexual scandals and suicide are plaguing state Labour governments**. What would require a novel or two to cover effectively, with some chapters yet to be written, we simply make the point that if this behaviour is occurring in the highest levels of the public sector, we can only hope that this does not reflect on the private sector. As it happens, Australia is seen as the least corrupt country amongst the G20 group of countries and 9th least corrupt amongst the 163 countries ranked by the Transparency's 2006 corruption perceptions index. It is believed that the AWB scandal is yet to have an impact. Indonesia was ranked the most corrupt of the G20 group, with Haiti rated the most corrupt country in the world (Transparency International 2006).

**Tourism MP jailed following attempted blackmail:** A former Queensland tourism minister was sentenced to 18 months jail following her threats to make public damaging evidence against "someone" that would cause them to "suffer and lose everything", unless the Premier organised her an executive position with Tourism Queensland. The name of the person to whom the threats were directed was suppressed (*The Age*, May 31, 2007).

**Australian Labour member accused of bullying staff:** A staff member is reported to have received A$35,000 following a workplace bullying claim, settled by the Department of Premier and Cabinet. The bullying is alleged to involve yelling and threatening behaviour, harassment, work overload and stress causing the staffer to develop a mood and anxiety disorder (*West Australian* 2008).

**Health Department director-general resigns under cloud:** Dr. Neil Fong resigned as director-general following the release of a report by the West Australian Corruption and Crime Commission (CCC). The CCC report found that Dr. Fong knowingly misrepresented the true nature of his contact with former disgraced state Premier Brian Burke and was "untruthful" in his evidence to the CCC over the recollection of 33 emails between the two men. Dr. Fong is known for his immense capacity to absorb information and it is alleged that Dr. Fong deliberately tried to remove or distance himself from Brian Burke (Corruption and Crime Commission, January 25, 2008).

## CORRUPTION AND BRIBERY

**World Bank releases report on corruption:** Industrialised, wealthy nation-states struggle with corruption and bad governance with a World Bank report concluding that the average quality of governance worldwide over the last decade has not improved much. The World Bank's database recorded governance on over 200 nation-states and measured not only corruption and democracy, but also for civil liberties, press freedom, human rights and openness of government operations (*Australian Financial Review* 2007).

**Former Thai president's wife arrested:** The wife of Thai's ousted prime minister has been charged with corruption over conflict of interest and malfeasance. The couple also face charges for alleged concealment from the Thai Stock Exchange over his ownership of shares worth millions of dollars (*West Australian* 2008).

**Bali jail security chief charged:** The security chief of Bali prison faces charges in Denpasar for drug and ammunition possession, and is facing the death penalty (*West Australian* 2008).

**State corruption:** Taiwan's ruling party will be investigated for corruption, a day after the opposition party's head was charged with corruption. Several presidential aides have already been indicted for suspected misuse of a confidential state affairs fund (*West Australian* 2008).

**Chinese Communist Party corruption:** Nearly 100,000 members of the Chinese Communist Party, including the party chief, were punished for corruption last year, in an attempt to stamp out widespread bribery. It has been shown that 80 percent have taken bribes and violated the party's financial and economic rules (*West Australian* 2008).

**22 Chinese company executives detained for bribery:** Company executives for major multinationals, including McDonalds and Whirlpool have been detained by Chinese authorities in connection to a bribery investigation. The probe comes amid a proposed wider crack-down into corruption allegations against city leaders that resulted in the sacking of the Communist Party's secretary. Bribes were allegedly paid to seven companies by local computer network operators in return for orders (Chinadaily, January 1, 2007).

**UN and World Bank launch corruption recovery scheme:** The Stolen Asset Recovery Initiative, released by the UN and World Bank, is in response to some estimates that as much as US$40 billion is corruptly flowing from developing countries per year. The UN's Office on Drugs and Crime reported that the global proceeds from criminal activities, corruption and tax evasion crossing borders every year from all countries is estimated at up to US$1.6 trillion. The initiative will focus on making public assets safe by creating independent anti corruption agencies and ensuring high standards of integrity and financial disclosing among civil servants. In developed countries, which usually receive the stolen funds, financial institutions need to be aware that banking secrecy is no longer an obstacle to money laundering investigations (The World Bank 2007).

**Lawyer charged with perverting the course of justice:** A prominent Australian defence lawyer has been charged after a recorded phone conversation he had with an imprisoned witness is alleged to have resulted in him recanting his evidence and declining to be a witness in the case (*West Australian* 2007).

**Indian police ordered to resume bribery inquiry:** An Indian Court has ordered police to resume an investigation into allegations that a French company paid millions of dollars in bribes to Indian middlemen to secure E2.4 billion sale of Scorpone submarines to the Indian Government (*West Australian* 2007).

**Japan in defence corruption scandal:** Defence Ministry offices have been searched following the arrest of a top military bureaucrat, amid allegations that defence officials were bribed by contractors, including one linked to General Electric. Y200,000.00 cash is alleged to have been paid as a birthday gift and a dozen free golf trips, in return for favourable contract agreements (*West Australian* 2007).

## SUPPLY CHAIN AND RESILIENCE BREAKDOWN— BUSINESS CONTINUITY

**Need for an executive protection plan:** Larger organisations should have an executive succession plan of who would take the CEO's place if they had to be replaced in the short and perhaps longer term. However, few organisations are likely to have an executive protection plan in the event key personnel are at imminent risk or under threat from litigation (criminal or civil), competitive forces or criminal activity. Such strategy may include personal crisis, kidnap, extortion, whilst travelling and importantly also, the protection of their families. There are numerous and regular cases of senior executives, company directors and high flyers that come under intense scrutiny from the media. Scandal involving senior executives can have a negative impact on an organisation's reputation. Having a well tested response plan adds confidence in management and mitigates any risk to corporate reputation and brand recognition.

**Lack of testing disaster recovery plans:** Robert Flux from the Websense engineering department believes businesses approach disaster recovery (DR) is an insurance-like purchase and see it only as an "expense you have to spend in the hope you never cash it in". Davis, senior vice president of storage management for CA, said what brings organisations unstuck the most is failing to test the disaster recovery scenario regularly and as a result, most organizations are less well prepared than they think. "We [CA] did a survey of a user group, which was representative of about 50 of the top 200 companies in the world; 70 percent of them were not confident they could recover in the event of a disaster and a lot had to do with the fact they did little to test their scenarios," Davis said. "Creating a 'virtual' disaster to see if you can recover from such an event seems to be the status quo, but those that do [test] maybe have one or two simulations a year, and ultimately they don't feel comfortable about the plan. A big part of testing is understanding that disaster recovery is not about an event, but about setting up processes and getting people in place to manage it on a regular basis" (Crawford, *Computerworld*, September 28, 2006).

**Real scenarios for testing disaster recovery:** Barbary, strategic initiatives manager for an Australian University, was directly involved in a disaster recovery exercise last year. Barbary said it is hard to test all scenarios of a disaster recovery plan and that is the critical problem. "You need to do real testing and it is great to do a benchmark exercise, but there is nothing like a real-life scenario," Barbary said. "Organizations think they are prepared, but a very big client of ours rang me a few months back and said it was having a simulated disaster and would be at its disaster recovery site (Adelaide University) in about 20 minutes; two-and-a-half hours later the team rolled up. "Everyone in the organization was given a little plastic card with an address of where to go in the event of a disaster, then four streets away from us they burst into the wrong building. The disaster recovery exercise fell apart progressively after that and about three hours later the company cancelled the whole exercise and hoped it never had a real disaster." Salant, vice president of IT for Millennium Copthorne Kingsgate Hotels, said a common issue with disaster recovery plans is packaged solutions some vendors offer. Salant said before kits can be sold to an end user, vendors should have a thorough understanding of their business. "For us in the hotel industry, a disaster means I cannot check a guest in and out, so in a disaster recovery plan all I want to do is have an SQL server located somewhere so in the event of a disaster I can just re-route a telecommunications link" Salant said (Crawford, *Computerworld*, September 28, 2006).

**Understanding an impact of a significant event:** Business should have an understanding of the potential impact terrorist attacks such as these would have on their business and how they would react if it directly or indirectly impacted on them. A crisis plan should be developed to cater for the worst scenario. Companies do not necessarily need to plan for every scenario, but what is needed is a plan that encompasses the worst, then it can be adapted and downgraded as situations arise. Every crisis is unique, so it's very hard to plan for a specific crisis. What is needed are processes that are already established to deal with crises in general. You need pre-agreed, clearly defined lines of responsibility and delegation. There are also simple operational issues of ensuring you have adequate communications, with enough phones, email, operators and 24-hour access. You do not want to be working this out in the heat of a crisis and if so, it's probably already too late (Schaefer n.d.).

## WORKPLACE VIOLENCE

**Workplace violence statistics appear low:** A study conducted by Massey University in New Zealand indicates that a third of employees have suffered violence in the workplace; however the number suffering violence in the workplace could be even higher. Haydn Olsen stated that the findings of the university study, which found a third of employees suffered violence at work, seemed a little low. "I think we have a real issue with violence in New Zealand at work, in society, at homes ... Violence is not just physical ... it can be physical it can be psychological—so bullying is a form of psychological violence.

The Massey University surveyed 96 organisations and found nearly a fifth of the 2,466 cases of workplace violence they reported involved physical injury and 175 cases led to lost time and/or hospitalisation. These cases accounted for a total of 572 lost working days directly attributable to workplace violence. The health sector had the highest rate of workplace violence, with 42 of the 175 most serious cases of physical assault and is five times the magnitude of the next highest sector. "I think the employer needs to take some responsibility for leadership in this area. It's about creating the kind of workplace culture that inhibits this sort of thing happening," Olsen said. "Unfortunately, too often it's tolerated or accepted or people say 'that's just the way things are' and we've really got to stop doing that" (TVNZ, July 8, 2011).

**Workplace bullying affects witnesses too:** Workplace bullying has a ripple effect; hurting not only victims, but their colleagues who witness bullying. The study consisted of more than 1,700 New Zealand workers and illustrated a clear link between people being exposed to bullying and poor perceptions of their work environment. "The greater exposure a person had to bullying, both directly and indirectly, the more negative their perception of the work environment was," said Dr. Cooper-Thomas. While she said that the effects of bullying on witnesses have not been well studied, almost 10 percent of the study's participants said they had been a witness to bullying. "When you think of the ripple effect across a workforce from all those who are touched by bullying, the impact is significant," Cooper-Thomas said. She also noted that the company's organizational climate and leadership style had an effect on the incidence of bullying. In the study, those who experienced some sort of bullying often came from companies with less constructive leadership and a laid back management style (AAP News, June 28, 2011, cited in ASIS, *Security Management Weekly*).

**What employers need to know about workplace bullying:** Recognizing victims is as important as recognizing abusers, expert says. "Status-blind harassment"—more commonly known as workplace bullying—is a growing concern to employers and their employment practices liability insurers. While the costs of having bullies in the workplace are clear, appropriate steps to recognize and rein in the problem are not always obvious. Experts use the term "status-blind" or "equal-opportunity harassment" to distinguish workplace bullying from harassment targeted at classes of workers protected under state statutes. "It's the boss who abuses his or her power not because someone is a woman over the age of 40 or a Hispanic, but rather because the boss wants to bully and is a bully, and anyone who gets in the way is going to be a victim of that bullying", states Maatman. The experts say there are other consequences to consider, such as employee turnover and sick days.

**Workplace violence may start with bullying:** Adele states that "Workplace violence starts with bullying", citing a case where an individual shot his co-workers. "The back-story was that he was bullied at work and no one listened." Training managers "to be good at mitigating the risk of bullying does not just involve focusing on the bully's behaviour, but really [means] carefully gauging the emotional state of all their employees to get a sense of whether they are victims." More generally, he explains that risk mitigation in this area really involves two components: pre-hire assessment and performance management. "There are things that can be done to assess perspective employees for the tendency to express anger, to be aggressive, to show excitability—all factors that can lead to bullying." What if bullying tendencies are revealed during the hiring process? "It would be perfectly legitimate in my view not to hire somebody who poses a reasonable risk," Adler says, noting that he speaks from the perspective of an organizational psychologist, not a lawyer. "Bullying can result in lawsuits, loss of talent, creating a hostile environment for employees that would cause them to leave," he says (Sclafane 2011).

**Screening employees and contractors crucial in reducing workplace violence:** A comprehensive background screening program is key strategy to reducing violence in the workplace, considering the best prognosticator of future violence is a review of the past. Background screening is now a common practice and the check process can include county criminal record and national criminal file searches, drug testing, prior employment and education verification, license verifications, and other investigations that could uncover potential warning signs. Comprehensive background screening can take up to a week to complete, but the failure to rigorously check employees could lead to problems such as workplace violence, employee theft or fraud that could leave organizations vulnerable to employee injury or death, unsafe working conditions, brand and reputation damage and lawsuits for negligent hiring. Also, all vendors or temporary employees who come in contact with an organization's personnel and customers should be screened, including service and repair professionals, construction workers and food service workers.

In addition, employees and contractors should be re-screened annually. For example, an employee might have joined the organization with a clean record, but new information about a domestic dispute would be critical because such problems are sometimes brought into the workplace. Employees and contractors will better understand the need for such screening when it is properly communicated and presented as part of an organization's larger effort to maintain a violence-free workplace. Comprehensive screening typically does not bother people with clean backgrounds, and it may prompt people who have committed reckless acts to 'self-select' out of the interview process (Tate, *Security Magazine*, July 2011).

## FOOD AND PRODUCT CONTAMINATION

**Seven people die of Tylenol laced with cyanide:** One of the most highlighted case of product tampering occurred in 1982 when seven people died in Chicago after ingesting capsules of the pain reliever Tylenol, laced with cyanide. Autopsies showed cyanide poisoning but, at first, no one could see the connection between victims. Later, it was noted that they had all purchased Extra-Strength Tylenol, which had been contaminated with cyanide. At the time, psychological profilers were fascinated by the case because this was a new crime, with no apparent motive. As the victims were random and probably unknown to the attacker, it was a crime involving great psychological distance probably motivated by rage at society and seeking power through fear. The crimes aroused great public anxiety, yet the incidents stopped suddenly and no one was arrested or convicted. However, one man was imprisoned after trying to blackmail the manufacturers of Tylenol. Following the Tylenol incidents, over-the-counter drugs have been sold in tamper-proof packaging.

Such packaging may deter the impulsive criminal, but those with the motivation could find a way around the packaging. The Food and Drug Administration (FDA) recently expressed some concern that al Qaeda might tamper with the domestic food and drug supply, and may find a way of targeting illegally imported prescription drugs. The FDA has a special unit dedicated to the forensic investigation of product tampering. Recent incidents included the contamination of baby food with ground castor beans, which contain the deadly poison ricin. In what may have been a hoax, a shipment of lemons from Argentina was said to be impregnated with an unspecified biological toxin (Product Tampering 2011, http://www.enotes.com/forensice-science/product-tampering, accessed September 2, 2011).

**Tampered products contain many contaminants:** A wide variety of contaminants have been found in products that have been tampered with, including mice, syringes, cyanide, needles, liquid mercury and glass. A forensic laboratory must take a look at the physical and chemical nature of the contaminant, using a range of techniques. If the contaminant is an organic compound, then infrared spectroscopy and gas or liquid chromatography, in conjunction with mass spectrometry, can rapidly provide an identity. Chromatography experiments against an uncontaminated sample, in the case of a soft drink, will reveal the proper composition of the product. Extra components could be contaminants and these will be analysed more closely. Inorganic contaminants, such as acids or sodium hydroxide, can be examined with techniques such as atomic absorption, which can show the elements involved (Product Tampering 2011, http://www.enotes.com/forensice-science/product-tampering, accessed September 2, 2011).

**Baby-food makers confront British contamination scare:** Britain is grappling with its worst-ever case of food tampering as jars of baby food were contaminated across the country. Outbreaks of this alarming strain of crime, which can have devastating consequences for the consumer-products companies involved, have been less frequent in Britain than in the US. Britain has never experienced catastrophic product-tampering cases like the one in Chicago (1982), when seven died after taking doses of Tylenol, a Johnson & Johnson pain reliever (Lohr, special to the *New York Times*, May 2, 1989).

**FDA finds traces of poison in jars of baby food:** Tiny amounts of the poison ricin have been detected in two jars of baby food, which had been tampered with before being sold by a Southern California supermarket. Nevertheless, the authorities said the contaminant was ground-up castor beans from which ricin is derived, not the purified form of the toxin that is far deadlier. Two babies who ate some of the food were not harmed. "There is a big difference between purified toxin and crude castor beans," said Dr. Acheson, chief medical officer at the Food and Drug Administration's Center for Food Safety and Applied Nutrition (Pollack, *New York Times*, July 29, 2004).

**Tampered Nurofen tablets found in Northern Ireland:** One of the packets of Nurofen Plus which led to a recall of the painkiller was found in Northern Ireland. The strip of tablets had been substituted with a prescription medicine for epilepsy. Four packets in the London area contained a common drug used in the treatment of mental illnesses. Police are investigating the possibility of sabotage. A member of the Pharmaceutical Society and a community pharmacist, said what had happened was "extremely worrying". "What we are concerned about is why this happened or how this happened to make sure, first of all, that we fully understand it and, secondly, to ensure it does not happen again," he said. The police are involved and investigations are ongoing. No other types of the brand are affected and all stocks of Nurofen Plus have also been recalled from pharmacy shelves in the Republic of Ireland (BBC News, August 27, 2011, http://www.bbc.co.uk/news, accessed September 2, 2011).

**Dead patient named in "medicine tampering" case:** One of three people reported to have died after what UK police suspect were multiple cases of medicine tampering was confirmed to be a 44-year-old mother who had previously been responding well to treatment, but died at hospital. Two male victims aged 71 and 84, who both had serious health problems, died the previous week. Police are investigating three deaths at the hospital after saline solution was deliberately contaminated.

The alarm was raised after insulin was discovered in a batch of 36 saline ampoules in a hospital storeroom. A nurse had reported seeing a higher than normal number of patients with unexplained low blood sugar levels. Detectives believe the insulin was deliberately injected into saline containers used by at least two wards, but say the deaths remain unexplained as they await the results of post-mortems. "We are no longer treating the tampered medication as a sole contaminated batch, because we cannot be sure that this was the only incident of its kind," a police source said. "We will be interviewing all those who became ill from the contaminated saline to find out if they can shed any light on who is responsible" (McCorkell and Youde, *Independent Newspaper*, July 17, 2011).

## FAILINGS AND BREACHES OF TECHNOLOGY

**Bank attacks surge in past year:** Leading financial institutions experienced a huge surge in the number of security attacks over the past year and specifically from external sources, according to the Deloitte 2006 Global Security Survey. Phishing and pharming accounted for more than half (51 percent) of the external attacks, followed by spyware or malware utilization (48 percent). "Insider fraud (28 percent) and leakage of customer data (18 percent) were cited by respondents as among the top three most common internal breaches."

While 96 percent were concerned about employee misconduct involving IT systems, only a third (34 percent) have provided their staff with some form of information security and privacy training over the past 12 months. The most common mediums that financial institutions use for security training and awareness are Web page alerts and e-mails (63 percent). Other, perhaps more effective methods, such as orientation training (35 percent) and recognition of exemplary behaviour (9 percent), ranked low in use (*Computerworld*, June 19, 2006).

**Auditor General still finding poor information security standards in Government:** After warning several Australian Government departments in the past concerning secure data management, the Auditor General has again found cases of second-hand state government computers on sale publicly, which contain sensitive and confidential information. Four in ten computers purchased at public auctions and computer stores were found to contain information that should have been appropriately disposed of, including employee performance reviews, resume, photographs, emails, letters and contact details. Such information can potentially be used to design social engineering attacks, identity theft and fraudulent transactions (*West Australian* 2008).

**Secure mobile data means not taking it with you:** The surge of mobile workers has prompted increasing data security concerns. While a majority of companies neglect to encrypt and backup sensitive data, refusing to store important data on mobile devices is the first step to preventing a disastrous data loss. Firms should set up a VPN for enabling employees to share data among themselves; Windows Vista and Windows 7 users already have built-in VPN capabilities. Secondly, since remote access software allow users to run applications from office PCs, employees need not store critical data on removable devices. LogMeIn Free and Windows Live Mesh are among the free remote access offerings, with a number of remote access programs designed for smart phones and tablets. Lastly, online storage is the most secure method of remote backup. The advantages to cloud storage are manifold and they include minimizing the risks associated with viruses, data theft, and lost devices (Pacchiano, *Small Business Computing*, April 19, 2011, cited in ASIS, *Security Management*).

**Android malware jumps 400 percent as all mobile threats rise:** Cyberthieves are targeting Google's Android as they take advantage of a user base that is "unaware, disinterested or uneducated" in mobile security, according to the Malicious Mobile Threats Report 2011 from the Juniper Networks Global Threat Centre. Malware developers are increasingly targeting mobile devices, and Android malware has jumped 400 percent since summer 2010, the study state. The spike in malware is a result of users not thinking about security, a large volume of downloads from unknown sources, and the dearth of mobile security software, Juniper found. About 17 percent of all reported infections were from SMS Trojans sending text messages to premium rate numbers, the report says. Spyware capable of monitoring phone calls and text messages from the device accounted for 61 percent of reported infections. One hundred percent of reported infections on Android phones were of this type of spyware. Consumers can anticipate seeing more sophisticated malware attacks against the Android platform, the study suggests. These attacks include "command and control zombies and botnet participators, devices that are remotely controlled to execute malicious attacks." Enterprises and users must be aware of the growing hazards of going online using mobile devices and safeguard them the same way they protect desktops, laptops and servers (Rashid, eWeek, May 17, 2011, cited in ASIS, *Security Management*).

**On-line miscreants targeted 500 key business executives in what is believed to be the first mass-targeted malicious-software attack:** MessageLabs intercepted more than 500 individual e-mail attacks targeted at individuals in senior management positions in a variety of organizations around the world. Normally, MessageLabs reported to only seeing approximately 10 targeted attacks per 200 million e-mails per day. The malicious e-mails contained the name and job title of the victim in the subject line. The vertical sector most targeted was banking and finance, with chief investment officers being targeted in 30 percent of the attacks. However, other verticals were also targeted. Eleven percent of the intended victims were chief executive officers, while 6 percent were chief finance officers.

The executives being targeted were perhaps "not that tech-savvy." In the attacks, an executable file was embedded in a Microsoft Word document. If the victim opened the document and clicked on a link, the file would have run a data-stealing Trojan horse that relied on creating buffer overflow conditions in Office documents. MessageLabs stated they did not know who had perpetrated the attack. "It's a certainty that some executives were compromised." The intended victims' spouses and relatives were also targeted by name, in attempt to infect other computers related to the victim. The intent was to indirectly gain access to confidential correspondence and intellectual property relating to the target, MessageLabs suspected that the hackers harvested the information using search and social-networking sites (Espiner, February 7, 2007, ZDNet UK).

**Google fraud and security hacking:** The future will make search technology only more dangerous. Bell Canada's Garigue points out that search technology is still in its very infancy, barely scratching the surface of what he calls the shallow Web. "Google is the first generation of tools," Garigue says. As these tools get more sophisticated, the shock waves will only grow stronger as search engines find systems vulnerabilities. Hackers can use carefully crafted searches to find things like open ports, overly revealing error messages or even password files on a target organization's computer systems. Any search engine can do this; blame the popularity of the somewhat imprecise phrase "Google hacking" on Johnny Long, author of *Google Hacking for Penetration Testers.* Long hosts a virtual swap meet where members exchange and rate intricately written Google searches. Perhaps make Google and other search engines part of your company's routine penetration testing process? In addition, Bhalla recommends focusing on two things, which ports are open and which error messages are available (Scalet, May 5, 2006).

## LOSS AND MISUSE OF INFORMATION

**Thailand still on US piracy list:** The Thai government is disappointed that the US decided to keep the country on its Priority Watch List for intellectual property piracy in its yearly Special 301 report, Deputy Commerce Minister Alongkorn Ponlaboot said. The country has made large efforts to put an end to products that violate intellectual property rights, according to Ponlaboot. However, the US report states that while the country has "shown a continuing commitment to improving protection and enforcement," it has "failed to make substantial progress." Enforcement in Thailand against piracy is both weak and non-deterrent, said the US Trade Representative. The US biggest concern is Thailand's failure to ban the use of video cameras in movie theatres, which are often used to create pirated movies. Other countries on the Piracy Watch List include China, Russia, Algeria, Argentina, Canada, Chile, India, Indonesia, Israel, Pakistan and Venezuela. The naming of Thailand as a top pirate could open it up to punitive trade measures; however, there has been no action taken against the country in the past (*Bangkok Post*, May 5, 2011, cited in ASIS, *Security Management*).

**76 percent of energy utilities breached in past year:** A survey revealed that roughly three-quarters of energy companies and utilities experienced at least one data breach in the past 12 months. The average clean-up cost for each breach was US$156,000, according to the survey of 291 IT security practitioners at utilities and energy companies conducted by Ponemon Institute. Seventy-one percent of respondents said that "the management team in their organization does not understand or appreciate the value of IT security." Moreover, only 39 percent of organizations were found to be actively watching for advanced persistent threats, 67 percent were not using "state of the art" technology to stop attacks against SCADA (supervisory control and data acquisition) systems, and 41 percent said their strategy for SCADA security was not proactive.

The survey also concluded that the leading threat for energy utilities was not external attackers, but rather insiders. Forty three percent of utilities cited "negligent or malicious insiders" as causing the highest number of data breaches. The report also suggested that a "lack of leadership and absolute control over the security program could be contributing to this threat." Just 18 percent of utilities said a security leader had overall responsibility for information security, while 29 percent of organizations had no specific person with overall responsibility (Schwartz, *Information Week*, April 6, 2011).

**Failure to encrypt portable devices inexcusable, say analysts:** BP recently revealed that an employee lost a laptop containing the personal information of roughly 13,000 people who had submitted claims associated with the Gulf of Mexico oil spill. The data on the laptop, which included names, social security numbers and dates of birth was unencrypted. The fact that such data was stored on an unencrypted laptop has floored analysts, who said that it is inexcusable that many companies are still not using encryption to protect information stored on mobile devices. Many companies have chosen not to encrypt laptops and other mobile devices because of the costs involved, though Gartner analyst Avivah Litan says that cost should not be an issue given the fact that a laptop can be encrypted for as little as US$15. Analysts also noted that the rising cost of data breaches should convince companies to use encryption.

According to a report released by the Ponemon Group, a data breach can cost a company an average of US$214 per compromised record. Government agencies, meanwhile, have been slow to comply with a 2006 US Office of Management and Budget memo that called for all agencies to use encryption on portable devices containing sensitive data. The average rate of compliance among government agencies currently stands at just more than 54 percent (Vijayan, *Computerworld*, March 31, 2011).

**Private sector officials decry lack of cybersecurity info sharing:** Several private sector officials testified before the House Homeland Security subcommittee on cybersecurity, infrastructure protection and security technologies to discuss what they said was a lack of sharing of information about cyber attacks with the federal government. Among those who testified at the hearing was AT&T Chief Security Officer Ed Amoroso, who said that there is not a good way to share such information in real time. He added that there are a number of obstacles to the government and the private sector sharing information about cyber attacks, including the need for a large number of lawyers when sharing information. Amoroso also said that a lack of legal authority prevents the private sector from using information from the government about attack signatures because the use of such information would raise questions about whether the company was acting as an agent of the government. Meanwhile, Sean McGurk, the director of the Homeland Security Department's National Cyber Security and Communications Integration Centre, said that the government is publishing a subset of signature data called indicators that can be used to generate signatures that are specific to certain types of equipment (Fierce Government IT, April 19, 2011, cited in ASIS, *Security Management*).

## REFERENCES

ABC News. 2006. Centrelink staff sacked for privacy breaches. Retrieved April 19, 2012, from http://www.abc.net.au/news/2006-08-23/centrelink-staff-sacked-for-privacy-breaches/1245368

ASIC. 2007. Former Pan Pharmaceuticals CEO pleads not guilty. Australian Securities & Investment Commission. Retrieved April 18, 2012, from http://www.asic.gov.au/asic/asic.nsf/byheadline/07-23+Former+Pan+Pharmaceuticals+CEO+pleads+not+guilty?openDocument

ASIC. 2007. Promina pays $100,000 fine Australian Securities & Investment Commission. Retrieved April 18, 2012, from http://www.asic.gov.au/asic/asic.nsf/byheadline/07-69+Promina+pays+$100,000+fine?openDocument

ASIS International. 2011. Rs9m Robbed in Biggest Bank Heist of the Year. Security Management Weekly. Retrieved April 18, 2012, from http://security-world.blogspot.com.au/2011/04/security-management-weekly-april-15.html#516838

Bowler, J. in a statement as Minister for Employment Protection to the WA Legislative Assembly, Bogus WorkSafe Inspectors. Hansard, p. 6340b-6341a. Retrieved May 5, 2012 from http://www.google.com.au/url?sa=t&rct=j&q=&esrc=s&frm=1&source=web&cd=5&ved=0CF4QFjAE&url=http%3A%2F%2Fparliament.wa.gov.au%2FHansard%255Chansard.nsf%2F0%2F289e809af9e07308c8257570003a5d89%2F%24FILE%2FA37%2520S1%252020060920%2520p6340b-6341a.pdf&ei=79ekT-v2L4uRiQfEqYykAw&usg=AFQjCNEykq24dAwWMUJrY4jCVkv3keLofg

Channelnewsasia. February 16, 2007. http://www.channelnewsasia.com/stories/technology-news/view/258966/1/.html

Chinadaily. 2007. Top multinationals caught up in Chinese graft probe. Retrieved May 25, 2011, from http://www.chinadaily.com.cn/china/2007-01/20/content_788320.htm

Corruption and Crime Commission. 2008, Report on the Investigation of Alleged Misconduct concerning Dr Neale Fong, Director General of the Department of Health. Perth: Corruption and Crime Commission.

Daily Mail Reporter. 2009. Fake forensic scientist jailed for string of child attacks. Mail Online. Retrieved May 25, 2011, from http://www.dailymail.co.uk/news/article-1235071/Fake-forensic-scientist-jailed-string-child-sex-attacks.html

Espiner. February 7, 2007. ZDNet UK. http://www.usatoday.com/tech/products/cnet/2007-07-02-top-execs-email-attacks_N.htm

Gettler, L. 2007. Qantas hit with $200m class action. *The Age Newspaper*. Retrieved April 17, 2012, from http://www.theage.com.au/news/business/qantas-hit-with-200m-class-action/2007/02/01/1169919472132.html

Identity Crawler. n.d. http://www.identitycrawler.com/cb/index.html

Lawyers Weekly. 2006. ABL in AWB bid for professional privilege. Retrieved May 25, 2011, from http://www.lawyersweekly.com.au/deals/abl-in-awb-bid-for-professional-privilege

Litterick, D. 2006. Coca-Cola is still the real thing, thanks to Pepsi. *The Telegraph*. Retrieved April 17, 2012, from http://www.telegraph.co.uk/news/worldnews/northamerica/usa/1523329/Coca-Cola-is-still-the-real-thing-thanks-to-Pepsi.html

Mission and Justice. 2006. PNG's police chief facing inquiry. Retrieved May 25, 2011, from http://www.missionandjustice.org/pngs-police-chief-facing-inquiry/

Rivers and Prapanya, CNN World. (September 16, 2006). http://articles.cnn.com/2006-09-16/world/thai.bombs_1_bombs-yala-hat-yai?_s=PM:WORLD

Rossi, S. 2007. HSBC Australia exposes sensitive customer data. Computerworld. Retrieved April 19, 2012, from http://www.computerworld.com.au/article/179967/hsbc_australia_exposes_sensitive_customer_data/

Rowley, C. and R. Tonkin. 2006. Follow the Big Money: Bad Business with Baghdad. webdiary – Independent, Accountable and Transparent. Retrieved April 17, 2012, from http://webdiary.com.au/cms/?q=node/1206

Scalet, S. May 6, 2006. Ways Google is shaking the security world. *Computerworld*. Retrieved April 19, 2012, from http://www.computerworld.com/s/article/9000540/Ways_Google_is_shaking_the_security_world

Sclafane, S. 2011. What employers should do about workplace bullying. Property Casualty 360. Retrieved May 25, 2011 from http://www.propertycasualty360.com/2011/04/01/what-employers-should-do-about-workplace-bullying

Schaefer, A. n.d. Management Crisis: How GlaxoSmithKline managed its extortion crisis. CEO Forum Group. Retrieved April 22, 2012, from http://www.ceoforum.com.au/article-detail.cfm?cid=6336&t=/Alan-Schaefer-GSK-Consumer-Health-Care/Management-Crisis-How-GlaxoSmithKline-managed-its-extortion-crisis

Stoyeck, R. n.d. Stock investing: Bank of America, Morgan Stanley, UBS, and Bear Stearns Swept up in latest Insider. Retrieved May 25, 20111, from http://www.approvedarticles.com/Article/Stock-Investing-----Bank-of-America--Morgan-Stanley--UBS--and-Bear-Stearns-Swept-up-in-latest-INSIDER/4841

Sunday Times - Pickworth, C. & Tovia, J. (September 12, 2006). Cheats cause for hiring care. *The Sunday Times*. Retrieved May 5, 2012 from http://www.dailytelegraph.com.au/cheats-cause-for-hiring-care/story-e6frez89-1111112196635

*The Age*. Oxfam may sack 10 over tsunami aid fraud. Retrieved April 18, 2012, from http://www.theage.com.au/news/National/Oxfam-may-sack-10-over-tsunami-aid-fraud/2006/05/05/1146335917613.html

*The Age*. May 31, 2007. http://www.theage.com.au/news/national/three-months-jail-for-blackmail-minister/2007/05/31/1180205390962.html

*The Telegraph*. November 20, 2007. http://myreader.co.uk/msg/13791653.aspx

The World Bank. 2007. Stolen Asset Recovery (StAR) Initiative: Challenges, Opportunities, and Action Plan. The International Bank for Reconstruction and Development. Washington: The World Bank.

Transparency International. 2006. http://www.transparency.org/policy_research/surveys_indices/cpi/2006

Urban, R. August 8, 2006. Malaysian police nab 'prince' Omar, The Age newspaper. Retrieved May 5, 2012 from http://www.theage.com.au/news/business/malaysian-police-nab-prince-omar/2006/08/07/1154802820268.html

*West Australian*. 2007. Gods Garbage Motorcycle gang members arrested for extortion - http://www.perthnow.com.au/news/top-stories/bikies-charged-with-death-threat/story-e6frg12l-1111113393704

White, A. n.d. EU charges Intel with monopoly abuse. ABC News. Retreived April 17, 2012, from http://abcnews.go.com/Technology/story?id=3428255&page=1

WikiLeaks. 2012. WikiLeaks Rational. Retrieved April 18, 2012, from http://rationalwiki.org/wiki/WikiLeaks

# 7 External Corporate Threats and Risks

## INTRODUCTION

The following chapter presents a selection of recent external security vignettes, sorted by case type and circumstances (Table 7.1). Such vignettes should provide the corporate security manager with a breadth of events that have occurred elsewhere and therefore have a likelihood of occurring against his or her own corporation.

## TERRORISM AND POLITICALLY MOTIVATED VIOLENCE

**Reliance executive is killed in India:** An India company executive was killed on Wednesday in a shooting that was committed by leftist militants opposed to industrial development. The general manager of Reliance Power's operations in India's Jharkhand state, was travelling with other Reliance executives to scout land for a company project in Jharkhand's Chatra district when Maoist rebels opened fire on their convoy. In addition to Ojha, several other Reliance employees were injured in the shooting. Local police are investigating the exact circumstances of the shooting, though one official said that Ojha likely got caught in the crossfire between warring rebel groups. Nevertheless, the shooting came at a time when Maoist rebels in India have become increasingly violent in protecting tribal lands from being encroached on by industry (*Wall Street Journal*, July 4, 2011).

**Terrorist cells in Indonesia:** Australian and Indonesian Police are reported to have foiled a terrorist cell operating in East Java. One man was shot dead and in further raids police seized 20 bombs, explosive materials, detonators and more than 1000 rounds of ammunition (*West Australian* 2007).

**Army plot to kill prime minister:** A Thai army sergeant arrested in an investigation into an alleged plot to kill the prime minister has admitted his involvement. The alleged plot has been the object of intense speculation in Thailand, which has been in political turmoil since the beginning of the year because of an active popular movement demanding that Thaksin step down because of alleged corruption and abuses of power (Associated Press 2006).

**Six bombs explode in Thailand:** Six bombs exploded, one every five minutes, in a southern Thailand city, killing at least four people and wounding 30. The evening attacks in Hat Yai came just hours after a government-sponsored peace rally in the nearby town of Yala and on the 21st anniversary of the founding of the GMIP—Gerakan Mujahedeen Islami Pattani—separatist movement. The six bombs were placed about every 500 yards along the main commercial street (Rivers and Prapanya, CNN World, 2006).

**TABLE 7.1**
**External Threats and Risks**

| External Corporate Incident | |
| --- | --- |
| Terrorism and politically motivated violence | Kidnapping and extortion |
| Civil unrest | Piracy |
| Regional conflict | Economic espionage |
| Organized transnational crime | Community and street crime |
| Cyber and electronic crime | Natural disasters and catastrophic incidents |

**Wave of political violence sweeps Karachi:** Nearly three dozen people have been killed in an apparent wave of political violence in Karachi, Pakistan, over the last 24 hours. Among those killed was a former Pakistani lawmaker from the country's ruling Pakistan People's Party, reportedly shot and killed. Some of the other 32 people who were killed in the violence were tortured and shot. The violence was part of a rash of killings that began in late June after the Muttahida Qaumi Movement—the most powerful political party in Karachi—announced its intention to leave the federal coalition and join the opposition. More than 300 people were killed in political violence in Karachi last month. Many of those killings have been blamed on gangs with ties to political parties in Karachi (Associated Press, cited in ASIS, *Security Management Daily*, August 18, 2011).

**Pakistani militant group a global terror threat:** There are fears that the Pakistani terrorist organization Lashkar-e-Taiba could attack Western targets. Current and former members of Lashkar-e-Taiba, which is believed to have been responsible for carrying out the 2008 terrorist attacks in Mumbai, have said that the group's only goal is to reunite Kashmir, the territory whose control is disputed between India and Pakistan. However, experts have said that Lashkar-e-Taiba could be on the verge of broadening its reach beyond the South Asia region. According to European intelligence officials, Lashkar-e-Taiba had plans to attack several targets in Australia, including a nuclear reactor south of Sydney or a military base near Alice Springs. In addition, the intelligence officials also said that Lashkar-e-Taiba has recruited members from existing terrorist organizations in Europe and has radicalized Western Muslims.

Meanwhile, documents filed in US courts and an internal Indian government dossier on the Mumbai attacks indicate that Lashkar-e-Taiba members have been found in the US, Europe, Australia and East Asia. But a former Pakistani government official with ties to the military and the intelligence agency ISI has said that Lashkar-e-Taiba is divided over whether to attack the West, with senior leaders of the group saying that the timing for such attacks is not right (Gannon, *Kuwait Times*, May 4, 2011).

**Top JI operative in custody in Pakistan:** Pakistan arrested a top Indonesian Jemaah Islamiah (JI) terrorist Umar Patek, one of Indonesia's most wanted and involved in the 2002 Bali bombing which killed 202 people. The arrest followed a tip from the US Central Intelligence Agency (CIA). Patek would be eventually returned to Indonesia. Patek is a skilled explosive expert and senior member of JI network, having escaped Indonesia in 2003 (*Straits Times*, April 2, 2011).

**Suicide blasts kill 41 at Pakistan shrine:** Two suicide blasts outside a shrine in the central Pakistani province of Punjab killed at least 41 people. The blast took place outside the shrine of Sufi saint Ahmed Sultan in Dera Ghazi Khan district. Sunni extremists, including the Taliban, are vehemently opposed to the Sufi strand of Islam. More than 4,500 people have been killed in suicide attacks and bomb blasts, blamed on home-grown Talban and other Islamic extremist networks, since government troops stormed a radical mosque in Islamabad in July 2007 (*Straits Times*, April 4, 2011).

## CIVIL UNREST

**Uighur violence in China leaves at least 19 dead:** At least 19 people were killed in far Western China in two violent incidents that Chinese authorities blamed on militant members of the country's Uighur minority. Chinese media reported that the first attack took place before midnight on Saturday, when the perpetrators hijacked a truck that was stopped at a stop light in the city of Kashgar and killed the driver. The attackers then reportedly drove the truck into a crowd of people, jumped out of the truck, and began stabbing people randomly with knives.

The second attack took place on Sunday afternoon, when a bomb exploded at a restaurant in downtown Kashgar. After police officers and fire fighters arrived on the scene, five attackers rushed out and began stabbing civilians, the local government said. A total of 11 people were killed in that attack, including the five attackers; however, a spokesman for the World Uyghur Congress disputed the accounts given by the Chinese media and the local government, saying that there was a brawl between Uighur residents of Kashgar and city police officers. The spokesman added that most of the people who were killed were police officers and that the violence was caused by "repressive Chinese rule". There could be additional violence as the Muslim holy month of Ramadan approaches (Demick, *Los Angeles Times*, August 1, 2011, cited in ASIS, *Security Management Daily*).

**China stamps out southern unrest:** Order has been restored in the Chinese jeans-manufacturing centre of Zengcheng following days of rioting. The rioting was sparked by an incident in which security guards pushed a pregnant migrant street vendor to the ground when they tried to move her food stall from the street. The incident outraged migrant workers, who make up about half of the population of Zengcheng. Following the riots, thousands of riot police armed with tear gas and shotguns were deployed to Zengcheng and were tasked with patrolling major thoroughfares, manning checkpoints at intersections, and checking the identity papers of drivers and pedestrians.

Although the city appeared calm, the atmosphere remained tense amid warnings that rioting could resume if officials do not address concerns among migrant workers about difficult working conditions, long hours and rising food prices (Page, *Wall Street Journal*, June 15, 2011, cited in ASIS, *Security Management Daily*).

**Caution in Thailand as national general election approaches:** A national general election was scheduled in July 2011 and there was possibility of further civil unrest and violence in the period surrounding the election and formation of a new government. Past large scale political demonstrations and related incidents in Bangkok and other parts of Thailand have resulted in fatalities and injuries in recent years. Firearms, grenades and small explosive devices have been used at various locations. In 2010, a number of small explosive devices were detonated in Bangkok and some other provinces, including Chiang Mai. The political situation remains unpredictable and further political unrest and violence cannot be ruled out in Bangkok and other provinces (Department of Foreign Affairs and Trade, Australian government, July 4, 2011).

**Malaysia protest lifts opposition:** Malaysia's opposition movement has gained momentum following a rally of 20,000 protesters in Kuala Lumpur that police broke up using tear gas and water cannons. The protesters say that the country's electoral system is unfair, favouring the ruling coalition that has been in power since the country gained independence from Britain in 1957. Reports indicate that police detained approximately 1,600 people, all of whom were subsequently released. That has not stopped government criticism from building.

While officials maintain that the protesters do not represent the majority of Malaysians, the opposition says that the rally would have been much larger if the government had not closed down roads and public transit to keep people away. Malaysia has become increasingly fractured in recent years as groups from conservative Islamists to secular progressives seek reform to give them a better voice in the government and to prevent corruption. Rally leaders said they do not plan to stage another major protest any time soon, though they said that they are planning to organize government opponents outside of Kuala Lumpur (Barta and Fernandez, *Wall Street Journal*, July 11, 2011, cited in ASIS, *Security Management*).

## REGIONAL CONFLICT

**Philippines stir waters of the Spratlys:** Upgrading a military runway and recent gas exploration sparked renewed territorial claims between China and the Philippines. The Philippines army is upgrading facilities to maintain a presence within the territory, spending S$200 million. China, Malaysia, Taiwan, Brunei, Vietnam and the Philippines all contest all or part of the Spratly Islands, which are believed to have huge hydrocarbon deposits (*The Straits Times*, March 31, 2011).

**Pakistan plays hardball:** The counterterrorism partnership between Pakistan and the US has been strained in recent months. Pakistan is critical of the US's current strategy in Afghanistan and objects not only to the presence of CIA operatives, but also the use of agency drones to kill terrorists in tribal regions. The country's top army and intelligence officials say that they want a return to 1980s relationship rules between the CIA and Pakistan's Inter-Services Intelligence Directorate (ISI), when the US took a "hands-off" approach.

However such a shift is unlikely, as Pakistan's President Asif Ali Zardari accuses the ISI and the army of playing both sides in the war on terror. For example, Pakistan's army continues to fund the terrorist group Lashkar-e-Taiba, which was responsible for the 2008 attack on Mumbai, India, that killed 164 people. Still, Pakistan also faces a constant threat from terrorist groups and it currently has more troops on the ground in its tribal regions than NATO has in Afghanistan. Despite these contradictions, observers say the US must preserve its relationship with Pakistan if its continued pursuit of al-Qaida operatives in the area is to succeed (Riedel, *Newsweek*, April 17, 2011, cited in ASIS, *Security Management*).

**Taliban more dangerous than al Qaeda:** Pakistani President Pervez Musharraf warned the West that Taliban insurgents are a more dangerous terrorist force than al Qaeda, because of the broad support they have in Afghanistan. Five years after the 9/11 attacks on the US and the subsequent US invasion of Afghanistan to topple the Taliban,

Musharraf said Taliban fighters had regrouped in southern Afghanistan. "The centre of gravity of terrorism has shifted from al Qaeda to the Taliban," he told EU lawmakers who quizzed Musharraf on Pakistan's counterterrorism efforts. "This is a new element, a more dangerous element, because it (the Taliban) has its roots in the people. Al Qaeda didn't have roots in the people," he said.

**Middle East instability second highest risk to cause global catastrophe:** A risk analysis on the most likely causes of global catastrophe in the next ten years, presented at the recent World Economic Forum in Davos, Switzerland, identified the top three risks as a global asset price collapse, Middle East instability and a fiscal crisis.

## ORGANIZED TRANSNATIONAL CRIME

**Drug trafficking surges in Indonesia:** Drug trafficking has surged in Indonesia, say authorities, who are cracking down on more smugglers, dealers and producers than ever before. Data from the National Narcotics Agency (BNN) estimates that at least four million people, or 1.7 percent of Indonesians, are drug abusers and that in 2010 drug busts have doubled to 28,801. Drug syndicates use Indonesia due to its porous borders and 17,000 islands. Indonesia mandates the death penalty for drug trafficking; however, the penalties for production and usage are still relatively lenient (*Straits Times*, April 4, 2011).

**KL busts huge tax evasion syndicate:** In one of the biggest joint operations involving several law enforcement agencies in Malaysia, customs offices and more than 100 businesses nationwide have been raised in connection with tax evasion and money laundering activities. The syndicate had siphoned away billions of (Singapore) dollars. 25 customs offices, forwarding agents, a holding company and 24 related companies were raided. The customs officers were detained under offences relating to the Customs Act, Income Tax Act, the Anti-Money Laundering Act and Anti-Terrorism Act. Some 150 bank accounts have been frozen, including overseas accounts. This investigation was one of the biggest in Malaysia's history (Star/Asia News Network, April 4, 2011).

**Outlaw motorcycle gangs: breaching security, but still safe:** "Sex, drugs, sackings at Observation City: staff orgies in vacant rooms." It is alleged that managerial, security and other staff members used vacant rooms for parties with prostitutes and use of illicit drugs. The article also alleged that the security company employed on security duties for the hotel is associated with an outlaw motorcycle gang. Follow-up reports indicated that internal theft and misuse of hotel assets were rife (*Sunday Times* newspaper, April 9, 2006). In contrast, "feel safer near bikies expert" suggested that bikie club houses should be allowed in Perth residential areas as they "should" make residents feel safer. Arthur Veno claimed that the bikies have a policy of "not tolerating criminals in or near their club" and that "petty criminals" were kept away (*West Australian*, April 15, 2006).

**Organised crime in business:** The Australian Crime Commission (ACC) has warned the business community to examine operating models for areas of risk to infiltration or attack from organised crime. The ACC has observed organised crime groups moving into the insurance and telecommunication sectors, and increasingly using professional service providers, such as accountants and lawyers to assist in fraud offences and money laundering (*Australian Financial Review*).

**Broker admitted to money laundering:** A former Lehman Brothers broker has admitted to laundering US$11 million in drug proceeds through company accounts for a Mexican drug cartel. Accounts were established in the British Virgin Islands (*Australian Financial Review* 2005).

**Flight attendant caught as a drug mule:** A 26-year old female Malaysian Airlines flight attendant was caught by customs and charged with trafficking a kilogram of crystal methylamphetamine in three packages concealed in her underwear. The case is one of West Australian's biggest international 'ice' importations. She was not a member of the cabin crew (*West Australian* 2008).

## CYBER AND ELECTRONIC CRIME

**Spam is at a two-year high:** Spam has significantly increased and reached a two-year apex that includes the jump in late 2010, according to M86 Security Labs. A Commtouch study states that a jump in email-attached malware has just stopped; however, additional waves are expected. M86 suggests that most of the spam is generated by the Cutwail botnet and pernicious spam accounted for 13 percent of the mix, which spiked to 24 percent. A significant portion of the malicious spam was concealed in phony correspondence from UPS, which corroborates Commtouch's findings that UPS spam was much of what Cutwail and Festi are issuing (Greene, *Network World*, cited in ASIS, *Security Management*, August 2011).

**Application vulnerabilities chief among federal cybersecurity concerns:** Of the 145 C-level executives who took part in a Frost & Sullivan on-line survey earlier this year, 73 percent said that application vulnerabilities were their biggest concern when it came to cybersecurity. Mobile devices were the second biggest concern, cited by 66 percent, followed by viruses and worm attacks at 64 percent. Cloud-based services were only cited by 43 percent of respondents as being their biggest concern. The survey also asked C-level executives about their main concerns with regard to the security of cloud computing. Ninety-four percent cited the loss or leakage of confidential or sensitive data, while 90 percent said that that their biggest concern was the exposure of confidential or sensitive information to unauthorized systems or personnel. Finally, Frost & Sullivan found that the number of federal cybersecurity employees will increase from roughly 27,000 in 2010 to 61,299 by 2015 (Perera, May 11, 2011, cited in ASIS, *Security Management*).

**Australian CIOs rate employee security threats above outsiders:** An estimated 49 percent of local businesses now perceive cybercrime as a greater threat than physical crime to their business. At the same time, the perception is that perpetrators of cybercrime are becoming increasingly sophisticated; 84 percent of global CIO's believe that lone hackers are increasingly being replaced by organised and technically proficient criminal groups. Significant numbers of CIO's also pointed out the administrative losses from cybercrime, such as the costs of investigating the breach (41 percent), notifying customers and suppliers (31 percent) and legal fees (18 percent) (*Computer World*, March 14, 2006).

**Growing use of Internet to spread terror and hate:** Terrorists and extremists are turning to the Internet to spread their views and incite readers to take action, according to a report issued by a Jewish human rights group. Called "Digital Terrorism and Hate

2006," the report was issued by the Simon Wiesenthal Centre and focuses on more than 6,000 Web sites that raise money for terrorist groups and teach related skills, such as bomb building. In particular, the report details Middle Eastern-run Internet forums that encourage attacks on Christians and Jews with tips on, for example, how to use a cell phone as a bomb detonator. It also highlights European online news groups used by sports fanatics to incite racial activity at sporting events. There's also a transnational Internet network used by North American, European, and Middle Eastern extremists to share ideas, the report says (CSO Online).

**Cybercrime fighters using bogus websites:** Bogus websites have been set up by Australian police and military intelligence officers in order to track and monitor for extremists who use the internet to recruit and plan attacks. Similar programs, also operated by US and British agencies, include tracking child pornography and financial fraud.

## KIDNAPPING AND EXTORTION

**Neck bomb hoax was a "very serious" plot:** Australian police investigated what was an attempted extortion that took place at the Sydney home of the CEO of an information technology company. The incident began when a masked man broke into the home of William Pulver in the upscale Sydney suburb and chained what appeared to be a bomb to the neck of his 18-year-old daughter Madeleine. The man then fled. When authorities arrived on the scene, they found a list of the attacker's demands attached to the device, primarily the need to contact an e-mail address. Homes in the area were then evacuated and streets were closed as bomb squad specialists spent 10 hours removing the device from Madeleine's neck, which they later determined did not contain any explosives (MSNBC, August 5, 2011, cited in ASIS, *Security Management*).

**Gods Garbage motorcycle gang members arrested for extortion:** The president and two members of the outlaw motorcycle gang (OMCG) Gods Garbage have been arrested by Australian police for allegedly threatening a businessman over a reported A$45,000 debt. They collected A$9000 from the businessman, before the arrests were made (*West Australian* 2007).

## PIRACY

**Piracy costs world shipping industry US$9B a Year:** The Indian National Ship Owners Organization (INSO) reports that piracy currently costs the global shipping industry more than US$9 billion each year with increased insurance costs, longer travels times to avoid pirate-infested waters, salaries for armed guards and ransoms paid for the release of captured vessels and crew. Pirates in Somalia currently hold 26 hijacked vessels and 600 crew. In order to combat this problem, the INSO has called on the United Nations to create an international maritime force, much like its peacekeepers, to supplement the work of national navies attempting to protect ships in the area. The force would be empowered to board suspicious ships, have armed soldiers to protect ships at sea, and be able to attack pirate vessels. The association has also proposed that the UN create a "no ship zone" off the Somali coast to prevent pirate ships from entering or leaving the area (Nirmala, Associated Press, October 3, 2011, cited in ASIS, *Security Management Daily*).

**Report finds increase in global sea piracy, but less successful attacks:** According to the International Maritime Bureau (IMB), the number of piracy incidents around the world increased this year as pirates extended their reach to attack merchant ships from Asia and the Middle East. The bureau said there were 266 pirate attacks across the globe in the first half of 2011, a 36 percent increase from 2010. Most of the pirate attacks occurred off the coast of Somalia, near the Horn of Africa. The group also noted that despite the increased number of attacks, the rate of success has actually decreased.

IMB Director Mukundan said that Somali pirates have increased their area of attacks to include the trade routes from the Arabian Gulf and from Asia, where more vulnerable vessels carry expensive goods. Somali pirates make up approximately 60 percent of the globe's total incidents. The bureau says the region's naval presence needs to be increased to deal with the rising number of attacks; however, Mukundan said that a naval presence is not the only solution. Mukundan said that action must be taken in south central Somalia to improve living conditions, which would help minimize the incentive for young Somalis to take to the sea in order to commit piracy (Schearf, Voice of America News, July 20, 2011, cited in ASIS, *Security Management*).

**Indian Navy thwarts piracy attempt, 16 pirates held:** The Indian Navy and the Coast Guard captured 16 Somali pirates after preventing another piracy attempt in the Indian Ocean. Sixteen hostages were also freed in the operation. During the operation, the Navy responded to a distress call from the merchant ship *MV Maersk Kensington*. The pirates' ship was identified as *Morteza*, a previously-hijacked Iranian trawler. "The pirate vessel *Morteza* opened fire on the naval ship. *INS Suvarna* then engaged the pirate vessel in self-defence, resulting in *Morteza* catching fire due to fuel drums. The pirates and hostages jumped overboard," officials reported (*Economic Times of India*, March 29, 2011, cited in ASIS, *Security Management Daily*).

**German shippers see no let-up in piracy:** According to a 2011 study by PricewaterhouseCoopers (PWC), German shippers are increasingly turning to private security suppliers in an attempt to fight off the threat of piracy. Shippers believe pirates are becoming more professional and are targeting bigger areas and 27 out of the 100 shippers surveyed said they now use private, armed security services that can cost up to A\$6,000 a day. Insurer Munich Re has warned that using armed services could actually increase the chance of violence. Despite attempts by international navies to reduce attacks, Somali pirates continue to make millions of dollars in ransoms from seizing ships in the Indian Ocean and Gulf of Aden.

A senior British navy officer announced recently that efforts to fight piracy off the Somali coast have reduced the number of successful attacks on merchant ships. However, the study showed that only 17 percent of German shippers believe the EU mission, Operation Atlanta, was contributing a significant amount to the fight against piracy, down from 40 percent last year. In addition, 80 percent felt that ransom payments had only made piracy worse and that there were no signs that the problem was easing (Bryan, Reuters, July 29, 2011).

**India plans new law to deal with piracy:** Faced with repeated instances of piracy in the high seas with Indians' wellbeing at stake, New Delhi is putting together a robust mechanism to deal with the menace, contemplating and working on not just a new domestic law against piracy but also negotiating with the littoral states of Somalia and some independent ones within it to ensure that acts of piracy do not go unpunished because of logistical, legal or diplomatic issues.

The law, according to senior officials, has been in the works for some months now with the ministries of shipping, external affairs, defence, law and home affairs working in close cooperation. The legislation will put together some of the vital points of international laws against piracy, provisions of the IPC and the admiralty laws. It will, however, not be of any help in the negotiation process after Indians aboard a ship have been taken hostage which, according to experts in the field, often proves to be a major hurdle especially when the liners belong to smaller shipping companies.

"It will be a comprehensive piece against piracy. For example, now our domestic laws do not even define piracy. This has made it difficult to try the 120-odd pirates who are at present in our custody. The importance of international cooperation is immense. The reason we are trying to involve countries like Kenya, Tanzania and Seychelles is because if our Navy captures pirates in the Gulf of Aden, it is hardly feasible for them to bring them all the way back to be tried and prosecuted. Impunity is the biggest bane of piracy and it is important to resolve that," explained a senior official involved with the process of both the drafting of the law and the international negotiations.

Many countries have already put together a law and have understanding with the nations surrounding Somalia on prosecution of pirates as per a resolution adopted in the United Nations Security Council. Seychelles has an agreement with Somalia based on which Seychelles can try pirates and send them back home to serve the punishment. India too is planning something on these lines. Officials say it is a matter of some relief that no Indian-flagged ship has ever been targeted by pirates but the government does not want to sit back but tackle the menace with active cooperation from the international community (Ghosh, *Times of India*, April 28, 2011).

**Somaliland struggles in effort to fight piracy:** Over the last several years, piracy has become a growing problem off the coast of Somalia. In 2010, Somali pirates took more than 1,000 people hostage, which set a new record. So far this year, Somali pirates have hijacked 15 ships, including an American yacht whose four passengers were murdered. In response to this problem, Somaliland, an autonomous part of Somalia, is taking steps to fight piracy. However, the region's government is facing a number of obstacles in its efforts to stem piracy. For instance, Somaliland's coast guard is made up of just eight working vessels, despite the fact that the region has more than 500 miles of coastline. According to Somaliland Admiral Osman, boats are the primary item his coast guard needs in order to be effective. But Somaliland has limited space to detain pirates even if it had enough boats to catch them all.

The United Nations attempted to help by recently building a new prison in Somaliland's capital that has the capacity to handle 400 inmates. Nevertheless, prosecuting suspected pirates remains difficult because it is difficult to catch them in the act and collect evidence against them, and because Somaliland does not currently have any anti-piracy laws (Langfitt, National Public Radio, April 4, 2011).

## ECONOMIC ESPIONAGE

**New espionage warning issued by US Department of Defense:** Coins containing hidden radio transmitters were allegedly planted on contractors with classified security clearances on at least three occasions in 2005 and 2006 in Canada. Intelligence experts have nominated China, Russia or France as potential suspects (*West Australian* 2006).

**In China, business travelers take extreme precautions to avoid cyber-espionage:**
Security experts are warning travelers to avoid bringing electronic devices carrying
important company contacts and confidential information to China if at all possible.
This warning stems from the pervasive electronic surveillance and cyber-espionage
undertaken by the Chinese government and other regional sources. Although experts
have also posted similar warnings about other nation-states, China stands out because
of its focus on using cyber-espionage aimed at improving the country's economy by
stealing information. In order to prevent such attacks, some corporate travelers bring
disposable cell phones or temporary laptops that have been stripped of all classified
data. Others do not take any electronic devices at all or hide files on a thumb drive that
they only use on off-line computers. A few will even take detours to Australia instead
of risk taking in a bugged Chinese hotel room or purchase iPads or other devices for
one-time use on a trip (Nakashima, *Washington Post*, September 27, 2011, cited in
ASIS, *Security Management Daily*).

## COMMUNITY AND STREET CRIME

**Frenchman suffers acid attack in KL:** A French couple has become the first foreigners to fall victim to a string of acid attacks plaguing the Malaysian capital, Kuala
Lumpur. The couple was attacked by two men on a motorcycle with corrosive liquid
thrown into the man's face. At least 15 other people have been attacked in this way,
mostly students and teachers within the Bangsar area. Police believe this is an isolated
incident by a person of unsound mind, but more recent cases indicate that there is a
gang of copycats (*Straits Times*, April 2, 2011).

**Heroic intervention during armed robbery sparks Worksafe investigation:** A
pizza shop owner has been interviewed by Worksafe after reports he overpowered an
armed robber who threatened staff with a handgun. Worksafe reiterated that it was not
safe to tackle the offender and it would investigate what procedures the store had to
deal with violent situations (*West Australian*).

**Office worker assaulted by intruder:** A 17 year old female office worker was inde-
cently assaulted at a business by a strange man who sneaked into the office and found his
way to an upstairs archive room. Intruders, including those with mental illness, should
be managed with access control systems or procedures. Providing a secure workplace is
a requirement under the Occupational Health and Safety Act, the new Code of Practice
for Workplace Violence, and Risk Management Standard.

**Gun fired in an armed robbery after victim refused to comply:** A gun was fired in
an armed robbery after a service station attendant refused to comply with demands of
the offender. Staff who are at risk of armed robbery need to be sufficiently trained in
how to deal with offenders to minimise risk of injury to themselves and other patrons
(*West Australian* 2009).

**Uniform and identity card stolen:** A Fisheries Department identity card and uniform
were stolen from a staff member's car whilst parked outside his home last week. Staff
should be regularly advised not to keep identity cards and any other company assets,
including laptop computers, unsecured in their vehicles (*West Australian* 2005).

# NATURAL DISASTERS AND CATASTROPHIC INCIDENTS

**Japan's tsunami:** Toll of dead and missing from Japan's March 2011 quake and resulting tsunami exceeded 10,000 from a massive earthquake and tsunami. The quake and tsunami killed people in more than a dozen of Japan's 47 prefectures (Reuters, March 14, 2011). Note: 4863 people were killed on Japan's roads in 2010, down 1 percent from 2009, the first year since 1952 that the toll fell below 5,000 (JapanToday.com).

**Japan's N-crisis "under control" after nine months:** Japan has finally brought the leaking reactors at the Fukushima nuclear plant under control, nine months after the crisis began. The government hopes the announcement will bring relief to a disaster weary public, still haunted by the monster tsunami. Decommissioning will take 40 years and will require sealing the reactor and fuel in concrete (Agence France-Presse, December 17–18, 2011, *West Australian* 2005).

**Kashmir was rocked by a powerful earthquake:** The Pakistani-controlled Kashmir was rocked by a powerful earthquake measuring 7.6 on the Richter scale. About 73,000 people were killed, 130,000 injured and 2.8 million displaced.

**Industry shut down:** Australian racing industry shut down following the release of equine flu from a NSW quarantine holding facility. A national ban was in place on the movement of all horses (*West Australian* 2006).

**Bio-security virus outbreak:** Bird flu began spreading in more than 10 Asian countries and regions, including Vietnam, Indonesia, Thailand and China. Later in the year, Russia, Ukraine, Romania, Britain, Colombia and Turkey were also hit by avian flu. In some countries, human beings were infected and killed by the virus. The United Nations and other international organizations convened a string of meetings calling for international cooperation to address the issue (Xinhua, December 30, 2005, The China).

**Bird flu outbreak could cost US\$2 trillion:** The global cost of a bird flu pandemic could total more than US\$2 trillion, according to World Bank officials (*West Australian* 2007).

**Impact on HDD production due to severe flooding in Thailand:** Western Digital Corp. announced that production of hard drives in its facilities close to Bangkok, Thailand, would be constrained due to the severe flooding in Thailand. The flooding is causing problems with the region's infrastructure, including transportation and utilities, and has resulted in the inundation of some supplier facilities and employee homes.

In the quarter ending July 1, 2011, WD shipped approximately 54 million hard drives from its facilities in Thailand and Malaysia, with approximately 60 percent coming from its Thailand sites. The company's Thailand operations source much of its supply of components from local suppliers. While WD's facilities in Thailand were operational, production was suspended on a temporary basis to protect its employees and its facilities and equipment against water ingress. The company indicated that conditions associated with the continued flooding evolved quickly and the extent of the impact on its operations in Thailand cannot yet be fully determined (Western Digital Corp., *Australian Security Magazine*, Dec./Jan. 2012).

## REFERENCES

Xinhua. December 30, 2005. News Digest: Xinhua picks top 10 world stories of 2005. The China. Retrieved April 19, 2012, from http://thechina.biz/china-economy/xinhua-picks-top-10-world-stories-of-2005/

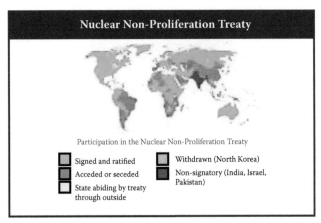

**FIGURE 1.1** Nuclear Non-Proliferation Treaty of Nation-States. From "Asia Pacific Ramifications of the Arab Spring & Israel National Security," 2011. *Australian Security Magazine*, October/November 2011. With permission.

**FIGURE 1.2** Corruption Perceptions Index 2010 results. Transparency International, 2010. With permission.

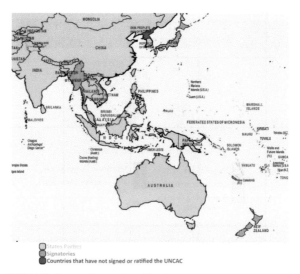

**FIGURE 1.3** UNCAC signatories and ratification status—Asia Pacific. From UNDOC, November 2011. With permission.

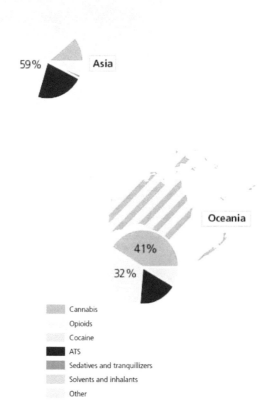

**FIGURE 1.4** Main problem drugs as reflected in treatment demand, by region, 2009. From UNODC, 2011. With permission.

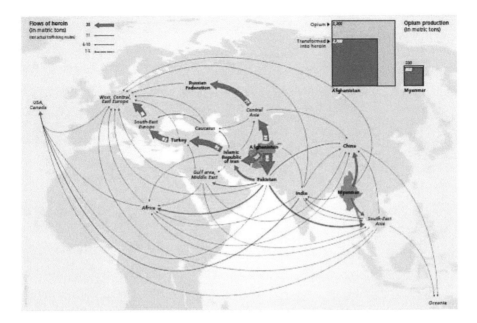

**FIGURE 1.5**  Global heroin flows from Asian points of origin. From UNODC, *World Drug Report 2010*. With permission.

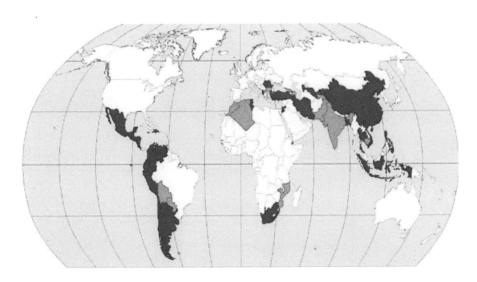

**FIGURE 4.1**  World states vulnerable to two or more hazards. Note: Red = high threat; orange = medium threat. From Independent Evaluation Group, 2006. With permission.

# 8 Asia-Pacific Country-Specific Overview

## INTRODUCTION

This chapter introduces country-specific Asia-Pacific regional nation-states, encompassing 41 nations. The region, as discussed, comprises a heterogeneous group that extends from the west with India to the east with Japan, and from the north with China to the south with New Zealand.

The chapter presents a synopsis of each nation-state, in alphabetical order. The synopsis provides a brief introduction, profile summary table, government structure, political nature, foreign affairs, details on the geography and economy. Each in-country synopsis ends with a security section, providing an overview of what foreign nationals may need to consider before visiting the nation-state. The chapter concludes with a list of useful websites for current and changing threats and risks.

## IN-COUNTRY OVERVIEWS

### Australia

Australia is a constitutional monarchy, with three political parties that center in the spectrum. Its lands are sparsely populated, and it has significant resource exports to the Asia-Pacific region. After federation in 1901, Australia has been and continues to be an active participant in international affairs. There are limited security issues for foreign nationals working in Australia.

### Profile Summary

| | | |
|---|---|---|
| Landmass | 7.7 million km$^2$ | |
| Population | 22.6 million | |
| Ethnic groups | | |
| Religions | Catholic 26% | Anglican 19% |
| | Other Christian 19% | Buddhist 2.1% |
| | Islam 1.7% | No religion 19% |
| | Not stated 12% | |
| Languages | English | |
| Education | Literacy 99% | Years compulsory: to age 16 |
| Current GDP | US$1.3 trillion | |
| Per capita | US$55,672 | US$39,764 PPP |

## Government

Australia is a constitutional monarchy with a democratic federal and state system, gaining independence in 1901 from the British.

## Geography

Australia is considered the world's smallest continent or the world's largest island and the sixth-largest country by total area. The continent is located between the Indian and Pacific Oceans, separated from Asia by the Arafura and Timor Seas. Australia is the flattest continent, with a large desert or semiarid area in the center making up the largest portion of the land. The climate is relatively dry and subject to drought, ranging from temperate in the south to tropical in the far north. The majority of people live along the coast.

## Political Conditions

In Australian politics there are three parties: the Liberal Party, representing urban business interests, and the Nationals, representing rural interests; these two parties are the center-right parties. Center left is the Australian Labor Party representing workers and left-of-center groups. The current Australian government foreign policy shows strong continuation with that of its predecessors so little is expected to change in the short to medium term.

## Economy

Australia's economy is dominated by the service sector, although the agricultural and mining sectors account for the bulk of Australia's exports. Australia's small domestic market has secured a steady 8.5 percent GDP rate in early 2011. Since the 1980s Australia's economy has dramatically transformed itself from an inward-looking, highly protected, and regulated marketplace. Australia enjoys one of the highest standards of living in the G20.

## Foreign Relations

After federation in 1901, Australia has been an active participant in international affairs. In 1944, Australia and New Zealand reached an agreement on security, welfare, and advancement of the people of the independent territories of the Pacific (the ANZAC pact). Australian has given firm support to the United Nations (UN) and is also active in the G20, the Commonwealth Heads of Government, the Pacific Islands Forum (PIF), the Cairns Group countries, and the World Trade Organization (WTO), also including APEC (Asia Pacific Economic Cooperation). In 2012, Australia joined the International Criminal Court. The country is also involved in ASEAN (Association of Southeast Nations), actively participating in promoting regional corporation on security issues.

## Security Issues

Some caution must be exercised when traveling to Australia, as robberies, burglaries, and auto theft are common in larger cities. Weapons are increasingly used in such crimes, and may also be associated with drug trafficking and usage. When drinking in public places, care must be taken as drink spiking and alcohol-related violence do occur.

## BANGLADESH

Bangladesh is parliamentary democracy, gaining independence in 1971 from Pakistan. Although one of the world's poorest and most densely populated countries, its lands are fertile but exposed to natural disasters and prone to political and civil unrest. There are significant security issues for working foreign nationals in all parts of the country, with trouble flaring rapidly.

### Profile Summary

| | | |
|---|---|---|
| Landmass | 147,570 km² | |
| Population | 156 million | |
| Ethnic groups | Bengali 98% | Other 2% |
| Religions | Muslim 83% | Christian 0.3% |
| | Hindu 16% | Others 0.9% |
| Languages | Bangla | English |
| Education | Attendance 61% | Literacy 47.5% |
| GDP growth rate | FY2008 6.2% | |
| Current GDP | US$84.2 billion | US$226.4 billion PPP |
| Per Capita | US$554 | US$1,500 PPP |

### Government
Bangladesh is a parliamentary democracy, gaining independence in 1971 from Pakistan.

### Geography
Bangladesh is a low-lying, riparian country with a largely marshy jungle coastline of 710 kilometers on the northern littoral of the Bay of Bengal. Formed by a deltaic plain, Bangladesh's alluvial soil is highly fertile but vulnerable to flood and drought. Bangladesh has a subtropical monsoonal climate characterized by heavy seasonal rainfall, moderately warm temperatures, and high humidity. Natural calamities, such as floods, tropical cyclones, tornadoes, and tidal bores, affect the country almost every year. Bangladesh also is affected by major cyclones, on average 16 times a decade. Urbanization is proceeding rapidly, with the areas around Dhaka and Comilla the most densely settled.

### Political Conditions
Bangladesh is a democracy, although there are serious problems related to a dysfunctional political system, weak governance, and pervasive corruption. Bangladeshis regard democracy as an important legacy of their bloody war for independence and

vote in large numbers. However, democratic institutions and practices remain weak. Bangladesh is generally moderate in international forums and is a longtime leader in international peacekeeping operations, being the second-largest contributor to UN peacekeeping operations with 10,481 troops and police. Bangladesh became a member of the United Nations Human Rights Council in 2006; however, an explicit goal of its foreign policy has been to strengthen relations with Islamic states.

## Economy

Although one of the world's poorest and most densely populated countries, Bangladesh has made strides to meet the increasing food needs with greater domestic production. The country is largely self-sufficient in rice production; nevertheless, an estimated 13 percent of the population faces serious nutritional risk. Although improving, infrastructure to support transportation, communications, and power supply is poorly developed. Bangladesh is limited in its reserves of coal and oil, and its industrial base is weak. The country's main endowments include its vast human resource base, rich agricultural land, relatively abundant water, and substantial reserves of natural gas.

## Foreign Relations

Bangladesh pursues a moderate foreign policy that places heavy reliance on multinational diplomacy, especially at the UN. Geographic, cultural, historic, and commercial ties are strong, although Indo-Bangladesh relations are often strained due to India's power. Bangladesh's complex relationship with Pakistan is the legacy of their shared history and independence. Other links include China, Russia, and the United States.

## Security Issues

There needs to be a high degree of caution in Bangladesh due to the unpredictable security and political situation. It is necessary to be aware of personal security at all times, supported with media and local information sources for news about possible security risks.

Nationwide hartals (general strikes) may be called at short notice in response to political developments and can involve the shutdown of all activity, resulting in violent clashes between antigovernment groups and security forces. In the event of a hartal, avoid unnecessary travel and keep clear of all protests and large crowds.

Significant dates and anniversaries can attract violence, and public celebrations have been targeted for attacks in the past. Include a list of significant dates and anniversaries, and ensure employees are briefed on these dates.

There have been a number of terrorist incidents in recent years, and security agencies in Bangladesh continue to arrest people connected to terrorist organizations. Further attacks are possible, including those against Western interests.

Since the beginning of 2009, the number of reported crimes, including armed robbery and mugging, has increased in Dhaka. Travel to the Chittagong Hill Tracts region is dangerous due to the high risk of politically motivated violence and kidnapping.

## BHUTAN

Bhutan is a constitutional monarchy, formally adopting the constitution in 2008 to become a parliamentary democracy. The mountainous terrain, with lower lying foothills, provides one of the world's smallest economies. Bhutan relies heavily on India for trade and development, and is working with Nepal to resolve issues of Bhutanese refugees residing in Nepal. There are limited security issues for working foreign nationals in all parts of the country, with infrequent small-scale bomb attacks and protests occurring.

## Profile Summary

| | | |
|---|---|---|
| Landmass | 46,500 km² | |
| Population | 672,425 | |
| Ethnic groups | Drukpa 50% | Indigenous or migrant tribes |
| | Ethnic Nepalese 35% | 15% |
| Religions | Lamaistic Buddhist 75% | Indian- and Nepalese-influenced Hinduism 25% |
| Languages | Dzongkha (official language) | English (instruction) |
| | Bumthang-kha | Sharchop-kha |
| | Nepali | |
| Education | Years compulsory: 11 | Literacy 59.5% |
| | Primary school net enrollment rate 82.1% | |
| Real growth rate (2007) | 8.5% | |
| Current GDP | US$3.359 billion | |
| Per capita | US$5,200 PPP | |

## Government

Bhutan is a constitutional monarchy, formally adopting the constitution to become a parliamentary democracy in 2008.

## Geography

Bhutan is bordered by China to the North and India to the South, and is located at the southern slopes of the Eastern Himalayas. The mountainous terrain contrasts with the lower-lying foothills and some savannah. Approximately 64 percent of Bhutan is covered by forest. The terrain varies from 98 m (322 ft.) above sea level in the valley of Drangme Chhu to more than 7,000 m (23,000 ft.) above sea level in the mountainous regions. Eastern Himalayan subalpine conifer forests are found in the higher elevations of the central region with Eastern Himalayan broadleaf forests found in the lower elevations. The majority of Bhutan's forest production stems from these forests.

Bhutan experiences five seasons, including summer, monsoon, autumn, winter, and spring. The monsoon season generally runs between June and September. The climate in Bhutan varies with elevation, from a polar-type climate with all-year snow in the North, to temperate in the highlands and subtropical-type climate in the South. Heavy monsoon rains are experienced in the western regions of Bhutan, while hot humid summers and cool winters are experienced in the South. A drier climate is experienced in the central and eastern regions of Bhutan with warm summers and cool winters.

## Political Conditions

Approximately 35 percent of Bhutan's population is comprised of Nepali migrants, referred to as Lhotsampas. Between 1988 and 1993, ethnic Nepali refugees fled to Nepal alleging ethnic and political repression. Bhutan and Nepal have been working to resolve the refugee situation by repatriating refugees from Nepal. The situation is thought to improve with the transition to democracy, with officials expressing the issue as a priority.

The spiritual head of Bhutan is the Je Khempo, nominated by the monastic leaders and appointed by the king. The Je Khempo has authority over all religious institutions, with the monk body involved in advising the government on many levels. Bhutan is divided into 20 dzongkhags (districts) with each headed by an elected district officer. A group of villages form a constituency called gewog, administered by a local elected leader or gup. Bhutan contains 201 elected gups.

## Economy

Bhutan's economy is one of the world's smallest; however, it has grown since 2005, becoming the world's second-fastest-growing economy in 2007, with growth of 22 percent. The commissioning of the Tala Hydroelectricity Project assisted in Bhutan's economic growth through this period. Bhutan principally exports electricity, cardamom, gypsum, timber, handicrafts, cement, fruit, precious stones, and spices.

Agriculture, forestry, tourism, and the sale of hydroelectric power to India form the base of Bhutan's economy. Bhutan has not been able to benefit from significant trading of its products, as access to roads and the sea is difficult and expensive. A free-trade accord between Bhutan and India was signed in 2008. The majority of development projects, such as road construction, are undertaken by contracted Indian labor.

## Foreign Relations

In 2007, India and Bhutan signed a new Treaty of Peace and Friendship to govern relations between the countries and removed the clause stating India would "guide" Bhutan's foreign policy, which allowed Bhutan to purchase military equipment from other countries. Through a joint effort with the Indian military, Bhutan strengthened its border security and expelled the Indian insurgents of the United Liberation Front of Assam in 2003.

Bhutan does not have diplomatic relations with China; however, it has engaged in several high-level talks regarding three Chinese-built roads that the Bhutanese government believes intrude on its territory.

In 1983 Bhutan established diplomatic relations with Nepal and is currently negotiating a resolution to the refugee issue. Over 85,000 refugees reside in Nepal, with the majority claiming Bhutanese citizenship. The Bhutanese government alleges the refugees are "voluntary emigrants," who have forfeited any citizenship rights. Progress on the rectification of this issue remain slow. Several insurgent groups have stemmed from these refugee camps, including the Bhutan Communist Party (Marxist–Leninist–Maoist), the Bhutan Tiger Force, and the United Revolutionary Front of Bhutan.

Bhutan became a member of the UN in 1971; however, it does not share diplomatic relations with any of the permanent members of the UN Security Council. Bhutan shares diplomatic relations with Japan and seven European nations, forming the "Friends of Bhutan" group. These countries include Switzerland, Denmark, Sweden, Norway, the Netherlands, Finland, and Austria. Bhutan also has diplomatic relations with South Korea, Canada, Australia, Kuwait, Thailand, Bahrain, Bangladesh, the Maldives, Sri Lanka, and Pakistan.

## Security Issues

Several groups have formed in Bhutan, with the primary goal of repatriating Nepali-speaking Bhutanese refugees residing in Nepal camps. Between 2006 and 2008, Bhutan experienced a series of small bombs in the capital Thimphu; however, incidents were generally on a small scale. The majority of the other incidents occurred away from tourist destinations, near the southwestern border.

The capital Thimphu has seen a rise in burglary and drug abuse; however, incidents are still few. Bhutan experiences relatively little crime, with petty crimes such as pickpocketing and purse snatching occasionally reported.

## Brunei

Brunei is a sultanate (Malay Islamic monarchy), with the sultan as both head of state and prime minister, presiding over a 14-member cabinet. The country has a stable geographical, political, and legal environment, with the legal system based on English common law. There are some concerns with the current changing economy and heavy reliance on imported oil and gas. Brunei has a relatively low occurrence of serious crime, but be aware of the political situation.

## Profile Summary

| | | |
|---|---|---|
| Landmass | 5,765 km$^2$ | |
| Population | 406,200 | |
| Ethnic groups | Malay | Chinese |
| | Other indigenous groups | |
| Religions | Islam | |
| Languages | Malay | Chinese |
| | English | Iban |
| | Other indigenous dialects | |
| Education | Years compulsory: 9 | Literacy 94.7% |
| GDP growth rate | −1.9% | |
| Current GDP | US$12.0 billion | BND15.6 billion |

## Government

Brunei is a sultanate (Malay Islamic monarchy), which gained independence in 1984.

## Geography

Brunei is in southeastern Asia, bordering the South China Sea and Malaysia. Brunei is located close to vital sea lanes through the South China Sea, linking the Indian and Pacific Oceans. Seventy-seven percent of the population lives in the east of Brunei, while only 10,000 people live in the mountainous southeastern part (district of Temburong). Most of Brunei is located within the Borneo lowland rain forests that cover most of the island, with areas of mountain rain forests inland. Brunei has a tropical equatorial climate, high temperatures, humidity, and rainfall with an annual average temperature of 26.1°C. Natural hazards such as typhoons, earthquakes, and severe flooding are quite rare, even though Brunei sits within the Pacific Ring of Fire earthquake regions.

## Political Conditions

Brunei is a Malay Islamic monarchy, with the sultan being both the head of state and the prime minister. The country has been under martial law, following a rebellion in the early 1960s that was put down by British troops from Singapore. Brunei's legal system is based on English common law, with an independent judiciary enacted by the sultan. Brunei has arrangements with the United Kingdom, where judges for the Brunei High Court are appointed by England. Final appeals can still go to the Privy Council in London.

## Economy

Brunei's economy maintained moderate growth in the mid-2000s. Its economy is subject to fluctuations in the global oil market, and is heavily dependent on oil and gas production. In recent years, Brunei's growth has dramatically decreased and it continues to have one of the lowest gross domestic product rates of any ASEAN nation. However, the country has one of the highest rates of macroeconomic stability in the world and the highest in Asia. Brunei's government encourages foreign investment; however, investment outside the oil and gas industry is limited.

## Foreign Relations

Brunei is a member of many international associations. After becoming independent, Brunei joined ASEAN, giving the membership the highest priority in foreign affairs. Later, Brunei joined the UN. The country has high import rates from the United States, Singapore, and Malaysia.

## Security Issues

Brunei has a relatively low occurrence of serious crime, although it is advised to frequently check the news for any changes in political issues. In the event that issues arise, it is advised to avoid protests and large crowds. Local offenders occasionally target tourists for petty crime such as burglary and theft. Breaking road rules is not harshly penalized—running red lights, speeding, and unlicensed drivers are common in Brunei. Capital punishment applies for serious offenses such as murder and kidnapping. Corporal punishment applies for other serious crimes such as rape, robbery, and visa offenses.

## BURMA

Since the independence of Burma (now officially known as Republic of the Union of Myanmar) in 1948, the country continues to be a part of the longest-running civil war among ethnic groups, which still remains unresolved. For many years, Burma was under martial law until 2010, when former military groups were given the right to create a civilian regime. Security issues are broad, and foreign nationals are advised not to travel to Burma, which is prone to political unrest, a poor legal system, and ethnic unrest. Human rights violations in the country are repeatedly reported, including increasing cases of child labor and human trafficking.

### Profile Summary

| | | |
|---|---|---|
| Landmass | 678,500 km² | |
| Population | 53.99 million | |
| Ethnic groups | Burman 68% | Shan 9% |
| | Karen 7% | Rakhine 4% |
| | Chinese 3% | Mon 2% |
| | Indian 2% | Other 2% |
| Religions | Buddhist 89% | Christian 4% |
| | Muslim 4% | Animist 1% |
| | Other 2% | |
| Languages | Burmese English | Minority ethnic languages |
| Education | Male literacy 93.9% | Female literacy 86.4% |
| GDP growth rate | 3.2% | |
| GDP per capita | $2,989 | |
| Current GDP | $40.288 billion | |

### Government
Burma is a civilian regime ruled by former military groups after a 2008 national referendum that adopted a new constitution, though deep flaws are driving political unrest.

### Geography
Burma is located in Southeast Asia, bordered by the People's Republic of China, Laos, Thailand, and Bangladesh. One-third of Burma forms an untouched coastline. Burma is the 40th largest country in the world and the second largest in Southeast Asia. The climate ranges from tropical monsoon, hot, humid, and wet summers to scant rainfall and mild winters. There are some areas that suffer from prolonged drought conditions in central Burma. Central lowlands are surrounded by steep rugged highlands. Current environmental issues include deforestation, causing

significant air, soil, and water pollution. Inadequate sanitation and water treatment have caused an increase in related disease.

### Political Conditions

Burma remains an authoritarian country, ruled by former military with the aim of creating a civil regime. Political flaws create significant unrest for the Burmese society. Clashes between the Burma Army and the Independence Army continued through 2011, with a series of attacks by the Burmese Army. Fighting between the two groups began in the 2010 election, with the attempt to create a less military-controlled society. The unstable political situation decreases human rights, allowing little freedom of speech.

### Economy

Burma's resources are rich, but since the reformations in 1962 the Burmese economy has become one of the least developed in the world. Exports can be up to US$8.1 billion, which includes natural gas, agricultural products, precious and semiprecious stones, and forest products. The major markets for Burma are Thailand, Hong Kong, India, Singapore, China, and Malaysia. Imports are US$4.5 billion, ranging from refined material oil, machinery, and meats to vegetable oil, pharmaceuticals, and cement. Burma's major suppliers for imports consist of China, Singapore, Thailand, South Korea, Japan, Indonesia, and India. Burmese goods are prohibited for importation to the United States.

### Foreign Relations

The trade market for Burma generally consists of neighboring countries such as China, Singapore, Thailand, and Japan.

### Security Issues

Burma requires a high degree of caution. Areas bordering China, Laos, and Thailand are unsafe and should not be visited, as there are risks of ethnic conflicts, banditry, and unmarked landmines. Currently (2012), there is an uncertain security situation with possibility of civil unrest. Monitor the media for changing situations. Bomb attacks in Burma have increased, targeting tourist areas such as shopping malls, hotels, and markets. Terrorism continues in Burma, with further reports of planning attacks.

### CAMBODIA

Cambodia is a constitutional monarchy, formally adopting the constitution in 2008 to become a parliamentary democracy. The country borders Thailand, Laos, and Vietnam, and has approximately 443 km of coastline along the Gulf of Thailand. Areas surrounding the parts of the Cambodian–Thai border are unsafe and foreign nationals should not visit these areas; however, other parts of the country are relatively safe—just take normal precautions.

## Profile Summary

| | | |
|---|---|---|
| Landmass | 181,040 km$^2$ | |
| Population | 13.4 million | |
| Ethnic groups | Cambodian 90% | Vietnamese 5% |
| | Chinese 1% | Tribes, Cham, Lao 4% |
| Religions | Theravada Buddhism 95% | Islam |
| | Animism | Christian |
| Languages | Khmer (official language) | French |
| | English | |
| Education | Years compulsory: 9 Primary | Literacy 75.1% |
| | school enrollment rate 94.4% | |
| Annual economic growth rate | 5.9% | |
| (2010 est.) | | |
| Current GDP (2010 est.) | US$11.3 billion | |
| Per capita GDP (2010 est.) | US$830 | |

## Government

Cambodia is a constitutional monarchy, formally adopting the constitution to become a parliamentary democracy in 2008.

## Geography

Cambodia contains low-lying central plains surrounded by uplands, low mountains, and the upper reaches of the Mekong River delta. The Tonle Sap plain measures 2,590 km$^2$ in the dry season and 24,605 km$^2$ in the wet season, is densely populated, and is devoted to wet rice cultivation. Thinly forested transitional plains extend outward from the central regions. The southern limit of the Dangrek Mountains is marked by a sandstone escarpment located to the north of the Cambodian plain.

Cambodia experiences a monsoonal climate and contains a marked wet and dry season. Southwest monsoons blow inland carrying moisture from the Gulf of Thailand and Indian Ocean between May and October. The dry season is caused by northeast monsoons occurring between November and March. Cambodia experiences flooding almost every year.

## Political Conditions

Cambodia is a constitutional monarchy, with its constitution providing for a multiparty democracy. The executive branch of the government includes the king, who is the head of state, an appointed prime minister, 10 deputy prime ministers, 42 ministers, 206 secretaries of state, and 205 undersecretaries of state. The bicameral legislature includes a 123-member elected National Assembly and a 61-member Senate. The judiciary includes a Supreme Court, lower courts, and an internationalized court with jurisdiction over serious crimes of the Khmer Rouge era.

## Economy

The Cambodian economy has many natural resources including timber, gemstones, iron ore, manganese, phosphate, hydroelectric potential from the Mekong River, oil, gas, and bauxite. Agriculture accounts for 33 percent of GDP and covers 2.7 million hectares, producing rice, rubber, corn, meat, vegetables, dairy products, sugar, and flour. Manufactures of clothing and tobacco, and fishing total 21 percent of GDP. Services include tourism at 40 percent of GDP. The central government budget indicates revenue of US$1.5 billion, with expenditures amounting to US$2.2 billion in 2010.

### Foreign Relations

Cambodia is recognized as a member of most major international organizations, including the UN and ASEAN. The country has established diplomatic relations with most countries. Cambodia is also a member of the World Bank, the International Monetary Fund (IMF), the Asian Development Bank (ADB), and the 148th member of the WTO.

Thai military and Cambodia are engaged in an ongoing border dispute that has led to injuries and fatalities, with landmines being reported.

### Security Issues

A visit to Cambodia requires an awareness of personal safety and security at all times, even though the country is relatively safe. Areas surrounding the Preah Vihear, Ta Krabei, and Ta Moan temples on the Cambodian–Thai border are unsafe for travel.

### CHINA

China is a Communist party-led state with an extremely large population. It has a large landmass, and the climate ranges from very hot summers to cold winters. Economically, China has overtaken Japan and almost the United States, with predictions it will become the leading world economy. In general, it is safe for foreign nationals to travel to most parts of China; however, there are significant security issues in Tibet and Xinjiang. In addition, security briefings should be provided to address industrial espionage and restricted confidential data carried to China.

### Profile Summary

| | | |
|---|---|---|
| Landmass | 9,596,961 km² | |
| Population | 1,330,141,295 billion | |
| Ethnic groups | Han Chinese 91.5% | Other nationalities 8.5% |
| Religions | Atheist | Daoist |
| | Buddhist | Christian |
| | Muslim | |
| Languages | Mandarin (Putonghua) | |
| Education | Years compulsory: 9 | Literacy 93% |
| GDP growth rate | 8.7% | |
| Current GDP | US$4.814 trillion | |
| Per capita GDP | US$3,678 | |

## Government

China is a Communist party-led state, adopting its constitution in 1982.

## Geography

China has an extremely large population of 1.3 billion in an area of 9,596,961 km², being one of the most populous countries in the world. The climate varies greatly, ranging from summer temperatures reaching to 30°C and winters of Arctic severity. Central China has very hot summers and very cold winters, differentiating from the south where the summers are hot and winters are mild. There are many plains, deltas, and hills in the east with mountains, high plateaus, and deserts occupying the west. In the south, China is home to Mount Everest, the Earth's highest point. Modern China is separated from Burma, Laos, and Vietnam by the southwest border of high mountains and deep valleys. Dust storms have become very frequent in spring due to prolonged drought and poor agricultural practices.

## Political Conditions

China had difficulty in restraining abuse by official authority and revolutionary excesses. The government's efforts are continuous in promoting rule of law. China is constantly in violation of human rights according to international recognized norms. Reported abuses peak around three major anniversaries, namely the founding of the People's Republic of China, the Tiananmen Square incident, and the Tibetan uprising. Abuses include torture, forced confessions, irrational long-term detention, mistreatment of prisoners, as well as severe restrictions on freedom of speech, religion, privacy, and workers' rights.

## Economy

Economic statistics (2010) indicated that China was the third-largest world economy, projected to overtake Japan later that year. Currently, China has more than doubled Japan's economic activity with predictions that it will overtake the United States. Over the past two decades, China's market reforms significantly reduced poverty and increased income levels. The government not only promoted agricultural activities but also encouraged nonagricultural activities and self-management for state-owned enterprises.

## Foreign Relations

China has worked extremely hard to gain international support after the establishment of the People's Republic. The country holds a seat in the UN, becoming increasingly active in multilateral organizations. In addition, China has increased efforts to reduce tension in Asia, creating a cooperative relationship with members of ASEAN.

## Security Issues

The risk of terrorism, civil unrest, crime, and natural disasters creates the need to exercise a degree of caution when traveling to China overall. It is necessary to be aware of personal security at all times, and consult the media and local news for any possible security warnings.

In certain areas such as Xinjiang and Tibet, there must be a high degree of caution. Heightened ethnic tensions in Xinjiang cause a volatile situation, where protests and bombings have occurred, killing and injuring people. Tibet also has continuous protest by the Tibetan monks turning violent, resulting in deaths and injuries. The Chinese authorities must grant travelers permission to enter Tibet. Little warning of protest events is given.

Industrial espionage is prevalent, and limited commercial electronic data should be taken into China by foreign nationals. Only new and blank mobile phones and laptops should ever be used.

## COMOROS

Comoros is one of the smallest countries in the world. The country is a federal presidential republic after gaining its independence in 1978 from France. Comoros is under the system of Islamic laws. There are many security issues for foreign nationals in Comoros, as there is civil and political unrest, and it is a very poor country with a significantly high levels poverty and unemployment.

### Profile Summary

| | | |
|---|---|---|
| Landmass | 2,171 km² | |
| Population | 752,438 | |
| Ethnic groups | Antalote | Cafre |
| | Makao | Oimatsaha |
| | Sakalava | |
| Religions | Sunni Muslim 98% | Roman Catholic 2% |
| Languages | Shickomoro | Arabic |
| | French | |
| Education | Attendance 60% Primary | Literacy 56.5% |
| | 34% Secondary | |
| GDP growth rate | 0.5% | |
| Current GDP | $741.4 million | |
| GDP per capita | US$1,000 | |

### Government

Comoros is a republic.

### Geography

Comoros is one of the smallest countries in the world, with only 2,253 km² of landmass. The island has a rugged terrain varying from steep mountains to low hills. The climate is generally tropical and mild. The islands are rarely subject to cyclones.

Comoros was formed by volcanic activity and is located east of Africa and northwest of Madagascar in the Indian Ocean.

## Political Conditions

Politics takes place in a framework of a federal presidential republic, where the president is both head of state and head of government. The Comoros legal system is based on Islamic laws. Comoros was French territory and gained its independence in 1978. Since 2002, the island has been led by elected leaders, with the presidency rotating every four years between the three main islands. Citizens running for presidency must defer to those originating from Moheli. In recent years, it has been decided that in 2014 people from Grande Comoros can run for president. Elections are deemed generally free and fair.

## Economy

Comoros is one of the world's poorest countries, with an extremely high 14 percent unemployment. In recent years, the government's main focus has been economic growth and poverty reduction. Agriculture (fishing, hunting, and forestry) is the primary sector of employment, but only 38 percent work in this field. Agriculture occupies over 80 percent of the population and 40 percent of GDP. Comoros is the world's leading producer of essence of ylang-ylang, for manufacturing perfume. The country lacks modern infrastructure, with some villages not accessible by road.

## Foreign Relations

Comoros's neighbor is Madagascar, which hosts the U.S. embassy along with other foreign relations. Comoros became the 143rd member of the UN, and is part of the African Union, the Arab League, the European Development Fund, the World Bank, the IMF, the International Labour Organization, the World Health Organization, the Indian Ocean Commission, the Common Market for Eastern and Southern Africa, and the African Development Bank.

## Security Issues

Security conditions of Comoros can change rapidly. Occasional strikes can occur, along with violent clashes between police and demonstrators. An extremely high degree of caution needs to be taken, as civil and political unrest has been a significant issue since the country became independent. There is a history of sudden, violent, and illegal seizure of power from a government.

## COOK ISLANDS

The Cook Islands are a self-governing parliamentary in free association with New Zealand. Located in the South Pacific Ocean, the islands were made from volcanic activity. The isolation of the islands results in a struggling economy, as foreign markets are far. Natural resources are difficult to maintain as the climate is prone to cyclone seasons. New Zealand and China provide aid to the Cook Islands. Security issues are limited—just take normal precautions—but natural disasters are relatively frequent in the cyclone season.

---

**Profile Summary**

| | | |
|---|---|---|
| Landmass | 240 km² | |
| Population | 752,438. | |
| Ethnic groups | Maori 87.7% | Part Maori 5.8% |
| | Other 6.5% | |
| Religions | | |
| Languages | | |
| Education | | |
| Current GDP | US$183.2 million | |
| GDP per capita | US$9,100 | |

---

### Government

The Cook Islands are a self-governing parliamentary democracy, with free association with New Zealand.

### Geography

Located in the South Pacific Ocean, the 15 separate Cook Islands were created by volcanic activity. The climate is moderate to tropical.

### Political Conditions

Politically, the islands are a representative democracy with a parliamentary system associated state relationship with New Zealand. The country is part of the Commonwealth, heavily relying on the Queen of England, who is represented in the islands by a Queen's Representative.

### Economy

The Cook Islands' economy struggles significantly, which is affected by its geography. The islands are isolated from foreign markets and depend on natural resources, which suffer from natural disasters. The 15 islands are focusing on expanding tourism, banking, mining, and fishing sectors.

### Foreign Relations

The Cook Islands have many international alliances as the country struggles to operate independently. The banking sector is linked to an offshore financial sector, where Australia and New Zealand have a significant involvement. New Zealand works closely with the Cook Islands to provide aid when needed and China has also contributed foreign aid. Cook Islanders are considered New Zealanders, whereas not all New Zealanders are citizens of the Cook Islands.

## Security Issues

Foreign nationals must be alert to their own security when visiting the Cook Islands.
  Natural disasters are relatively frequent with the cyclone season from November to April.

## Fiji

The islands were formed by volcanic movement and are located north of New Zealand. Cyclones interrupt the agriculture continuity, occurring on average once a year. Fiji is a parliamentary democracy, overthrown in 2006 by a military coup. This coup has affected all sectors of the islands. Economically, exports have decreased, and due to the political unrest, international aid has become difficult. Security issues include high crime and violent assault against foreign nationals. In addition, political tension may lead to civil unrest. A high degree of personal security awareness must be maintained

## Profile Summary

| | | |
|---|---|---|
| Landmass | 18,376 km$^2$ | |
| Population | 851,745 | |
| Ethnic groups | Indigenous Fijian 57% | Indo-Fijian 37% |
| Religions | Christian 52% | Hindu 33% |
| | Muslim 7% | |
| Languages | English | Fijian |
| | Hindu | |
| Education | Literacy 93% | |
| Current GDP | $3.269 billion | |
| GDP per capita | $3,773 | |

## Government

Fiji became independent from the United Kingdom in 1970 as a parliamentary democracy that was overthrown by military coup in 2006.

## Geography

The islands of Fiji were formed by volcanic movement and are located north of New Zealand. The 322 islands range in size dramatically. Heavy rains on the southeastern islands create a dense tropical forest, whereas lowlands on the western islands have a dry season sheltered by the mountains. Although winds are moderate, cyclones tend to occur once a year with 10 to 12 per decade.

### Political Conditions

From the time of independence until 1987, Fiji was a parliamentary democracy, combining the traditional Fijian system and elements of European communities. Political unrest began after the 1987 election, when extremists feared the domination by the Indo-Fijian community. This resulted in a military coup, beginning the "coup cycle." In 2007, the most recent prime minister was appointed, pursuing a "cleanup campaign" in an attempt to minimize corruption.

### Economy

Fiji is one of the more developed of the Pacific island economies. For many years, the most successful exports were sugar and textiles; however, the coup affected many organizations and exports have declined. In 2010, fish was the leading export along with gold from Fiji's only mine, with both expected to increase. The European Union is actively involved in relations with Fiji, promising a large amount of financial aid; however, after the coup, this aid was put on hold until it improves its human rights situations.

### Foreign Relations

Traditionally, Fiji has shared close foreign relations with the neighboring countries of Australia and New Zealand. In recent years, Fiji has pursued closer relations with Asian countries, including China, Indonesia, and India. Fiji is actively part of the UN, becoming a member in 1970 and participating in many peacekeeping missions.

### Security Issues

Overall, traveling to Fiji requires a high degree of caution, particularly in Suva. Crime is prevalent and civil unrest may arise. Political tension, due to the unresolved political situation, gave police and military extensive powers that undermine the rule of law. Robbery, theft, and violent assault occur around the Fijian islands against tourists and foreign nationals. A high degree of personal security awareness must be maintained.

### INDIA

India is a federal constitutional republic, governed under a parliamentary system. It is one of the five BRICS nations. India is the most populous democracy in the world. The country is located on top of the Indian tectonic plate and occupies a major portion of the Indian subcontinent. There are significant security issues in Jammu and Kashmir, as political unrest has led to many terrorist attacks and sexual assaults against foreign women.

## Profile Summary

| | | |
|---|---|---|
| Landmass | 3.29 million km² | |
| Population | 1.17 billion | |
| Ethnic groups | Indo-Aryan 72% | Dravidian 25% |
| | Others 3% | |
| Religions | Hindu 80.5% | Muslim 13.4% |
| | Christian 2.3% | Sikh 1.9% |
| Languages | Hindi | English |
| Education | Literacy 61% | Years compulsory: 10 |
| GDP growth rate | 6.5% | |
| Current GDP | US$1.095 trillion | |
| GDP per capita | US$3,100 | |

## Government

India is a federal republic, gaining independence in 1947.

## Geography

India covers a major portion of the Indian subcontinent, lying on top of the Indian tectonic plates. The terrain varies from the Himalayas to flat river valleys and deserts in the west. The climate ranges from alpine to subtropical monsoon. India's climate is strongly influenced by the Himalayas and the Thar Desert, both of which drive the monsoons.

## Political Conditions

Federalism in India accounts for the power distribution between the federal government and the states. After a long history of single political dominance, India has declined in stability during the previous 12 years. The Maoist-inspired parliamentary republic has six recognized national parties and more than 40 regional parties. When India first became a republic in 1950, the Congress party held the majority in the Parliament; currently, the Congress is considered center-left or liberal. Political turmoil and unrest became apparent two years after the 1996 election, with several short-lived alliances sharing power in the center.

## Economy

India is the world's tenth-largest economy by market exchange rates, with US$1.53 trillion. India is one of the fastest-growing economies in the world. Out of its 1.7 billion people, there are 467 million workers, which is the second-largest labor force in the world.

India averaged a steady 7.5 percent growth rate in 2010 and has shown evidence of doubling hourly wages during the last decade. The economy has made major improvements, moving 432 million of its citizens out of poverty. India has become a major exporter of software services and workers, but there is still more than half the population that depends on agriculture to survive.

## Foreign Relations

India has a prominent voice in international affairs, with its foreign policy now recognized as a leader of the developing world and the Non-Aligned Movement (NAM). India is an active member of the UN and is now seeking a permanent seat on the UN Security Council. In addition, India is strengthening political and commercial ties with the United States, Japan, the European Union, Iran, China, and ASEAN.

## Security Issues

There needs to be a high degree of caution in India overall as there is political unrest causing an increase in terrorist activity, in particular in its major cities. Reports of sexual assault and harassment against foreign women have also increased. Violent protests and demonstrations are a frequent occurrence, and major secular and religious holidays provide opportunities for terrorist attacks.

## INDONESIA

Indonesia is an independent republic, being one of the largest countries in terms of land area. Indonesia is struggling to maintain a strong economic system. The government has significant control over most private enterprises. Security issues include civil and political unrest, which creates an unsafe environment in most parts of Indonesia. Bombing and terrorist attacks are also predicted to continue.

## Profile Summary

| | | |
|---|---|---|
| Landmass | 2 million km² | |
| Population | 240.3 million | |
| Ethnic groups | Javanese 40.6% | Sundanese 15% |
| | Madurese 3.3% | Minangkabau 2.7% |
| | Other 38.4% | |
| Religions | Muslim 86.1% | Protestant 5.7% |
| | Catholic 3% | Hindu 1.8% |
| | Others 3.4% | |
| Languages | Indonesian | Javanese |
| Education | Literacy 90.4% | Years compulsory: 9 |
| GDP growth rate | 6.1% | |
| Current GDP | $707 billion | |
| GDP per capita | $4,394 | |

## Government

Indonesia is an independent republic.

## Geography

Indonesia is one of the largest countries in terms of area, containing 17,508 islands that are scattered over each side of the equator. Indonesia shares land borders with Malaysia, Papua New Guinea, and East Timor. The country is located in the Pacific, Eurasian, and Australian tectonic plates, making it vulnerable to volcanic activity and frequent occurrences of earthquakes. Indonesia contains 150 active volcanoes, two famously erupting in the nineteenth century with worldwide outcomes. The climate is equatorial, but cooler in the highlands. The large islands consist of coastal plains, with mountainous interiors.

## Political Conditions

Indonesia is a republic, with a presidential system based on the 1945 constitution that provided separation of executive, legislative, and judicial powers. Political reform was established in 1999 that formally set up new rules for the electoral role. As of 2004, the president may serve a maximum of two consecutive five-year terms.

## Economy

The government plays a significant role in Indonesia's market-based economy, with 139 state-owned enterprises and government-administrated prices. The financial crisis in 1997 to 1998 led the government to take more custody of private-sector assets. Capital markets then improved by the recapitalization of the banking sector. Despite the global financial crisis, poverty and unemployment have declined. The country is one of the largest economies in Southeast Asia.

## Foreign Relations

Since gaining independence, Indonesia has had an active foreign policy; nevertheless, it separates itself from any conflict between rival countries. The separation of East Timor strained Indonesia's relations with the international community. Indonesia's contemporary foreign policy is in participation with ASEAN and as a major trade partner with Japan.

## Security Issues

Careful consideration of the need to travel to Indonesia is highly recommended. Security issues include civil unrest and political tension, with many violent attacks occurring. Threats of terrorist attacks in Indonesia, including Bali with its many tourists, make it unsafe to travel. Night clubs, bars, and restaurants should be avoided. There are continuous threats of terrorism.

## JAPAN

Japan is a constitutional monarchy, with a parliamentary government. The country contains four main islands located on the eastern or Pacific coast of Asia. Japan suffered economic and political turmoil after the earthquake and subsequent tsunami of March 2011. There are limited security issues, such as being aware of personal safety. Japan is vulnerable to earthquakes, tsunamis, and volcanic activity.

## Profile Summary

| | | |
|---|---|---|
| Landmass | 377,835 km$^2$ | |
| Population | 127.08 million | |
| Ethnic groups | Japanese | Korean 0.5% |
| | Chinese 0.4% | |
| Religions | Shinto and Buddhist | Christian |
| Languages | Japanese | |
| Education | Literacy 99% | |
| GDP growth rate | 3% | |
| Current GDP | US$5.391 trillion | US$4.338 trillion (PPP) |
| GDP per capita | US$34,200 | |

## Government

Japan is a constitutional monarchy, with a parliamentary government after enacting the constitution in 1947.

## Geography

Japan is a country of four main islands, extending along the eastern or Pacific coast of Asia. The Japanese islands contain mountainous terrain, with only 25 percent being flat. Situated on a volcanic zone, Japan is vulnerable to earthquakes, tsunami, and volcanic activity. Temperatures range from warm summers to cold long winters with heavy snowfall. The heavy rain season begins in early May, gradually moving from south to north.

## Political Conditions

For many years Japan was embodied in the emperor; in the present day, the country is a constitutional monarchy with a parliamentary government. The prime minister has the power to appoint or remove ministers. Japan follows the Anglo-American common law and civil law, consisting of many levels of courts.

## Economy

Japan has an industrial, free-market economy. The economy is linked to international trade, creating the third largest in the world. Japan has few natural resources. The economy had one of the highest growth rates in the world from 1960 to 1980. After the 2011 earthquake, the pace of business dramatically slowed as many areas became contaminated, and food and water were affected.

More than 320,000 became homeless, with millions of households left with no running water.

## Foreign Relations

Japan has diplomatic relations with nearly all independent nations. Becoming an active member of the UN in 1956, Japanese foreign policy aims to promote peace and prosperity. Japanese and U.S. relations have been seen as an important part in maintaining stability in eastern Asia. China and Japan share close relations in the WTO; however, in recent years Japan has become increasingly concerned about the Chinese exploitation of the gas fields in the East China Sea.

## Security Issues

It is necessary to be aware of personal security at all times and use media and local information sources for news about other security risks. This is especially the case in the coastal areas of northern Honshu, which were affected by the 2011 earthquake and following tsunami. A precautionary zone of 80 kilometers around the Fukushima nuclear power plant was created after the disaster.

## KIRIBATI

Kiribati is a republic, having gained independence from the United Kingdom. Located in both the eastern and western hemispheres, it consists of 30 coral islands and a single main island. The political situation consists of informal parties and elections. Kiribati is one of the least developed countries in the world and relies heavily on services such as tourism for economic stability. The islands have a low level of crime, but natural disasters such as undersea earthquakes and resulting tsunamis should be considered.

## Profile Summary

| | | |
|---|---|---|
| Landmass | 719 km$^2$ | |
| Population | 102,697 | |
| Ethnic groups | Micronesian 99% | |
| Religions | Roman Catholic 55% | Kiribati Protestant 36% |
| | Other 9% | |
| Languages | English (official) | Gilbertese/I-Kiribati |
| Education | Literacy 92% | |
| Current GDP | US$163 million | |
| Per Capita | US$1,636 | |

GOVERNMENT

Kiribati is a republic, gaining independence from United Kingdom in 1979 and adopting a constitution on the same day.

## Geography

Kiribati consists of 31 coral islands and 1 main island. Located on both the eastern and western hemispheres, the Line Islands are the first area to enter the new year. Agriculture and cultivation are extremely difficult on these islands, as the soil is destroyed by high levels of salinity. Kiribati's terrain is an archipelago of low-lying coral atolls surrounded by reefs. The climate is maritime equatorial or tropical, with climate change expected to increase sea levels, causing many of the reefs and islands to be at risk of inundation.

## Political Conditions

Political parties exist, but they are more similar to coalitions on behavior. Parties do not have official platforms or structures, and most candidates formally present themselves as independents. Campaigning is by word of mouth and information gatherings held in traditional meeting houses. As these islands are experiencing a growing population and crowding is prevalent, the focus is on employment opportunities.

## Economy

Kiribati is one of the least developed countries in the world, with an extremely low GDP rate of US$1,600 per capita. Even with a low GDP, 64 percent of the population are economically active. Sixty-four percent of revenue is generated by the service sector, relying heavily on tourism. Kiribati also gains a large portion of its income from abroad including fishing licenses, development assistance, and worker remittances.

## Foreign Relations

Kiribati maintains friendly relations with most countries, in particular its neighboring countries Japan, Australia, New Zealand, and Fiji. Australia, Taiwan, New Zealand, and Cuba maintain resident diplomatic missions in Kiribati and also provide the majority of foreign aid.

Kiribati became a member of the UN in 1999, but does not maintain a resident ambassador in New York and New Zealand, casting a proxy vote arrangement. Kiribati is also a member of PIF, ADB, the Commonwealth Heads of Government, the IMF, the Pacific Community, and the World Bank.

## Security Issues

It is necessary to be aware of personal security at all times, supported with media and local information sources for news about possible security risks. Although there is a low crime rate on the islands, large groups and protests should be avoided if civil and political unrest arises. As Kiribati is located in an area of high seismic activity undersea earthquakes and destructive tsunamis may occur.

# LAOS

Laos is a Communist state, with its economy heavily dependent on its neighbors, Thailand, Vietnam, and the north of China. As civil unrest is prevalent and criminal activity is common, foreign nationals are warned to consider the need to travel in areas in the Xaisomboun district, east of Vang Vieng.

## Profile Summary

| | | | |
|---|---|---|---|
| Landmass | 236,800 km² | | |
| Population | 6.5 million | | |
| Ethnic groups | Tai-Kadai 66.2% | Austro-Asiatic 22.8% | |
| | Hmong-Yao 7.4% | Tibeto-Burman 2.7% | |
| Religions | Buddhism 65% | Christianity 1.3% | |
| Languages | Lao (official) | English | |
| Education | Literacy 69% | | |
| GDP growth rate | 8.5% | | |
| Current GDP | US$6.9 billion | | |
| Per Capita | US$986 | | |

## Government

Laos is a Communist state, with the Lao People's Revolutionary Party (LPRP) the only legal party.

## Geography

Laos consists of rugged mountains, plateaus, and alluvial plains. The Mekong River forms a large part of the western boundary with Thailand, where the mountains form most of the eastern border with Vietnam. There are three seasons—rainy, cold, and hot. The rainy season is from May to November, followed by a dry season from December to April.

## Political Conditions

There is one legal party in Laos, the Lao People's Revolutionary Party (LPRP). The head of state is President Sayasone and the head of government is Prime Minister Thammavong. Laos adopted its constitution in 1991, amending it in 2003. The National Assembly approves all new laws.

## Economy

The Laos economy depends heavily on its neighbors, Thailand, Vietnam, and the north of China, for investment and trade. The country is poor, with inadequate infrastructure and a large unskilled workforce, and it relies heavily on foreign assistance.

The economy of Laos is essentially a free-market system with active central planning by the government, similar to China and Vietnam.

## Foreign Relations

After assuming power in December 1975, Laos aligned itself with Vietnam and the Soviet bloc, adopting a hostile posture toward the West. Laos has maintained these close ties to the present day. After the collapse of the Soviet Union, Laos has sought to improve relations with its regional neighbors. Laos was admitted into ASEAN in 1997. The country maintains a special relationship with Vietnam and formalized a 1977 treaty of friendship, which created tensions with China.

## Security Issues

Civil unrest is prevalent and criminal activity is common; foreign nationals are warned to consider carefully the need to travel in areas in the Xaisomboun district, east of Vang Vieng. This particular area is experiencing many attacks by bandits. Isolated incidents of civil unrest, including armed attacks and bombings, have occurred in Laos. Curfews can be enforced, which can lead to roadblocks, spot roadside checks, and occasional house raids.

## MALAYSIA

Malaysia is a federal parliamentary democracy, with a constitutional monarch. It is a relatively open state and a newly industrialized market economy. Security issues include a high threat of kidnapping by terrorists and criminals in particular tourist areas. Malaysian authorities have increased security in these regions in response to these incidents. Crime is common, although violent crime against foreign nationals is uncommon. Drink spiking, robbery, credit card fraud, and assaults occur.

## Profile Summary

| | | |
|---|---|---|
| Landmass | 329,847 km$^2$ | |
| Population | 28.3 million | |
| Ethnic groups | Malay 53.3% | Chinese 26% |
| | Indigenous 11.8% | India 7.7% |
| Religions | Islam 60.4% | Buddhism 19.2% |
| | Christianity 9.1% | Hinduism 6.3% |
| Languages | Bahasa Melayu | Chinese |
| | English | |
| Education | Literacy 93.5% | Years compulsory: 6 |
| GDP growth rate | 7.2% (2010) | |
| Current GDP | $255.3billion | |
| GDP per capita | (GNI) $8,126 | |

## Government

Malaysia is a federal parliamentary democracy, with a constitutional monarch after gaining independence in 1957.

## Geography

Malaysia is the 66th-largest country by total land area in the world. It borders with Thailand in the west and Indonesia and Brunei in the east. Malaysia has a narrow causeway linking it to Singapore. The capital of Malaysia is Kuala Lumpur. The terrain consists of coastal plains and an interior that is jungle-covered mountains.

## Political Conditions

Malaysia's predominant political party, the United Malays National Organisation (UMNO), has continuously held power since its 1957 independence. After the coalition's share of the vote declined in 1969, riots broke out in Kuala Lumpur between the Malays and the ethnic Chinese, which resulted in many being killed and injured.

## Economy

Malaysia is a relatively open state-orientated and newly industrialized market economy. The economy peaked in the early 1980s to mid-1990s, averaging an 8 percent annual growth rate. In 2010, Malaysian banks were well capitalized and the country maintains a high level of foreign exchange reserves with little external debt. Malaysia has a managed float currency exchange regime, being flexible in adjusting to global economic and financial developments.

## Foreign Relations

Malaysia is a founding member of ASEAN, an active member of the APEC forum, and member of the Organisation of Islamic Cooperation (OIC), the NAM, and the UN.

## Security Issues

Overall, caution must be exercised in Malaysia. Islands, dive sites, and coastal areas of the Eastern Sabah have posted security warnings alerting foreign nationals to consider carefully the need to travel. There is a high threat of kidnapping by terrorists and criminals in these particular tourist areas. Malaysian authorities have increased security in this region in response to these incidents. Crime is common, including drink spiking, robbery, credit card fraud, and assaults.

## MALDIVES

The Maldives is a republic, which consists of over 1,100 coral islands grouped into 26 atolls. The Maldivian economy is based on servicing tourism and fishing. More than 700,000 tourists visit annually. Security caution must be exercised, with regular monitoring of political developments that might affect the republic.

| Profile Summary | | |
|---|---|---|
| Landmass | 298 km² | |
| Population | 314,000 | |
| Ethnic groups | Maldivians | |
| Religions | Sunni Islam | |
| Languages | Dhivehi (official) | English |
| Education | Years compulsory : 7 | Literacy 97% |
| GDP growth rate | 4.8% | |
| Current GDP | US$1.48 billion | |
| Per capita GDP | US$4,770 | |

## Government

The Maldives is a republic, after gaining independence in 1965 and adopting a constitution in 2008.

## Geography

The Maldives consists of over 1,100 coral islands grouped into 26 atolls. These islands spread over 90,000 square kilometers along the north–south direction, making this one of the most dispersed countries in the world. The terrain is described as flat atolls, with a hot and humid climate affected by the Indian Ocean. The Maldives is the lowest country in the world, with more than 80 percent of the landmass at less than one meter above sea level.

## Political Conditions

Maldives is a republic, with a president and government. In 1988, a Sri Lankan group tried to overthrow the Maldivian government, with the Indian military suppressing the coup attempt within 24 hours. President Nasheed was elected in 2008, promising to strengthen democracy and increase media freedom. Several of Nasheed's cabinet ministers have faced "no confidence" votes and have also been unable to advance legislation. The previous government kept a tight rein on expressions of Islamic extremism. There has been a growing trend in Islamic conservatism since the advent of democracy and free speech.

## Economy

The Maldivian economy is based on servicing tourism and fishing as the "backbone" of the economy. More than 700,000 tourists visit annually. The economy struck difficult times with the 2004 Indian Ocean tsunami devastating many islands. The Maldives engaged in post-tsunami reconstruction, with a rebound in tourism, which is expected to continue to grow. The country was approved a US$93 million loan in 2009, but after the first initial payments the loan was put on hold as the Maldives were seen as unfit to repay. The country is facing a foreign exchange shortage.

## Foreign Relations

Maldives follows a nonaligned policy and is committed to maintaining friendly relations with all countries. The country has a UN Mission in New York and embassies in the United States, Sri Lanka, China, the UK, Bangladesh, India, Japan, Singapore, and Malaysia. The Maldives is also part of the United Nations Children's Fund, the World Health Organization , OIC, and NAM.

## Security Issues

Caution must be exercised in the Maldives, with regular monitoring of the political developments that might affect personal security. Protests were anticipated to occur during the 2011 elections. Drug-related crime is known to occur, as are petty crimes including thefts from beaches and hotels.

## MARSHALL ISLANDS

The Marshall Islands are a parliamentary democracy in free association with the United States, consisting of 29 low-lying coral atolls. A relatively new democratic political system, combined with a hierarchical traditional culture, is prevalent. The government employs almost 50 percent of the salaried workers, making it the largest employer. Security issues are minimal, as there is a relatively low crime rate.

## Profile Summary

| | | |
|---|---|---|
| Landmass | 181 km² | |
| Population | 61,300 | |
| Ethnic groups | Bengali 98% | Other 2% |
| | 90% Marshallese | 10% U.S., Filipino, Chinese, New Zealander, Australian, other Micronesian (FSM) |
| Religions | | |
| Languages | Two major Marshallese dialects from Malayo-Polynesian family | English |
| Education | Literacy 98%—based on the question "Do you read the Bible?" | |
| Current GDP | $161.7 million | US$226.4 billion PPP |

## Government

The Marshall Islands are a parliamentary democracy in free association with the United States, gaining independence 1986.

## Geography

The Marshall Islands consists of 29 low-lying coral atolls and five single islands. The islands are located north of Nauru and Kiribati, east of the Federated States of Micronesia, and south of the U.S. territory of Wake Island. The climate is generally tropical, with a wet season from May to November. The islands occasionally suffer from typhoons, many starting in the islands and growing stronger as they move west toward the Mariana Islands and the Philippines.

## Political Conditions

A relatively new democratic political system, combined with a hierarchical traditional culture, is prevalent with the first two presidents being chiefs. Democracy has functioned well after a number of local and national elections.

## Economy

The government employs almost 50 percent of the salaried workers, making it the largest employer in the islands. The economy combines a small subsistence sector such as fishing, breadfruit, banana, and pandanus cultivation, and a modern urban sector. The modern sector consists of wholesale and retail trade, restaurants, banking, construction, professional services, fisheries, and copra processing. The largest exports of the Marshall Islands are fresh caught fish exported to Japan and Hawaii, and frozen fish exported to Asia.

## Foreign Relations

Under the terms of the Compact of Free Association, the government of the Marshall Islands Is free to conducts its own foreign relations. The island has established relations with 67 nations, including most other Pacific Islands nations. The country became a member of the UN in 1991, maintaining embassies in the United States, Fiji, Japan, and Taiwan.

## Security Issues

Security issues are limited, as the Marshall Islands have a relatively low crime rate. The most common crimes are break-ins and thefts from homes, hotel rooms, and vehicles. Fights and assaults occasionally occur at night clubs and bars.

## MAURITIUS

Mauritius is a republic, after becoming independent and adopting a constitution in 1968. Mauritius is part of the Mascarene Islands, and its politics are vibrant and characterized by the coalition and alliance building. All parties support democratic politics and an open and private economy. The country has strong relations with the West, as well as India and other south and east African countries. Security issues are limited with low crime levels, although petty crime, such as pickpocketing, bag snatching, and robbery, is on the rise and some areas are a greater threat. Natural disasters and severe weather must be considered between November to May, when widespread damage and disruption can occur

## Profile Summary

| | | |
|---|---|---|
| Landmass | 2,040 km² | |
| Population | 1,284,264 | |
| Ethnic groups | Indo-Mauritians 68% | Creoles 27% |
| | Sino-Mauritians 3% | Franco-Mauritians 2% |
| Religions | Hindu 48% | Roman Catholic 23.6% |
| | Muslim 16.6% | Christian 8.6% |
| Languages | Creole English | French |
| Education | Years compulsory: 11 | Literacy 84.4% |
| GDP growth rate | 2.1% | |
| Current GDP | US$9.156 billion | |
| GDP per capita | US$12,400 | |

## Government

Mauritius became a republic in 1992, after becoming independent and adopting a constitution in 1968.

## Geography

Mauritius is part of the Mascarene Islands formed by a series of undersea volcanos. The islands are tropical in the coastal regions, with forests in the mountainous areas. Seasonal cyclones are destructive to the flora and fauna; however, they recover quickly. The clime is tropical, modified by southeast trade winds. Winter is warm and dry from May to November and summer is hot, wet, and humid from November to May.

## Political Conditions

Mauritian politics are vibrant and characterized by the coalition and alliance building. All parties support democratic politics and a relatively open economy, with a strong private sector. The Mauritian Labor Party (MLP) ruled from 1947 to 1982 and returned to power in 1995. Elections in 2000 saw the reemergence of the Militant Socialist Movement (MSM) and the Mauritian Militant Movement (MMM) as a winning alliance. The year 2005 brought the first Catholic head of government, which created a historic precedent of having a non-Hindu member lead the national government.

## Economy

The Mauritius economy contains no natural resources. Agriculture is 4.5 percent of GDP with products including sugar, tea, tobacco, vegetables, fruits, flowers, cattle, and fishing. Manufactured goods including export processing are 19 percent of GDP. The tourism sector covers 9 percent of GDP and the financial services 11 percent. Exports amount to US$2.055 billion, while imports cover US$3.552 billion.

Mauritius's major suppliers are India, France, South Africa, China, Japan, Spain, Italy, Germany, Malaysia, and Thailand.

## Foreign Relations

Mauritius, considered part of Africa geographically, has friendly relations with many regional African states, in particular, South Africa. Mauritius also has strong relations with the West, as well as India. Mauritius is part of the African Union, the WTO, the Commonwealth Heads of Government, La Francophonie, the Southern African Development Community, the Indian Ocean Commission, the Common Market for Eastern and Southern Africa, and the Indian Ocean Rim Association.

## Security Issues

There must be some awareness of security issues. Crime levels are low, though petty crime such as pickpocketing, bag snatching, and robbery has been increasing. The rate of crime is higher in downtown Port Louis, and the coastal tourist centers of Grand Bay, Perebere, and Flic an Flac. Security risks increase after dark, particularly on beaches and in poorly lit areas. Natural disasters, severe weather, and climate must also be considered from November to May, when widespread damage and disruption to essential services can occur.

## MICRONESIA

Micronesia is a constitutional confederation, in free association with the United States. The nation consists of 607 islands, extending 1,800 miles. Economically, the fishing industry is highly important with foreign commercial fishing fleets paying for the right to operate in territorial waters. Foreign relations have been established with most of its Pacific neighbors. Threats to security are high in some states and care must be taken to be aware of the local environment.

## Profile Summary

| | | |
|---|---|---|
| Landmass | 702 km² | |
| Population | 102, 624 | |
| Ethnic groups | Micronesian | Polynesian |
| Religions | Roman Catholic 50% | Protestant 47% |
| | Others 3% | |
| Languages | English | |
| Education | Literacy 89% | |
| Current GDP | US$253.5 million | |
| GDP per capita | US$2,347 | |

## Government

Micronesia is a constitutional confederation in free association with the United States, after becoming independent in 1986 and constituted in 1979.

## Geography

Micronesia consists of 607 islands, extending 1,800 miles across the archipelago of the Caroline Islands east of the Philippines. The four states are the island groups of Pohnpei, Chuuk, and Yap, and the island of Kosrae. The terrain is low-lying coral atolls, with a tropical climate.

## Political Conditions

Micronesia is governed under a 1979 constitution, which guarantees fundamental human rights and established a separation of governmental powers. There are four senators, one for each state, who serve four-year terms. There are no formal political parties. Micronesia has a weak central government, with each four states having separate constitutions, and their own legislation and governor.

## Economy

Between 1986 and 2001, the United States provided Micronesia US$2 billion in grants and services with the aim of encouraging sustainable development in addition to federal grants totaling US$35 million annually. The fishing industry is highly important, with foreign commercial fishing fleets paying over US$16.985 million annually for the right to operate in Micronesia territorial waters. The revenue gained from the licensing fees amounts to 28 percent of national government revenues. Exports of marine products to Japan account for nearly 85 percent of export revenues.

## Foreign Relations

Micronesia has diplomatic relations with most of its Pacific neighbors, such as Japan, Australia, and the People's Republic of China. Micronesia became a member of the UN in 1991.

## Security Issues

Threats to security are high in some states of Micronesia. In Yap, there are dozens of World War II-era aerial bombs in shallow depths located in the channels of Yap harbor. Crime is higher in Chuuk than in other states, and it is advised to stay off the streets after dark in Weno (the main island). Occasionally, national foreigners are subject to and possibly singled out for theft and abuse, sometimes violent.

## MONGOLIA

Mongolia is a mixed parliamentary/presidential government and the world's 19th‑largest nation, with a terrain that consists of deserts and mountains. Economic activity has been based on herding and agriculture, moving toward greater development of extensive mining of mineral deposits. Security issues include an increase in crime, in particular in Ulan Bator, with foreigners being robbed and assaulted.

## Profile Summary

| | | |
|---|---|---|
| Landmass | 1,566,500 km² | |
| Population | 2.735 million | |
| Ethnic groups | Mongol 95% | Turkic 5% |
| Religions | Buddhist Lamaism 50% | Muslim 4% |
| | Shamanist and Christian 6% | None 40% |
| Languages | Mongolian | |
| Education | Literacy 98% | Years compulsory: 9 |
| GDP growth rate | 7% | |
| Current GDP | US$ 6.8 billion | 8.25 trillion Mongolian Tugruks/MNT |
| GDP per capita | US$2,008 | |

### Government

Mongolia's government is mixed parliamentary/presidential, after gaining independence in 1921.

### Geography

Mongolia is the world's 19th-largest country, with a terrain that consists of deserts to the south and cold mountainous regions to the north and west. The country is subject to hard climate conditions. Ulan Bator has the lowest average temperature of any national capital in the world. Mongolia is high, cold, and windy, with extreme climate consisting of long, cold winters and short summers. The continental climate has little precipitation and sharp seasonal fluctuations.

### Political Conditions

Mongolia is a mixed parliamentary/presidential nation-state, with the Parliament elected by the people and the president directly elected. The government has a four-year term. The president is the head of state, commander in chief of the armed forces, and head of the National Security Council. Constitutional changes were made in 2011, requiring the president to nominate the prime ministerial candidate proposed by a party with a majority of members.

### Economy

Economic activity has been based on herding and agriculture, with the development of mining extensive mineral deposits of copper, coal, molybdenum, tin, and gold. The Soviet assistance, which comprised one-third of GDP, disappeared and caused recession in 1990–91. Economic growth returned after the formerly state-run economy was privatized and became a free-market economy. The economy then again suffered after severe winter and summer droughts in 2000–2001, causing a massive die-off of stock in 2002. In 2010, the legal "investment agreement" with Rio Tinto and Ivanhoe Miles to develop a gold deposit came into force.

## Foreign Relations

Mongolia seeks cordial relations with its neighbors, Russia and China. After the disintegration of the former Soviet Union, the country developed relations with the new independent states. The country is part of ASEAN, ARF, APEC, and Shanghai Cooperation Organisation. The country also serves on the UN Economic and Social Council and has diplomatic relations with both North and South Korea.

## Security Issues

Caution must be exercised when traveling to Mongolia. Be aware of personal security and stay up-to-date with media coverage of issues that may arise. Demonstrations and crowded protests should be avoided. Crime continues to increase, particularly in Ulan Bator, with foreigners being robbed and assaulted.

## NAURU

Nauru is a republic, located in the western Pacific Ocean. A state of emergency due to a political standoff has been an extended political issue for the nation, which has just been resolved. The economy relies heavily on international grants and development funding. There is a low crime rate, but caution must be exercised with political protests.

## Profile Summary

| Landmass | 24 km² | |
|---|---|---|
| Population | 10,185 | |
| Ethnic groups | Nauruan 93% | Chinese 5% |
| | Other Pacific Islanders 1% | European 1% |
| Religions | Christian (66%) | |
| | Roman Catholic (33%) | |
| Languages | Nauruan | English |
| Education | Literacy 97% | |
| Current GDP | US$54.2 million | |
| GDP per capita | US$5,551 | |

## Government

Nauru is a republic, gaining independence and becoming a constitution in 1968.

## Geography

Nauru is located in the western Pacific Ocean, being a small oval-shaped island located just 42 km south of the equator. A century of mining has stripped and devastated four-fifths of the total land area and rehabilitation efforts have been unsuccessful. The island is surrounded by a coral reef, exposed at low tide with pinnacles. The highest point of the plateau is 65 meters above sea level. The terrain is rough beach rising to a fertile but narrow ring around the reef. The climate is equatorial, with a monsoonal rainy season (November to February) and unreliable rainfall that is prone to El Niño-linked droughts.

## Political Conditions

In recent decades, with the country's uncertain future and economic failures, many no-confidence votes have been common in government, forcing many dramatic changes. There was a political standoff between the government and the opposition in 2010, leading to a constitutional referendum. After a year of elections and the continuation of political standoff, the state of emergency was lifted and Marcus Stephen was reelected.

## Economy

The phosphate mines once gave the nation the second-highest per capita GDP in the world; however, mining on a commercial basis ceased in 2002, contracting the economy. Nauru now relies heavily on payments for fishing rights, grants, and development funding from Australia, New Zealand, Japan, China, and Taiwan.

## Foreign Relations

Nauru joined the Commonwealth Heads of Government as a Special Member, taking part in all activities except heads of government meetings. The country was also admitted to the UN in 1999, and became a member of PIF, South Pacific Regional Environmental Program, and the Secretariat of the Pacific Community.

## Security Issues

There is a low crime rate, but caution and awareness of political and civil protests must be exercised.

## NEPAL

Nepal is a representative democracy, bordering China and India. After a 10-year Maoist insurgency, Nepal has seen rapid political change in the past two decades. Nepal ranks as one of the poorest nations in the world, with more than 55 percent of the population below the poverty line. A high degree of caution is required, due to the uncertain political and security issues, and criminals targeting foreign nationals.

## Profile Summary

| | | |
|---|---|---|
| Landmass | 147,181 km² | |
| Population | 29.3 million | |
| Ethnic groups | Brahman | Chetri |
| | Newar | Gurung |
| | Magar | Tamang |
| | Rai | Limbu |
| | Sherpa | Tharu |
| Religions | Hinduism 81% | Buddhism 11% |
| | Islam 4% | Others 4% |
| Languages | Nepali | >100 indigenous languages |
| Education | No years compulsory | Literacy 57% |
| GDP growth rate | 4.7% | |
| Current GDP | $12.6 billion | |

## Government

Nepal is a representative democracy, as a federal republic.

## Geography

Nepal borders China and India, divided into three main areas of mountain, hill, and lowland plains. The mountain region makes up the northern part of Nepal, containing the highest elevations in the world including Mount Everest. Nepal has five climatic zones: the tropical and subtropical zones, the temperate zone, the cold zone, the subarctic zone, and the Arctic zone, all due to the corresponding levels of altitudes.

## Political Conditions

After a 10-year Maoist insurgency, Nepal has seen rapid political change in the past two decades. In 1990, a parliamentary monarchy was established with the king being both the head of state and prime minister. There has been further development, compared to other Asian countries, such as the abolition of the death sentence and the approval of same-sex marriage. No government has survived for more than two years since 1991. In 2007, a bill was passed making Nepal a federal republic, with a president head of state. Since 2009, the country has been in political deadlock with Maoist combatants.

## Economy

Nepal ranks as one of the poorest countries in the world, with more than 55 percent of the population below the poverty line. Agriculture remains the principal economic activity, with rice and wheat. In 2009–10, exports decreased by 6 percent and imports grew by 187 percent. Nepal is a tourist destination for hikers and mountain climbers.

## Foreign Relations

Nepal has good relations with its neighbors, India and China. The nation takes an active role in the formation of the economic development-orientated South Asian

Association for Regional Cooperation (SAARC), participates in a number of UN specialized agencies, and is a member of the WTO, World Bank, IMF, Colombo Plan, and ADB.

## Security Issues

A high degree of caution must be exercised, as there are uncertain political and security issues. There is a strong risk of violent clashes between demonstrators and security forces, and any protests should be avoided. Law and order have deteriorated, with foreigners and aid organizations targeted by criminals, armed groups, and politically affiliated gangs.

## New Zealand

New Zealand is a parliamentary nation with no formal constitution. The country is made up of two main islands and a number of smaller islands. In recent years the National Party has gained control, creating economic reforms from a period of recession. A degree of caution is advised in areas such as Christchurch and Lyttleton, and natural disasters, such as earthquakes, occur.

### Profile Summary

| | | |
|---|---|---|
| Landmass | 270,500 km$^2$ | |
| Population | 4.36 million. | |
| Ethnic groups | European 76.8% | Maori 14.9% |
| | Asian 9.7% | Other Polynesian Pacific peoples 7.2% |
| Religions | Christian 55.6% | No religion 34.7% |
| | Hindu 1.5% | Buddhist 1.3% |
| Languages | English | |
| New Zealand Sign Language | Maori | |
| Education | Literacy 99% | Years compulsory: ages 6–16 |
| GDP growth rate | 0.73% | |
| Current GDP | $139 billion | |
| GDP per capita | $27,500 | |

### Government

New Zealand is a parliamentary nation with no formal constitution. The country was declared a dominion in 1907.

### Geography

New Zealand is made up of two main islands and a number of smaller islands. The islands are located near the center of the water hemisphere. The south island is the largest and divided along its length by the southern Alps, steep mountains, and deep fiords. The north island is less mountainous, but is marked by volcanoes. The climate consists of temperate and subtropical.

## Political Conditions

New Zealand has a conservative National Party and left-leaning Labour Party, with both dominating politics. The Labour Party was reelected in 1984, when the government instituted a series of market-orientated reforms in response to mounting external debt. In recent years, the National Party has gained control, creating many economic reforms after a period of recession and recovery from the devastating 2011 Christchurch earthquake.

## Economy

New Zealand's modern, prosperous, and developed market economy was ranked the third most developed in 2012, according to the UN Development Program. Natural resources include timber, natural gas, iron, sand, and coal. Agriculture products include dairy products, meat, and forestry products. Primary exports of US$2.86 billion included meat, dairy, wine, wood, and medical devices. Imports amounted to US$3.34 billion and consisted of primary machinery, aircraft, medical and veterinary instruments, motor vehicles, and plastic resins.

## Foreign Relations

New Zealand is a member of the UN, WTO, World Bank, IMF, OECD, APEC, ADB, and the Australian, New Zealand, United States Security Treaty. New Zealand, as a charter member of the Colombo Plan, has provided Asian countries with technical assistance and capital. New Zealand also shares close relations with Australia and the United States.

## Security Issues

New Zealand is relatively safe, but caution must be exercised when traveling in areas such as Christchurch and Lyttleton. Also, New Zealand is prone to earthquakes.

## NIUE

## Profile Summary

A profile summary is not available.

## Geography

Niue is a raised coral atoll in the southern Pacific Ocean. There are three outlying coral reefs: Beveridge Reed, Antiope Reef, and Haran Reef. Niue is one of the world's largest coral atolls. The island consists of steep limestone cliffs along the coast with a central plateau. Most of the population resides close to the west coast. Niue has a tropical climate with most rainfall occurring between November and April.

### Political Conditions

Politically, Niue vests executive authority in Her Majesty the Queen and the Governor-General of New Zealand.

### Economy

Niue's economy is small, with most activity revolving around the government.

### Foreign Relations

Niue holds close ties with New Zealand, being self-governing in free association since 1974.

## NORTH KOREA

North Korea is a highly centralized Communist state, and such isolation restricts international trade. North Korea occupies the northern portion of the Korean Peninsula. The country has a strict policy on tourism, and visitors are not allowed in or out. Security issues need to include consideration of the Communist state approach to national visitors and the fact that abductions are common.

### Profile Summary

| | | |
|---|---|---|
| Landmass | 122,762 km² | |
| Population | 25.5 million | |
| Ethnic groups | Korean | Chinese |
| | Japanese | |
| Religions | Autonomous religious activities | |
| Languages | Korean | |
| Education | Literacy 99% | Years compulsory: 11 |
| Current GDP | US$28 billion | |
| GDP per capita | US$1,800 | |

### Government

North Korea is highly centralized Communist state, under the rigid control of the Communist Korean Workers Party (KWP).

### Geography

North Korea occupies the northern portion of the Korean Peninsula, sharing land borders with China and Russia to the north. To the west are the Yellow Sea and Korea Bar, with Japan lying to the east. The capital city is Pyongyang. Approximately 80 percent of the land area is moderately high mountains separated by deep, narrow valleys and small cultivated plains. The other 20 percent is lowland plains covering small scattered areas. The climate consists of long, cold, and dry winters with short, hot, and humid summers.

## Political Conditions

North Korea is divided into nine provinces and two provincial-level municipalities. All government officials belong to the Communist Korean Workers Party (KWP). North Korea became independent in 1945, establishing the Democratic People's Republic of Korea (DPRK) in 1948. The country adopted a constitution in 1948, revising it in 1972, 1992, 1998, and again in 2009.

## Economy

North Korea has a highly centralized command economy. With the country being one of the five remaining Communist states in the world, it is one of only two with a government-planned state-owned economy. North Korea's isolation policy highly restricts international trade. In 1948, the country passed a law allowing foreign investment through joint ventures, but failed to attract any significant investment. Exports amounted to US$1.997 billion in 2009 including minerals, metallurgical products, manufactures, textiles, and agriculture and fishery products. North Korea's major trading partners are China, Singapore, and India.

## Foreign Relations

North Korea has mixed foreign relations. The relationship with South Korea has determined much of its post-World War II foreign policy. The North and the South have had difficult relations since the Korean War. In recent years, North Korea has attempted to pursue a mixed policy, seeking to develop economic relations with the South and to win support of the public for greater North–South engagement. As international trade is limited, other foreign relations barely exist.

## Security Issues

North Korea has a strict policy on tourism. Being a Communist state, visitors are not allowed. Abductions in North Korea are common and have become a high risk, with many cases unsolved. The DPRK has been involved in abducting Japanese citizens, along with other foreign citizens. Terrorism is at a high-alert level. The United States has agreed with the DPRK to support an international legal regime combating international terrorism and cooperation. The North Korean government does not release statistics on crime. If you do something illegal in North Korea, you will not be immune to prosecution.

## PAKISTAN

Pakistan borders Afghanistan, India, and Iran, and is considered a low-income country. After September 11, 2011, Pakistan's prominence in the international community increased significantly as it pledged an alliance with the United States to counter terrorism. Security issues are significant, including a high risk of terrorist attacks, assassinations, and abductions.

---

**Profile Summary**

| | | |
|---|---|---|
| Landmass | 803,943 km² | |
| Population | 167,762,040 | |
| Ethnic groups | Punjabi | Sindhi |
| | Pashtun | Baloch |
| | Muhajir | |
| Religions | Muslim 97% | Christian, Hindus, and others |
| Languages | Urdu | English |
| | Punjabi | Sindhi |
| | Pashto | Baloch |
| | Hindko | Brahui |
| Education | Literacy 49.9% | |
| GDP growth rate | 2.7% | |
| Per Capita | US$2,600 | |

---

### Government

Pakistan is a parliamentary democracy, gaining independence in 1947.

### Geography

Pakistan borders Afghanistan, India, and Iran. The capital city is Islamabad near Rawalpindi. The geography of Pakistan is a blend of varying landscapes, from plains to deserts, forests, hills, and plateaus, surrounding the coastal areas in the south to the mountainous landscape in the north. The climate varies from tropical to temperate, with arid conditions existing in the south. The monsoon season results in frequent flooding.

### Political Conditions

The president is chosen for a five-year term by an electoral college consisting of the Senate. The prime minister is selected by the National Assembly for a four-year term. With the 18th Amendment in place, the president names the most senior Supreme Court justice to be chief justice. Each province has a high court.

### Economy

The Pakistan economy is considered a low-income country by the World Bank. Low levels of spending on social services and a high population growth have increased unemployment, and there is rising inflation. Pakistan's extreme poverty and underdevelopment are key concerns, in particular in the rural areas. The economy is classified as vulnerable to internal and external shocks, due to the security concerns and the global financial crisis.

## Foreign Relations

Pakistan has had difficult and volatile relations with India. The country has also had a long-standing close relation to China, and extensive security and economic interests in the Persian Gulf. Pakistan expresses a strong desire for a stable Afghanistan. After September 11, 2011, Pakistan's prominence in the international community increased significantly, as it pledged an alliance with the United States in their counterterrorism efforts.

## Security Issues

Security is currently a major issue in Pakistan and most travel is considered dangerous. In areas such as Baluchistan, Khyber-Pakhtunkhwa, and the border of Afghanistan and India, travel is not recommended. There is an extremely high threat of terror attacks against many places in Pakistan frequented by foreign nationals. Terrorist attacks are in the advanced stages of planning and there have been many deaths and injury to hundreds of people. Kidnapping and assassination of foreigners remain a threat throughout the country.

## PALAU

Palau is a constitutional republic, in free association with the United States. The country consists of eight principal and more than 250 smaller islands. Palau has a very high GDP rate, which makes it one of the wealthiest Pacific Island states. Security issues are minimal, as the crime rate is low except for occasional petty crime.

## Profile Summary

| | | |
|---|---|---|
| Landmass | 458 km² | |
| Population | 20,000 | |
| Ethnic groups | Palauans | |
| Religions | Roman Catholic | Protestant |
| | Modekngei | |
| Languages | English | Palauan |
| Education | Literacy 95.2% | |
| Current GDP | US$178.4 million | |
| Per Capita | US$8,941 | |

## Government

Palau is a constitutional republic, in free association with United States.

## Geography

Palau consists of eight principal and more than 250 smaller islands lying roughly 500 miles southeast of the Philippines. The capital is Melekeok, with a population of 391 people. The terrain varies from mountainous main island, to smaller reef-rimmed coral islands. The climate is tropical.

## Political Conditions

The government is stable, and national elections are held every four years in the executive branch and Congress. Elections are free and fair, and candidates rely heavily on media campaigns, town meetings, and rallies. There are no political parties in Palau, as candidates run on their own platforms.

## Economy

Palau's extremely high GDP rate makes it one of the wealthiest Pacific Island states. Tourism is Palau's main industry, drawing in foreigners with its island beauty. The number of visitors is constantly increasing, ranging from countries such as Japan, Taiwan, and Korea to the United States. The countries export markets are the United States, Japan, and Taiwan, shipping mainly fish and handicrafts. Imports of fuel and related minerals, machinery, transport equipment, beverages and tobacco, manufactured goods, and food and live animals are generally from the United States, Japan, Singapore, Taiwan, and Korea.

## Foreign Relations

Palau, as a sovereign nation, conducts its own foreign relations. Since independence, the country has established diplomatic relations with many of its Pacific neighbors. Palau joined the UN in 1994 and is a dependable supporter of U.S. positions in the UN.

## Security Issues

Security issues are minimal, as the crime rate is low with the occasional petty crime.

## Papua New Guinea

Papua New Guinea is a constitutional parliamentary democracy, and its politics are highly competitive, with most members elected on a personal and ethnic basis. The nation is rich in many natural resources with strong international investment, but many of the population live at a subsistence level. There are extremely high levels of crime including muggings, assault, and rape.

## Profile Summary

| Landmass | 462,8400 km² | |
|---|---|---|
| Population | 6.7 million | |
| Languages | English | Tok Pisin |
| | Motu | |
| Education | Years compulsory: 0 | Literacy 49.3% |
| GDP growth rate | 47.1% | |
| Current GDP | US$8.8 billion | PGK 21.84 billion |
| Per capita | US$1,180 | |

## Government

Papua New Guinea is a constitutional parliamentary democracy.

## Geography

Papua New Guinea is approximately the size of California and the capital city is Port Moresby. The terrain is mostly mountains, with coastal lowland and rolling foothills. The largest portion of the population lives in fertile highland valleys that were unknown to the outside world until the 1930s. The climate is tropical, with the northwest bringing the monsoonal season in December to March. The southeast has the monsoonal season from May to October.

## Political Conditions

Papua New Guinea's politics are highly competitive, with most members elected on a personal and ethnic basis within their constituencies rather than as a result of party affiliation. There are several parties, but none are strong and no single party has yet won a seat in its own right. During the Parliament's five-year terms, there has been a history of changes in government coalitions and leadership. In 2003, the electoral system was changed to limited preferential voting, encouraging politicians to strike alliances.

## Economy

Papua New Guinea is rich in natural resources, including minerals, oil, gas, timber, and fish, and produces a variety of commercial agricultural products. These substances are dominated by foreign investors. Approximately 75 percent of the country's population relies primarily on the subsistence economy. Manufacturing continues to be slow, but the service industry is stable with tourism showing potential and largely untapped. Australia, Singapore, and Japan are the principal exporters to Papua New Guinea.

## Foreign Relations

Papua New Guinea has close ties with Australia, primarily because of the imports/exports. Papua New Guinea has diplomatic relations with 56 countries, and in recent years formed greater relations with Asian nations. Australia is the largest bilateral aid donor to Papua New Guinea, offering approximately A$355 million a year in assistance. Papua New Guinea is part of APEC, WTO, Millennium Development Goals, and the Pacific Island Countries Trade Agreement.

## Security Issues

Security issues require a high degree of caution, as there are extremely high levels of crime including muggings, assault, and rape. Foreign nationals are warned of a high risk of HIV/AIDS. Popondetta in Oro Province, Port Moresby, and Lau require extreme care, as law and order have deteriorated. Carjacking is an ever-present threat, with dangers increasing at night.

## PHILIPPINES

The Philippines is situated in the western Pacific Ocean in Southeast Asia, with a representative democracy modeled on the U.S. system. After independence, the Philippines became a constitution to establish a presidential system of government and independent judiciary. The economy is the 12th largest in Asia and continues to grow rapidly, with many natural resources. A high degree of caution is required due to terrorism events, high crime, and the high level of civil and political unrest in the central and southern islands.

## Profile Summary

| | | |
|---|---|---|
| Landmass | 300,000 km² | |
| Population | 92.9 million | |
| Ethnic groups | Malay | Chinese |
| Religions | Roman Catholic 80.9% | Muslim 5% |
| | Evangelical 2.8% | Iglesia ni Kristo 2.3% |
| | Aplipayan 2% | Other, unspecified, and none 2.5% |
| Languages | Filipino | English |
| Education | Years compulsory: 6 | Basic literacy 93.4% |
| GDP growth rate | 7.3% | |
| Current GDP | US$188.7 billion | |
| GDP per capita | US$2,007 | |

## Government

The Philippines is a constitutional republic, with a presidential system of government.

## Geography

The Philippines is located in the Southeast of Asia, with no neighboring countries. The climate is dominated by a rainy season and a dry season, creating a tropical wet climate. Monsoons occur throughout the year but are not associated with high winds and waves. The Philippines contains 7,107 islands, with the 11 largest containing 94 percent of the total area. The nation is seen as a cultural crossroad, with a number of ethnic groups forming a racial blend. The islands are generally volcanic in origin, being part of the Pacific Ring of Fire. The Philippines have typically narrow coastal plains and numerous swift-running streams.

## Political Conditions

The Philippines is a representative democracy, with a presidential system of government. Like many Third World countries with a presidential government, the president is both the head of state and head of government. It is governed as a unitary state, with the exception of the largely free-from-government Muslim region. There are 278 members in the House of Representatives, with 226 representing single-member districts. The government is still at risk of terrorist threats and attacks.

## Economy

The Philippines economy is the 12th largest in Asia and continues to grow rapidly. Natural resources consist of copper, nickel, iron, cobalt, silver, and gold, with significant reserves of chromite, nickel, and copper. The economy struggles to act quickly, as laws are underdeveloped and the government still holds significant power over the exploitation of mineral resources. In 2010, levels of growth were up to 7.8 percent with the goal to minimize debt ratios.

## Foreign Relations

The Philippines cultivates constructive relations with its Asian neighbors, linked through its membership in ASEAN. The country is also a member of the UN and some of its specialized agencies. In relation to the United States, it has a shared history and commitment to democratic principles as well as economic ties. The United States is also one of the Philippines' top trade partners. Philippine soldiers and police have participated in civilian and peacekeeping operations in East Timor. The government has made active efforts to improve the poor relationship between the claimants of the South China Sea.

## Security Issues

A high degree of caution is required. Terrorism events and kidnappings continue to occur in the central and western Mindanao, and travel to these areas is not advised. Terrorist attacks, including bombings, have become more frequent, in particular in tourist areas including Manila. There is a high degree of civil and political unrest in the central and southern islands, increasing the already significant crime issue. Criminal gangs are known to drug and assault tourists in Manila. Acts of violence occur randomly and frequently; gun ownership is widespread and poorly regulated.

## SAMOA

Samoa is a mix of parliamentary democracy and "Fa'a Samoa" (Samoan traditional custom), which blends local tribal leadership with a national parliamentary system. Samoa consists of two large islands of Upolu and Savai'i and seven islets. The country has strong foreign relations with New Zealand and Australia. Consideration of security issues is required in Samoa, as there have been a number of violent assaults and robberies, with increasing crime.

## Profile Summary

| Landmass | 2,934 km² | |
|---|---|---|
| Population | 183,203. | |
| Ethnic groups | Samoan 92.6% | Euronesian 7% |
| | European 0.4% | |
| Religions | Christian 98.9% | |
| Languages | Samoan | English |
| Education | Literacy 98.6% | |
| Current GDP | US$709.2 | |
| Per Capita | US$3,791 | |

### Government

Samoa is a mix of parliamentary democracy and "Fa'a Samoa" (Samoan traditional custom), a system that blends local tribal leadership with a national parliamentary system.

### Geography

Samoa consists of two large islands of Upolu and Savai'i, and seven islets. The country was east of the International Date Line, before the prime minister announced that the Date Line would be moved so that Samoa would lie to the west of the line. Samoa has a volcanic terrain, with only one or two active volcanoes on Savai'i. The coastal plain is narrow and with a mountainous terrain, including many rain forests. The climate in Samoa is tropical, with an average of 115 inches of rain per year.

### Political Conditions

In 2011, the Human Rights Protection Party (HRPP) won 29 seats and joined with 7 independent seats to hold a total of 49 seats. The Tautua Samoa Party (TSP) won 13 seats, remaining in opposition. The HRPP has held a majority for the past seven consecutive five-year terms. Following the 2011 election, eight petitioners were charged in the Supreme Court for various counts of bribery, treating, or gifting during a campaign, with two motions withdrawn and one case dismissed.

### Economy

With only 18 percent of the Samoan population employed in a salaried position, the country operates in a predominantly informal economy. The economy is dependent on tourism, capital flows from abroad, and some agriculture and manufacturing exports. New Zealand is Samoa's principal trading partner, with 35–40 percent imports and 45–50 percent exports. Exports include coconut products, nonu fruit, and fish. The main imports consist of food and drinks, consumer goods, industrial supplies, and fuels.

## Foreign Relations

Samoa has strong foreign relations with New Zealand after signing a Treaty of Friendship in 1962 after independence. As the country's parliamentary democracy is modified to include traditional cultural ways, Samoa often aligns with countries with similar values. The country has growing ties with China, although it is characterized as conservative and pro-Western. Samoa also shares a close relationship with Australia, which is the largest donor to Samoa with a bilateral program.

## Security Issues

Consideration of security issues is required in Samoa. There have been a number of violent assaults and robberies, including sexual assaults, and crime is on the increase. Clashes between rival groups and youths have recently been on the increase, in particular in isolated nightspots.

## SINGAPORE

Singapore is a parliamentary republic and consists of 63 islands, including Singapore island. Singapore has a strategic location on major sea routes, which gives it an economic importance in Southeast Asia. The government adopts a pro-business, pro-foreign investment, and export-orientated economic policy, supported with state investments. Security issues are low, with a low-level risk of terrorism and some petty crime.

## Profile Summary

| | | |
|---|---|---|
| Landmass | 712.4 km² | |
| Population | 5.077 million | |
| Ethnic groups | Chinese 74.1% | Malays 13.4% |
| | Indians 9.2% | Others 3.3% |
| Religions | Buddhist | Taoist |
| | Muslim | Christian |
| | Hindu | |
| Languages | English | Mandarin |
| | Other Chinese dialects | Malay |
| Education | Literacy 95.9% | Years compulsory: 6 |
| GDP growth rate | 14.5% (2010) | |
| Current GDP | US$222.7 billion | |
| Per capita | US$43,867 | |

### Government

Singapore is a parliamentary republic, after adopting a constitution in 1959 and gaining independence later that year.

### Geography

Singapore consists of 63 islands, including the main island. Over 20 percent of the land area consists of forest and natural reserves, although recent urbanization has eliminated most primary rainforest. Singapore's terrain is classed as lowlands. There are ongoing projects in attempt to increase Singapore's land area, involving the merging of smaller islands. The country has a tropical rain forest climate with no distinctive season, but the monsoon season is from November to January.

### Political Conditions

The People's Action Party (PAP) has been the ruling political party, reelected continuously since 1959 and headed by Prime Minister Lee Hsien Loong. A left-wing group split off from the PAP but resigned from Parliament in 1961, making PAP the sole representative party. In more recent times, an opposition has been slowly building. In the 2011 election, opposition parties contested 82 of the 87 seats, the largest number ever.

### Economy

Singapore has a strategic location on major sea routes, giving the country an economic importance in Southeast Asia disproportionate to its small size. The Singapore government adopted a pro-business, pro-foreign investment, and export-orientated economic policy framework, combined with state-directed investments in strategic government-owned corporations. This strategy proved a success, even after the outbreak of severe acute respiratory syndrome (SARS) in 2003, as growth bounced back due to the high demand for electronics, pharmaceuticals, and other manufactured goods. The government is actively negotiating eight free-trade agreements and is also a current member of ASEAN.

### Foreign Relations

Singapore is nonaligned. The country plays an active role in ASEAN, and is a current member of the UN and several of its specialized and related agencies, and of NAM and the Commonwealth Heads of Government.

### Security Issues

Security issues are low in Singapore. There is a low risk of terrorism against Western interests, in particular in areas frequented by foreigners. Violent crimes against foreign nationals are rare, but petty crime such as pickpocketing and street theft can occur at the airport, tourist destinations, hotels, and on public transport.

### Solomon Islands

The Solomon Islands is a parliamentary democracy, located northeast of Australia. The political conditions in the Solomon Islands are characterized by weak political parties and unstable parliamentary coalitions. The economy is based on the international demand for timber, supported by some tourism and fisheries. Security issues need to include consideration of the risk of criminal activity, and from time to time some political violence, civil unrest, and protests coinciding with Parliament activities.

## Profile Summary

| | | | |
|---|---|---|---|
| Landmass | 27,556 km² | | |
| Population | 539,000 | | |
| Ethnic groups | Melanesian 93% | Polynesian 4% | |
| | Micronesian 1.5% | Other 1.5% | |
| Religions | Christian 92% | | |
| Languages | English | | |
| Education | Literacy 76.6% | Years compulsory: none | |
| GDP growth rate | 4% | | |
| Current GDP | $564 million | | |
| GDP per capita | $1,047 | | |

## Government

The Solomon Islands is a parliamentary democracy, within the Commonwealth of Nations.

## Geography

The Solomon Islands are located northeast of Australia. With a terrain ranging from rugged mountainous islands to low-lying coral atolls, they stretch from Papua New Guinea to the Coral Sea off Vanuatu. The smaller atolls are considered beautiful, whereas the main islands consist of rain forested mountain ranges of mainly volcanic origin, with deep narrow valleys and coastal belts lined with coconut palms and ringed by reef. This region is geologically active and earth tremors are frequent. The islands' temperatures are high and extremely humid throughout the year, with a cooler period from June to August.

## Political Conditions

The political conditions are characterized by weak political parties and unstable parliamentary coalitions. Votes of no confidence are frequent, and government leadership and cabinet changes are common. In 2011, widespread extortion, a prevailing atmosphere of lawlessness, and ineffective policing prompted a formal request by the Solomon Islands government for outside assistance.

## Economy

The economy is largely based on the international prices and demands for timber. Nevertheless, in recent years the islands' forests have been dangerously overexploited, leading to a proposed government reform of harvesting policies. Tourism and fisheries are also primary areas of the economy. Principal aid donors are Australia, New Zealand, the European Union, and the People's Republic of China.

## Foreign Relations

International nations with diplomatic missions in the Solomon Islands are Australia, the United Kingdom, New Zealand, Papua New Guinea, and Japan. The Solomon Islands are members of the UN, the Commonwealth Heads of Government, Pacific Community, PIF, Melanesian Spearhead Group, the IMF, and a party to the partnership agreement between the European Union and the African, Caribbean, and Pacific Group of States (Cotonou Agreement).

## Security Issues

Security issues have to consider the risk of criminal activity, and political violence, civil unrest, and protests coinciding with Parliament from time to time. Any protests, large gatherings, and political rallies should be avoided. There is a particular concern in Honiara, were criminal activity sometimes involves violence. Verbal harassment, intimidation, and assaults, including indecent assault, have been directed toward foreigners, typically when alcohol is involved.

## SOUTH KOREA

South Korea has a republic government and occupies the southern portion of the Korean Peninsula. An armistice agreement monitored by the UN has maintained general peace on the peninsula for the past 58 years. South Korea has achieved a high level of economic growth in the last several decades and maintains a strong economy. Security issues are minimal, as the crime rate is low, and only general caution needs to be exercised.

## Profile Summary

| | | |
|---|---|---|
| Landmass | 98,480 km² | |
| Population | 48,754,657 | |
| Ethnic groups | Korean | Chinese |
| Religions | Christianity | Buddhism |
| | Shamanism | Confucianism |
| | Chondogyo | |
| Languages | Korean | English |
| Education | Literacy 98% | Years compulsory: 9 |
| GDP growth rate | 6.1% (2010) | |
| Current GDP | US$1.459 trillion | |
| GDP per capita | US$17,074 | |

## Government

South Korea has a republic government, liberated in 1956, with powers shared between the president, the legislature, and the courts.

## Geography

South Korea occupies the southern portion of the Korean Peninsula. The country is surrounded by the Yellow Sea to the west and the Sea of Japan (East Sea) to the east. South Korea can be divided into four general regions with an eastern region of high mountain ranges and narrow coastal plains, a western region of broad coastal plains, river basins, and rolling hills, a southwestern region of mountains and valleys, and a southeastern region dominated by the broad basin of the Nakong River. The terrain is partially forested mountain ranges separated by deep and narrow valleys, and cultivates along the coast in the west and the south. The climate is temperate, with rainfall heavier in the summer than winter.

## Political Conditions

The Republic of Korea (South Korea) has been dominated by the president, but shared among the presidency, the legislature, and the judiciary. The president is chief of state and is elected for a single five-year term. Under the constitution, the judiciary is independent and comprises a Supreme Court, appellate courts, and a Constitutional Court. The county has nine provinces and seven administratively separate cities. Political parties include the Grand National Party (GNP), Democratic Party (DP), Liberty Forward Party (LFP), New Progressive Party (NPP), Pro-Park Alliance (PPA), and Renewal Korea Party (RKP).

## Economy

Since the Korean War, South Korea has achieved a high level of economic growth in the last several decades, leading it into the ranks of the Organisation for Cooperation and Development (OECD). Today, South Korea is the seventh-largest trading partner with the United States and the fifteenth-largest economy in the world. Economists are concerned that a decade-long decrease in GDP is due to an ageing population and structural problems that are becoming increasingly apparent.

## Foreign Relations

The Republic of Korea maintains diplomatic relations with more than 170 countries and a broad network of trading relationships. It joined the UN in 1991 and has an active role in many international forums. The country has hosted major international events, such as the 1988 Summer Olympics, the 2002 World Cup Soccer Tournament, and the 2002 Second Ministerial Conference of the Community of Democracies.

## Security Issues

Security issues are minimal, as the crime rate is low. Petty thefts such as pick-pocketing, purse snatching, assault, and hotel and residential burglary occur more frequently in major metropolitan areas. Incidents of sexual assault and rape have been reported in popular nightlife districts. An armistice agreement monitored by the UN has maintain general peace on the Korean Peninsula for the past 58 years, although tensions have occasionally risen.

## Sri Lanka

Sri Lanka is a republic government, located at the top of the Indian tectonic plate in the Indian Ocean. Sri Lanka's income inequality is severe, with a significant difference between rural and urban areas. The country still remains in a state of emergency, with a high risk of politically motivated violence.

## Profile Summary

| | | |
|---|---|---|
| Landmass | 65,610 km² | |
| Population | 21.3 million | |
| Ethnic groups | Sinhalese 74% | Tamils 18% |
| | Muslims 7% | Other 1% |
| Religions | Buddhism | Hinduism |
| | Islam | Christianity |
| Languages | Sinhala and Tamil | English |
| Education | Literacy 91% | Years compulsory: age 14 |
| GDP growth rate | 8% (2010) | |
| Current GDP | US$49.55 billion | |
| GDP per capita | US$2,400 | US$5,000. PPP |

## Government

Sri Lanka has a republic government, gained after independence in 1948 and constituting almost 30 years later in 1978.

## Geography

Sri Lanka lies on the top of the Indian tectonic plate, positioned in the Indian Ocean. A land bridge exists between the Indian mainland and Sri Lanka. The country's terrain consists of coastal plains in the northern third of the country, with hills and mountains in the south-central area rising to more than 2,133 meters. The tropical climate has a light rainy season in the northeast for the months of autumn and winter, with heavy rain in the southwest from summer through to autumn.

## Political Conditions

Sri Lanka consists of a multiparty democracy with considerable stability, despite the high levels of political violence during the 26 years of civil conflict. There are two major political parties, the UNP and SLFP. The UNP has historically embraced democratic values, and the SLFP led the coalition government aided by emergency regulations, consolidated political powers, limited media freedom, and the role of civil society in Sri Lankan politics.

## Economy

Sri Lanka's income inequality is severe, with a striking difference between rural and urban areas. Approximately 15 percent of the country's population remains impoverished. These are the effects of civil conflict, falling agriculture labor productivity, lack of income-earning opportunities for the rural population, high inflation, and poor infrastructure outside the Western Province. Sri Lanka is a lower-middle-income developing nation. Despite a brutal civil war that began 1983, economic growth has averaged around 5 percent in the last 10 years.

## Foreign Relations

Sri Lanka follows a nonaligned foreign policy, but since 2001 has gained closer relations with the United States. The country participates in multilateral diplomacy, in particular the UN. Sri Lanka is a member of NAM, the Commonwealth Heads of Government, SAARC, the World Bank, the IMF, ADB, and the Colombo Plan.

## Security Issues

Security issues should be great concern, as Sri Lanka remains in a state of emergency with a high risk of politically motivated violence. All large demonstrations and public gatherings should be avoided. In the Northern Province, travel is not recommended as there is a great deal of postconflict activity by the security forces including de-mining with many marked and unmarked landmines. There continues to be a heavy presence of military and security forces.

## THAILAND

Thailand is a constitutional monarchy, located between Laos, Cambodia, and Burma, and is the world's 20th-largest country in terms of population. The Thai legal system blends principles of traditional Thai and Western laws. The economy is heavily dependent on exports of goods and services equivalent to nearly 70 percent of GDP, which is only just showing signs of recovery. A high degree of caution needs to be taken due to targeting of international visitors; political demonstrations during certain times and armed conflict continue.

## Profile Summary

| | | | |
|---|---|---|---|
| Landmass | 513,115 km² | | |
| Population | 67.0 million | | |
| Ethnic groups | Thai 89% | Other 11% | |
| Religions | Buddhist 93–94% | Muslim 5–6% | |
| | Hindu, Brahmin, other | Christian 1% | |
| Languages | Thai | English | |
| Education | Literacy 94.9% (males) | Years compulsory: 9 | |
| GDP growth rate | 7.8% (2010) | | |
| Current GDP | US$317 billion | | |
| GDP per capita | US$4,716 | | |

## Government

Thailand is a constitutional monarchy, adopting its current constitution following a 2007 referendum. Thailand was never colonized based on a traditional founding date of 1238.

## Geography

Thailand is the world's 50th largest country in landmass, while it is the world's 20th largest country in terms of population. It is located between Laos, Cambodia, and Burma. The south of Thailand consists of narrow land bridges that widen into the Malay Peninsula. The north is mountainous, with the highest point at 2,565 meters. Thailand has a densely populated central plain, and the climate is characterized as tropical monsoon.

## Political Conditions

Thailand is a constitutional monarchy, with 77 provinces. Since the 1992–2006 coup, the country is generally defined as free and fair with multiparty elections. The king has little direct power under Thailand's constitution. The Thai legal system blends principles of traditional Thai and Western laws.

## Economy

The economy is heavily dependent on the exports of goods and services, equivalent to nearly 70 percent of GDP. The U.S. market is largely relied upon, in particular in the automobile, petrochemicals, and electronics sectors, which have weakened the economy by reducing both domestic and international demand. Nonetheless, economic growth is now at a steady increase with results showing 12 percent (2010) and 8 percent (2011).

## Foreign Relations

Thailand is a strong supporter of ASEAN's efforts to promote economic development, social integration, and stability throughout the region. Relations with China are steadily increasing. Thailand participates in international and regional organizations and has close ties with Indonesia, Malaysia, the Philippines, Singapore, Brunei,

Laos, Cambodia, Burma, and Vietnam. Thailand has contributed troops and UN force commanders to the international peacekeeping effort in East Timor.

## Security Issues
A high degree of caution needs to be taken. In areas surrounding Pra Viharn, Yala, Pattani, Narathiwat, and Songkhla, the need to travel must be reconsidered. There have been large-scale political demonstrations and related incidents in Bangkok and in other parts of Thailand. The political situation remains unpredictable and further violence cannot be ruled out. Food and drink spikes occur in Thailand, and visitors are targeted. In Preah Vihear renewed fighting and use of heavy weapons and artillery in the area and fatalities have been reported.

## TUVALU

Tuvalu, formerly known as Ellice Islands, is a constitutional monarchy located 4,000 km northeast of Australia. The country has no formal political parties, and election campaigns are generally based on family ties and reputation. Tuvalu's economy suffers due to its small size, remote location, and lack of natural resources. A degree of caution needs to be taken, although the country has a low crime rate.

## Profile Summary

| | | |
|---|---|---|
| Landmass | 26 km² | |
| Population | 11, 149. | |
| Ethnic groups | Polynesian 96% | Micronesian 4% |
| Religions | Church of Tuvalu | |
| Languages | Tuvaluan | English |
| | Samoan | Kiribati |
| Education | Literacy 95% | |
| GDP growth rate | 1.6% | |
| Current GDP | US$29.008 million | |
| GDP per capita | US$2,615 | |

## Government
Tuvalu is a constitutional monarchy, with a parliamentary democracy after becoming independent in 1978 from the UK.

## Geography
Tuvalu, formerly known as Ellice Islands, is located 4,000 km northeast of Australia. The nation consists of four reef islands and five atolls, with poor soil and a total land area of 26 km². The islands have tropical temperatures, and are very low lying with narrow coral atolls.

## Political Conditions

Tuvalu has strong democratic values, with free elections every four years. There are no formal political parties, and election campaigns are generally based on family ties and reputation. Members of the Parliament generally have very close ties to the islands they represent. Tuvalu has had a number of prime ministers, creating pressure on the small nation.

## Economy

The economy suffers greatly from its small size, remoteness, and lack of natural resources. Thirty-nine percent of the people are employed in the public sector. Subsistence farming and fishing remain the primary economic activities. Over 75 percent of the population works primarily in rural subsistence and livelihood activities. There is growing youth unemployment, with few new jobs being created. The Tuvalu Trust Fund (TTF), managed overseas as an investment fund, contributes roughly 11 percent of the annual government budget since 1990.

## Foreign Relations

The nation maintains its independence, but generally has a pro-Western foreign policy. Tuvalu has close relations with its neighboring countries of Fiji, New Zealand, and Australia. It has diplomatic relations with Taiwan, which maintains the only resident embassy in Tuvalu with a large assistance program. Tuvalu is a recent member of the UN, joining in 2000 and maintaining a mission in New York. The country is also an active member of PIF, and member of the ADB, IMF, and World Bank.

## Security Issues

Foreign nationals need to be cautious when traveling to Tuvalu, although the country has a low crime rate. Visitors should be alert to their own safety and unusual activity.

## TIMOR LESTE (EAST TIMOR)

East Timor is a parliamentary republic located in Southeast Asia northwest of Australia. In 2008, it declared a state of emergency after an attempt to kill the president. The UN has supplied peacekeeping efforts in East Timor. East Timor is one of the poorest countries in the world, with very basic income, health, and literacy levels. Security issues have to be considered high, as there are high and violent crime rates, an uncertain security situation, and the possibility of civil unrest.

## Profile Summary

| | | |
|---|---|---|
| Landmass | 15,007 km² | |
| Population | 1,066,582. | |
| Ethnic groups | | |
| Religions | Catholic 96.5% | |
| Languages | Portuguese | Tetum |
| | English | Bahasa Indonesia |
| Education | Literacy 50.1% | |
| GDP growth rate | | |
| Current GDP | US$590 million (nonoil, 2009) | |
| GDP per capita | US$542 | |

## Government

East Timor is a parliamentary republic, gaining independence from Portugal in 1975.

## Geography

East Timor is located in Southeast Asia, northwest of Australia. The highest mountain is Tatamailau, at 2,963 meters. Generally, the climate in East Timor is tropical, hot, and humid, with distinct rainy and dry seasons.

## Political Conditions

Parliamentary elections are generally fair and free. However, in recent times political unrest has been known to occur when a majority government could not be formed. In 2008, a fugitive attacked President Ramos-Horta, who sustained gunshot injuries and had to be airlifted to Australia. The government immediately imposed a state of siege, which temporarily imposed a curfew and gave security forces greater latitude for arrests and searches. Nevertheless, since 2008 the government has succeeded in restoring relative calm and maintaining stability.

## Economy

East Timor is one of the poorest countries in the world, with very basic income, health, and literacy levels. Infrastructure and resources lack in both rural and urban areas. Unemployment is at an extremely high rate of 70 percent and half of the population live below the poverty line. The economy is dependent on government spending and assistance from international donors. Oil and gas revenues surged since 2005, as major projects in the Joint Petroleum Development Area that East Timor shares with Australia came online.

## Foreign Relations

East Timor shares many diplomatic relations. The country joined the UN in 2002, is pursuing membership in ASEAN, and became a member of ARF. East Timor has a high priority on relationships with Indonesia, Malaysia, and Singapore, and donors such as Australia, the United States, the European Union, Japan, and Portugal. The UN has supplied peacekeeping efforts in East Timor.

## Security Issues

Security issues have to be considered as there is an uncertain situation and the civil unrest could occur with little warning. Large rallies and protests should be avoided. Armed robbery and assaults have been directed at foreign nationals, in particular individuals traveling alone or at night. There is a history of gang-related violence, robbery, arson, and vandalism in major towns, and sexual harassment and violence against women.

## TONGA

Tonga is a constitutional hereditary monarchy located directly south of Western Samoa. It is an archipelago comprising 171 islands. The social and political structure comprises the king, nobles, and commoners, and status and rank play a powerful social role. Tonga has close relations with its Pacific neighbors. The economy is largely nonmonetary, with a heavy dependence on remittances from its overseas nationals. Security issues are limited, with moderate crime levels.

### Profile Summary

| | | |
|---|---|---|
| Landmass | 747 km² | |
| Population | 103,365 | |
| Ethnic groups | Tongan 98% | Polynesian |
| | European | |
| Religions | Christian | |
| Languages | Tongan | English |
| Education | Literacy 50.1% | |
| GDP growth rate | −1.2% | |
| Current GDP | US$319.24 million | |
| GDP per capita | US$3,103 | |

### Government

Tonga is a constitutional hereditary monarchy, which gained independence in 1970.

### Geography

Tonga is an archipelago located directly south of Western Samoa, consisting of 171 islands with 48 currently inhabited. Most of the islands have a limestone base formed from uplifted coral, while others consist of limestone overlaying a volcanic base. Tonga has a tropical climate with two seasons, summer and winter. Tonga experiences heavy rainfall around February and April, and from November to April a tropical cyclone season.

## Political conditions

Tonga was seen as quiet, inward looking, and isolated from development elsewhere in the world. The social structure consists of three main social groups of the king, the nobles, and the commoners. Status and rank play a powerful role in personal relationships, even within families. Recently, there has been a rising demand for more rights for commoners and reduced influence for nobility.

## Economy

Tonga's economy is characterized by a large nonmonetary sector and a heavy dependence on remittances from the more than half the population that lives abroad. Much of the monetary sector of the economy is dominated by the royal family and nobles. The manufacturing sector consists of handicrafts and a few small-scale industries, amounting to 7 percent of GDP. Tonga's development plans emphasize a growing private sector and upgrading agricultural productivity.

## Foreign Relations

Tonga maintains cordial relations with most nation-states, but has close relations with its Pacific neighbors. The country is currently a member of PIF. The United States and Tonga enjoy close cooperation on a range of international issues.

## Security Issues

Security issues need to include consideration of common crime, which is moderate. There has been a recent rise in house break-ins and property theft, attributed to the economic downturn. Sexual assaults against foreigners have occurred. Females in particular should avoid going out alone at night or alone to isolated locations, including beaches.

## Vanuatu

Vanuatu is a parliamentary democracy that consists of 83 islands. Historically, the English and French political lines have and continue to divide the government. The primary economy is agriculture, with 80 percent of the population employed in these activities. Vanuatu has a positive foreign policy, with relations with over 65 countries. Security issues need to include consideration of the possibility of volcanic eruption and cyclones, but the crime rate is low.

## Profile Summary

| | | |
|---|---|---|
| Landmass | 12, 190 km$^2$ | |
| Population | 234, 023 | |
| Ethnic groups | Ni-Vanuatu 94% | European 4% |
| | Other Pacific Islanders 2% | Asian |
| Religions | Predominantly Christian 82% | |
| Languages | Bislama | English |
| | French | >100 tribal languages |
| Education | Literacy 84.8% | |
| GDP growth rate | 3.0% | |
| Current GDP | US$647 million | |
| GDP per capita | US$2,620 | |

## Government

Vanuatu is a parliamentary democracy, after becoming independent from the UK and adopting a constitution at the end of 1980.

## Geography

Vanuatu consists of 83 islands, located approximately 1,750 km east of Australia. The two main islands, Espiritu Santo and Malakula, are volcanic with sharp mountain peaks, plateaus, and lowlands. There is an ever-present danger of a major eruption. The climate is subtropical, with approximately nine months of warm to hot rainy weather and the possibility of cyclones. Vanuatu has a long rainy season, with the wettest and hottest months being from December to April.

## Political Conditions

Historically, the English and the French political lines divided the government. The French politicians favored continuing association with the colonial administrators, whereas the English politicians favored early independence. In 2004, most major parties experienced losses when the president organized a special election after a vote of no confidence within Parliament. Since 2008, elections have continuously ended in a vote of no confidence.

## Economy

The primary economy is agriculture, with 80 percent of the population involved in these activities. Coconut oil, copra, kava, and beef account for more than 75 percent of total agriculture exports. Tourism is also a key economic factor. The government has a wide range of off-shore financial banking, investment, legal, accounting, insurance, and trust-company services, maintaining status as a tax haven.

## Foreign Relations

Vanuatu's favors a friendly foreign policy with over 65 countries, including Russia, China, Cuba, and Vietnam. Only Australia, France, New Zealand, and China maintain embassies, high commissions, or missions in Port Vila. Vanuatu has joined the ADB, the World Bank, the IMF, and the Agence de Cooperation Culturelle et Technique. Since the 1980s, the nation has received development aid from neighboring countries such as Australia, the UK, and New Zealand. Vanuatu retains strong economic and cultural ties to Australia, New Zealand, and France.

## Security Issues
Security issues need to include consideration of the possibility of a major volcanic eruption and, in certain periods of the year, cyclones. The crime rate is low but slowly increasing. Robberies, assaults, and sexual assaults against foreigners have occurred. Females in particular traveling alone should avoid going out at night or to isolated locations, especially on foot.

## VIETNAM

The Socialist Republic of Vietnam is a single-party state. Vietnam has been one of the fastest-growing world economies, with an increase in its people's quality of life due to the move away from a central planned economy. Vietnam has formed diplomatic relationships with 172 countries, including the United States. Security issues are high, due to the unpredictable political situation.

## Profile Summary

| Landmass | 331,114 km² | |
|---|---|---|
| Population | 90 million | |
| Ethnic groups | Vietnamese 85.7% | Tay 1.89% |
| | Thai 1.8% | Muong 1.47% |
| | Khmer 1.46% | Chinese 0.95% |
| | Nung 1.12% | Hmong 1.24% |
| Religions | Buddhism 50% | Catholicism 8–10% |
| | Cao Dai 1.5–3% | Protestantism 0.5–2% |
| | Hao Hao 1.5–4% | Islam 0.1% |
| Languages | Vietnamese | English |
| Education | Literacy 94% | |
| GDP growth rate | 6.8% | |
| Current GDP | US$102 billion | |
| GDP per capita | US$1,168 | |

## Government
The Socialist Republic of Vietnam is a single-party state, following the Chinese Communist party.

## Geography

Vietnam varies from mountainous terrain to a coastal delta, with a tropical monsoon climate. The country is divided into 58 provinces, with five centrally controlled municipalities. The north consists mostly of highlands and the Red River Delta, and the south consists of plains that experience higher average temperatures than the northern mountains.

## Political Conditions

Vietnam continues to support the central role of the Communist Party of Vietnam (CPV) in politics and society. The nation has recognized the increasing importance of growing global economic interdependence and has made concerted efforts to adjust its foreign relations to reflect the evolving international economic and political situation in Southeast Asia. Vietnam has increased efforts to form international alliances to stabilize the political situation. Tensions between China and Vietnam continue to arise over maritime claims in the South China Sea.

## Economy

After reunification from 1975 to 1985, the Sixth Party Congress approved broad economic reforms introducing the nation to foreign investment. Vietnam became one of the fastest-growing economies in the world, transforming from a net food importer to the world's second-largest exporter of rice. In 2010, exports reached highs of US$71.6 billion. The quality of life has improved for many after the move away from a central planned economy, with many plans for reforming key sectors and privatizing state-owned enterprises.

## Foreign Relations

Since 2007, Vietnam has formed diplomatic relationships with 172 countries including the United States. The nation is also a part of the UN and over 63 other international organizations. U.S. relations with Vietnam have progressed, becoming increasingly cooperative since political normalization. Foreign relations between Vietnam and China remain unpredictable.

## Security Issues

Security issues are high, due to the unpredictable political situation. It is necessary to be aware of personal security at all times, supported with media and local information sources for news about possible security risks. There is capital punishment, with death sentences for drug and other serious offenses. Traffic conditions are also dangerous, with frequent accidents.

# Useful Websites

## TRAVEL SITES

U.S. Department of State
http://www.state.gov/misc/list/index.htm
Australia Smart travel: http://www.smartraveller.gov.au/zw-cgi/view/Advice
Singapore: http://app.mfa.gov.sg/


## NATION-STATE GOVERNMENTS

Asia-Europe Meeting (ASEM): http://www.aseminfoboard.org/page.
    phtml?code=About
Asia Pacific Center for Security Studies: http://www.apcss.org/
Council for Security Cooperation in the Asia Pacific: http://www.cscap.org/
Links to Intergovernmental Agencies (such as defense, intelligence services):
    http://en.wikipedia.org/wiki/List_of_intelligence_agencies


## PROFESSIONAL BODIES AND NGOS

Asia Crime Prevention Foundation: http://www.acpf.org/index_e.html
ASIS International: http://www.asisonline.org
Australia: http://www.asial.com.au
China Security and Protection Industry Association: http://www.21csp.com.cn/
Hong Kong: http://www.apsahk.org/
India: http://www.apsa-india.org/
Malaysia: http://www.apsa-malaysia.com.my/
Singapore: http://www.sas.org.sg/
Thailand: http://www.apsathailand.com/apsa_chapter.html


## MEDIA

MySecurity Media: http://www.australiansecuritymagazine.com.au
My Security TV: www.mysecurity.com.au/tv
Australian Security Magazine: www.australiansecuritymagazine.com.au
Hong Kong Security Magazine: www.hongkongsecuritymagazine.ccom

# Appendix

## SUMMARY OF ASIA PACIFIC NATION-STATES

| Country | Area (km²) | Population | Population Density per km² | GDP Millions of US$ (2009) | GDP per Capita USD (2009) | Capital |
|---|---|---|---|---|---|---|
| Australia | 7,617,930 | 22,462,842 | 3 | 920,000 | 41,500 | Canberra |
| Bangladesh | 147, 570 | 156,000,000 | | | | Dhaka |
| Bhutan | 46,500 | 672,425 | | | | Thimphu |
| Brunei | 5,765 | 407,000 | 70 | 14,700 | 36,700 | Bandar Seri Begawan |
| Burma | 676,578 | 50,496,000 | 74 | 26,820 | 500 | Naypyidaw |
| Cambodia | 181,035 | 14,805,000 | 82 | 10,900 | 800 | Phnom Penh |
| China | 9,671,018 | 1,339,530,000 | 138 | 4,911,000 | 3,700 | Beijing |
| East Timor | 14,874 | 1,171,000 | 76 | 599 | 500 | Dili |
| Hong Kong | 1,104 | 7,055,071 | 6,390 | 210,730 | 30,000 | — |
| Indonesia | 1,904,569 | 237,556,363 | 126 | 514,900 | 2,200 | Jakarta |
| Japan | 377,944 | 127,470,000 | 337 | 5,073,000 | 39,700 | Tokyo |
| Laos | 236,800 | 6,320,000 | 27 | 5,721 | 900 | Vientiane |
| Macau | 29 | 541,200 | 18,662 | 21,700 | 39,800 | |
| Malaysia | 329,847 | 28,318,000 | 86 | 191,399 | 7,525 | Kuala Lumpur |
| Mongolia | 1,564,116 | 2,736,800 | 2 | 4,212 | 1,500 | Ulan Bator |
| New Zealand | 268,021 | 4,357,437 | 16 | 109,600 | 25,500 | Wellington |
| North Korea | 120,540 | 23,906,000 | 198 | 27,820 | 1,200 | Pyongyang |
| Papua New Guinea | 462,840 | 6,732,000 | 15 | 8,200 | 1,200 | Port Moresby |
| Philippines | 299,764 | 91,983,000 | 307 | 158,700 | 1,700 | Manila |
| Singapore | 710 | 4,987,600 | 7,023 | 177,133 | 35,500 | City of Singapore |
| South Korea | 100,140 | 50,062,000 | 500 | 800,300 | 20,000 | Seoul |
| Taiwan | 36,191 | 23,119,772 | 639 | 379,400 | 16,400 | Taipei |
| Thailand | 513,120 | 67,764,000 | 132 | 263,510 | 3,900 | Bangkok |
| Vietnam | 331,210 | 88,069,000 | 265 | 97,119 | 1,100 | Hanoi |

*Note:* This table does not include all Asia Pacific nation-states.

# Index